Power
in Postwar
America

Advisory Editor

BARTON J. BERNSTEIN
Stanford University

POWER IN POSTWAR AMERICA

*Interdisciplinary Perspectives
on a Historical Problem*

Edited by
RICHARD GILLAM
Stanford University

LITTLE, BROWN AND COMPANY　　BOSTON

To My Parents

99253

Acknowledgments

Without holding them responsible for my own interpretations, I would like to acknowledge gratefully the aid of several scholars who, by example or advice, have helped to make this a better volume: Professors Barton J. Bernstein and David M. Potter of the Department of History, Stanford University; Professor William Kornhauser, Department of Sociology, University of California, Berkeley; Professor Allen J. Matusow, Department of History, Rice University; Professor Seymour Martin Lipset, Department of Social Relations, Harvard University; Professor Otis Pease, Department of History, University of Washington; Professor Michael Rogin, Department of Political Science, University of California, Berkeley; and Professor Stephan Thernstrom, Department of History, University of California at Los Angeles. I am also indebted to the Social Science Research Council for a fellowship that first made it possible for me to consider interdisciplinary approaches to historical problems.

Contents

Power
in Postwar
America

Introduction

"Power" is a word currently much in the public vocabulary. Today, the rhetoric of contending groups refers, increasingly, to a malign power structure or power elite and laments the power concentrated in a notorious military-industrial complex. Melancholy citizens sense that power has passed out of popular hands, and they ponder their resulting sense of helplessness and frustration. Even public figures — generally the most sanguine of our national critics — at times raise the hopeful possibility of a "new politics" able, somehow, to democratize the present power structure. American intellectuals and scholars, too, have long been troubled by the evident dilemmas of power. Since the end of World War II, for example, a sophisticated debate over the problem of power in postwar America has engaged the minds of scholars and filled the pages of learned journals. In view of the present national malaise, this dispute takes on added significance and merits further attention from students of American society.

The peculiar hold of power on the contemporary American mind is, in part, a result of specific historical developments that followed World War II. Power is a factor in all political life, and attention to it has distinguished the work of most important social analysts. Yet power also becomes a particular concern when force, coercion, and domination rise to the surface of social life; when existence, as Hobbes remarked, seems "but a ceaseless search for power after power unto death." The experience of total war, of course, marked the national psyche with an awareness of these dark forces. The war also promoted construction of a huge military establishment, and this, along with expansion of other governmental and corporate institutions, greatly altered the fabric of postwar society. Such developments inspired many scholars to focus on the question of power and to re-examine it with a variety of interdisciplinary tools. Similarly, the current turmoil in America, the unrest in our cities and on our campuses, and the divisive effects of an enervating foreign war have recalled previous fears and given new impetus to critical assaults on the problem of power in contemporary society.

The perceived tension between concentrated power and effective democracy has been a common thread in such analyses. What implications, postwar researchers seemed to ask, might the changing calculus of power have for traditional democratic theory and for the survival of a democratic social order? Frequently,

1

then, the questions asked about power in America have also been questions about democracy. For this reason, the several "pluralist," "ruling class," and "elite" theories of power represented in this volume have both a descriptive and an evaluative dimension. They not only describe postwar American society, they also measure it against the standards of an ideal democratic polity. In this context, the contemporary dispute over power can be understood as the child of concerns long resident in the American mind.

Although the actual term "power" was not used systematically in this country until the 1930's and 1940's when the American social sciences began to reach maturity, debates over its equivalents or correlates — coercion, force, rule, dominion, legitimate and illegitimate authority — are part of our intellectual legacy. Historian Bernard Bailyn, for example, has shown that a particular view of the nature and proper exercise of power underwrote the colonial rebellion against England. As Bailyn puts it, "power" to the colonists "meant the dominion of some men over others, the human control of human life: ultimately force, compulsion."[1] This fearsome image clashed with equalitarian expectations born during the colonial period when power in America gradually had devolved from central authorities to local constituencies. Thus, when the American colonists perceived that a British "conspiracy" to recentralize power and to deprive them of their liberties had reached intolerable proportions, they rebelled. At least one effect of this revolution was to instill in the public mind a vision of power as demonic, oppressive, often conspiratorial, and to legitimize the symbolic description of power as a "monster" or a "tyrant."

Widespread popular concern about the predaceousness of power survived the Confederation period and, eventually, was institutionalized in such constitutional devices as separation of powers and checks and balances. As James Madison remarked in *The Federalist*, No. 41, the next step after granting power to a central government was "to guard as effectually as possible against a perversion of the power to the public detriment." Even the strong nationalist Alexander Hamilton spoke about an innate "love of power" and suggested that it must be checked for the public good. Yet, despite the establishment of a legitimate national authority and the investment of proliferous safeguards in the Constitution, citizens continued to regard power with suspicion, to see it as something menacing that should be scrutinized warily and constantly defended against; the preservation of a democratic polity demanded no less. This endemic popular concern about the monstrousness of power may also be traced through the nineteenth century. It inhered in the Jacksonian assault on the "money power" and on the Second Bank of the United States (often called "the Monster"), while similar worries about a "slave power" or "anti–slave power" conspiracy colored the rhetoric of those caught up in the debate over slavery during the middle decades of the last century. In addition, after the Civil War victimized and angry Populists rose up to attack Eastern financial power and the "Wall Street Conspiracy," charging that the privileged few consistently oppressed the impotent many.

[1] Bernard Bailyn, *The Ideological Origins of the American Revolution* (Cambridge: Harvard University Press, 1967), p. 56.

Most scholarly work on power, however, springs from the fertile soil of Progressivism. During the Progressive era at the turn of this century, the establishment of an integrated national economy, the unparalleled concentration of economic power in a few large corporations, and the rise of finance capitalism wrote an epitaph to the days of economic individualism and laissez-faire capitalism. With this social and economic transformation came a corresponding period of intellectual ferment. In particular, the alarming economic hegemony of financial oligarchs like J. P. Morgan and of massive trusts like the Standard Oil Company called forth renewed public concern with foreboding aspects of power such as coercion and economic exploitation.

Among intellectuals, this reaction was especially vigorous. The acerbic iconoclast Thorstein Veblen wrote innumerable works on institutional economics, containing some of the most venomous and insightful attacks ever made on the emergent corporate order. The more journalistic muckrakers translated their own Veblenesque hostility into the vernacular and successfully infused popular opinion with a jaundiced view of power. Progressive historians too, among them Charles Beard, were overcome with doubts about concentrated economic power, and they fashioned their historical interpretations accordingly. Thus, Beard's characteristic vision of persistent conflict throughout United States history, of the immutable struggles for power between noble yeomen and acquisitive capitalists, "realty" and "personalty," victim and plutocrat, again mirrored the distinctive tendency of Americans to view power as an exploitative phenomenon and frequently to examine it in terms of its economic origins. Such interpretations received an apotheosis of sorts during the thirties when the Depression inspired growth of vigorous anticapitalist sentiments and redirected the interests of historians and other intellectuals toward subjects such as the rapacious economic power of American businessmen. Scholarly analyses of this genre stressed the clash of economic interests, or of classes, and chronicled the victimization and oppression of the powerless by the economically powerful.

Such conclusions also found support in the social sciences. During the twenties and thirties, Robert and Helen Lynd brought the perspectives of social anthropology to their exploration of "Middletown" (Muncie, Indiana) and produced two seminal volumes, *Middletown* (1929) and *Middletown in Transition* (1937). In these works, the Lynds emphasized a basic division between the working class and the business class, arguing that the polarization of these classes constituted "the outstanding cleavage in Middletown." In their second study, they contended not only that "the business class in Middletown runs the city," but that "the nucleus of business-class control is the X family," long established in the community.[2] Similarly, when W. Lloyd Warner and his colleagues analyzed the social structure of "Yankee City" (Newburyport, Massachusetts), they concluded that the community was stratified into six vaguely defined classes and that power was largely a function of class position. In addition, popular tracts like Ferdinand Lundberg's *America's Sixty Families*, a curious blend of social science and journal-

---

[2] Robert S. Lynd and Helen Merrell Lynd, *Middletown: A Study in Contemporary American Culture* (New York: Harcourt, Brace, 1929), pp. 23–24; and *Middletown in Transition: A Study in Cultural Conflicts* (New York: Harcourt, Brace, 1937), p. 77.

ism, described a national economic elite, or class, of great power, similar to that detected by the Lynds and by Warner in single communities. Finally, in his *Business as a System of Power* (1943), Robert Brady went further, tying power both to class and to the "rise of bureaucratic centralism." The power of business "peak associations" like the National Association of Manufacturers, Brady suggested, was subverting democracy and would lead to a totalitarian social order dominated by bureaucratic organizations of the privileged classes.

In the forties, this strong current of economic determinism began to abate. During the postwar period especially, scholars reacted strongly against earlier interpretations of power. New theories were catalyzed by the war itself and by the complex reactions of Americans to the exigencies of the postwar epoch. World War II quickened the pace of social change and hastened a further concentration of power, inspiring sober anxiety in the minds of some citizens. Moreover, the exceptional tragedy and destructiveness attending the war begot a Manichaean view of life that emphasized original sin, human depravity, and the innate combativeness of man. Yet, if this dismal world view sometimes darkened the national spirit, it also reconciled many intellectuals to the inevitability of power struggles, such as the developing Cold War, and enabled many to accept the increased concentration of power at home as a necessary response to the possibility of crises abroad. In addition, the prevailing interpretation of fascism and communism as mass movements that sprang from the people caused many intellectuals to re-examine the traditional American belief in the democratic distribution of power. They often concluded that power could, in fact, be too widely distributed and, as a result, that it might most safely and "democratically" be entrusted to certain specialized elites.

Characteristically, however, scholars tempered such dispirited intellectual reactions with a reassuring optimism. The concentration of power in economic, political, and military institutions, after all, had advanced the cause of Allied victory during the war, and this noble contribution often seemed cause to reassess the presumed destructiveness of power. Hence, analysts drew upon New Deal and war experiences to illustrate the creative potential of benevolent political power and the democratic virtues of coercive military power exercised in a righteous cause. There eventually followed, among large numbers of intellectuals, a general shift from "conflict" to "consensus" interpretations of American history and, in the social sciences, from "stratification" to "functional" or consensual analyses stressing status rather than class, social cohesion, integration, and order rather than conflict. Many analysts spoke warmly about an "end of ideology," a lessening of political passions, which encouraged social harmony instead of strife. Such scholars often saw power not as a subversive phenomenon, but as an element vital to the preservation of a stable social order. Conflict models of power, prevalent during the decades before World War II, gave way to more complex theories resting on pluralistic premises.

Borrowing freely from Alexis de Tocqueville and from early political scientists such as Arthur Bentley, many liberal commentators argued that the ideal democracy of autonomous individuals — destroyed by the growth of a complex, highly integrated industrial society — had been replaced by an equally satisfactory "pluralist" democracy of groups. Some of these theorists, like David Riesman, contended that power was not concentrated and dangerous, as the growth of bureaucracy and administration after the war suggested; rather, it was dispersed among innumerable voluntary associations or "veto groups," which balanced one another in a kind of rough equilibrium. In essence, this pluralist theory simply replaced the free individual of classical liberalism with the autonomous group. Self-checking mechanisms of the political market place were said to prevent the growth of monolithic power blocs and to safeguard democracy. From this pluralist perspective, American society was characterized by much competition, a great deal of give-and-take, but unlike the explosive conflict emphasized by Progressive historians and some stratification theorists, such rivalry was thoroughly circumscribed and posed no real threat to the general social order.

By contrast, other pluralist theorists, such as economist John Kenneth Galbraith in his book *American Capitalism: The Concept of Countervailing Power* (1952), admitted that power had, in fact, become highly concentrated. Like pluralists of Riesman's convictions, however, Galbraith also drew the comforting analogies of balance and equilibrium from the philosophy of classical liberalism. The abuse of concentrated economic power, he argued, was prevented by self-checking mechanisms, or "countervailing powers," which automatically grew up to restrain corporate activities and to protect the public. Big unions and big government, for example, restricted the power of big corporations, and, within the economy, the power of large retailers checked that of large producers. No longer, therefore, did bigness necessarily imply the abuse of power; indeed, it might sometimes be cultivated for the attendant gains in economic efficiency, which corporations could then pass on to consumers. This view shaded into still another variant of pluralist theory. Concurring with other pluralists, advocates of this third version expressed optimism about the compatibility of democracy and the current distribution of power. These theorists departed from a major convention of American thought, however, and specifically denied that power was intrinsically malign or that it would inevitably be misused if not balanced or checked. Power, rather, was a resource of great potential benefit to society as a whole. In its most extreme form, this generally unexceptionable interpretation made a virtue of necessity; its adherents argued that concentrated power in modern, industrial societies was both inevitable and desirable.

In this new climate of opinion, big business, previously the bête noire of American reform, lost much of its former sinisterness. Those who, like Galbraith, did not find the corporation in happy equilibrium with the state and the labor unions, often turned instead to ideas that A. A. Berle and Gardiner Means first suggested in their important work, *The Modern Corporation and Private Property* (1932), and developed in several later books. Despite a trend toward increasing economic concentration, Berle and Means contended, corporate power was becoming less malevolent. Corporations were no longer the ready instrument of scurrilous capitalists motivated only by self-interest and lust for profits. Instead, ownership was now separated from control and as a result power had passed to managers who, like responsible trustees cultivating a "corporate conscience," ran their businesses with an eye to the general welfare. Many concepts indebted to the original Berle-Means interpretation, such as James Burnham's "managerial revolution" and economist Carl Kaysen's "soulful corporation," have since also gained great legitimacy in pluralist circles.

These theories, however, were not free of anomalies, and at least one is especially significant. Although the several species of pluralism are generally contrasted with elite analysis, pluralists themselves often expressed an elitism of their own. Thus, they acknowledged that small numbers of men must inevitably wield disproportionate power and make the major decisions in any modern, industrial society. Pluralists contended, nevertheless, that the essence of democracy would be preserved by the healthy competition between different elites with different competences, and by the accountability of responsible elites to the body politic. The critical elite theorists, to whom we shall turn in a moment, tended, on the contrary, to reject such prophylactic notions as elite competition and responsibility.

Yet, whatever the veracity of pluralist assumptions, the theory was particularly appropriate to the decades of the Cold War. It restored faith in the munificence of power at home and, at the same time, enabled Americans to direct their enmity toward malevolent concentrations of power abroad. In addition, pluralism allowed thoughtful citizens to live with the challenge that the postwar industrial order presented to traditional democratic expectations and values. Such virtues, indeed, have made pluralism an indispensable tenet of American liberal ideology.

Agreement about the pluralist wisdom, however, was never entirely unanimous. A minority of social critics, especially some sociologists, continued to fear the oppressive hand of power, to distrust the soporific effects of pluralism, and to sound alarms about the loss of mastery overtaking the democratic majority. A few enthusiasts still tended the fires of class analysis, which had lighted the path of so many earlier scholars; and, occasionally, the specter of a ruling class danced amid the shadows of scholarly imaginations. Yet other dissenters forged theories deriving, in part, from Max Weber's work on bureaucracy and from that of lesser worthies, like Vilfredo Pareto, Gaetano Mosca, and Robert Michels, on the concept of elites.

The most influential of these insurgent intellectuals, sociologist C. Wright Mills, argued that power in postwar American society had an institutional rather than a solely political or class base. Those few hundred individuals who occupied the "command posts" of dominant economic, political, and military institutions increasingly came together as an integrated "power elite" and, on important questions, were able effectively to manipulate the helpless citizens of an emergent "mass society." Like class theorists, Mills believed that the undemocratic structure of power was inimical to the interests of most Americans. Unlike most proponents of ruling class analysis, however, those of Mills' persuasion stressed elite domination rather than class conflict, emphasized the corresponding insensitivity of American society to disruption from below, and rejected the working class as an effective agent of social change. In short, power elitists often agreed with pluralists that the postwar period was dominated by consensus and a dearth of ideological passion. Yet pluralists commonly interpreted the consensus as a sign of social health, as an indication that common American values manned the barricades in defense of social order. Those finding a power elite, conversely, believed the deplorable gap between elite and mass had created this consensus by discouraging conflict and eviscerating democracy. Elite coordination and irresponsibility, they suggested, were more evident than the "competition" and "responsibility" commonly mentioned by pluralists. Such conclusions clearly evidenced a good deal of heroic honesty, but they also contained a strong admixture of radical pessimism that characterized a great deal of dissenting thought throughout the fifties.

During the sixties, however, a rebirth of dissent over such issues as civil rights, racism, poverty, militarism, and the integrity of American universities quickened the national pulse and helped to reorient critical social thought. Intellectuals, influenced by the rise of a "New Left," revived the venerable work of Marxist and Progressive intellectuals and, with varying degrees of ardor, again embraced the concept of class. These scholars commonly rejected the popular pluralist belief that the liberal state had been a just arbiter of business power and the proper guardian of a democratic polity. Some young historians argued that a new order of "corporate liberalism" or "political capitalism" had emerged, in which the state, the corporation, and other powerful groups worked together in the mutual service of American capitalism. This analysis owed more than a small debt to the thought of Mills (and Veblen), but it departed from the notion of a power elite by emphasizing the primacy of economic power in the new corporate liberal coalition. Unlike many static and unhistorical elite models, moreover, this new interpretation accounted for social change by adding the dynamic of class conflict and imperialism. Hence, some theoretical adepts argued that a corporate ruling class dominated both state and military policy, manufacturing a military-industrial complex at home and promoting imperialism abroad.

Other academic leftists, viewing society through the eyes of the powerless rather than the powerful, amended this basic analysis. The apparent militancy of previously inarticulate groups buoyed their radical spirit and caused them to resurrect old faiths by reintroducing creative and progressive conflict into the equation of power. Many of these young intellectuals also departed from the prevalent liberal (and socialist) assumption that centralization was inherently progressive. They called, instead, for the decentralization of power and the return of vital institutions — schools, welfare organizations, law enforcement agencies — to the control of localities and neighborhoods united by class or ethnic interests. The struggle for black power in the ghettoes and the battle over "maximum feasible participation" of the poor in America's poverty program are only two examples of this recent effort to democratize the structure of power through decentralization.

The bedeviling doubts planted in academic and popular minds by discovery of power elites and ruling classes denote, among other things, a potential crisis of liberal ideology. Clearly, liberal pluralism still commands vast amounts of disputed intellectual territory; yet the ranks of orthodoxy have thinned, and today its triumph may not be so inevitable as it once seemed. Certainly it is time, then, to reassess the tide of battle and to calculate the current balance between the warring legions of class, elite, and pluralist persuasions. Few issues, in fact, could be of greater importance, for from its outcome will follow profound implications for the survival of democracy in the United States.

The problem of power in postwar America defies all disciplinary confines and calls for the collective wisdom of scholars with many competences. The essays in this volume, accordingly, represent various disciplines centrally involved in the recent debate over power. In assessing this hybrid approach, it may help to recall the complementary potential of history and the social sciences.

More than a decade ago historian Richard Hofstadter envisioned the development of "a somewhat new historical genre, which will be a mixture of traditional history and the social sciences." Through intellectual cross-fertilization, Hofstadter argued, the social sciences might "open new problems which the historian has generally ignored," thereby increasing the "speculative richness" of his craft.[3] The problem at hand clearly confirms this pregnant suggestion. Disciples of Clio may, for example, pirate the abstract and general concept of power from the social sciences and invest it with historical significance by probing its unique qualities in a particular society during a specific period of time. While the social scientist examines power in cross-section, at a given time, the historian may pursue it longitudinally through time. What the historian lends to the social sciences in expanded perspective, on the other hand, the social scientist may repay to history in conceptual and methodological sophistication. These different emphases clearly reinforce rather than contradict one another, and each, in a different way, enriches our understanding of power in American society. In studying this important subject, therefore, the idolatry of narrow disciplines pays homage to false gods.

A commitment to cross-disciplinary perspectives, however, complicates scholarly niceties and plunges the initiate into bewildering analytical and conceptual difficulties. Such troubles begin with the idea of power itself. "There is," as two social scientists have observed, "an elusiveness about power that endows it with an almost ghostly quality. . . . We 'know' what it is, yet we encounter endless difficulties in trying to define it. We can 'tell' whether one person or group is more powerful than another, yet we cannot measure power. It is as abstract as time, yet as real as a firing squad."[4] Power, in short, has been extraordinarily difficult to define and to analyze. Hence, it is quite important to understand precisely what a scholar means by the word, since this vital problem of definition may condition an entire analysis.

Many scholars, following Max Weber, have defined power as "potential," as "the chance of a man or of a number of men to realize their own will in a communal action even against the resistance of others who are participating in the action."[5] This vague, but inclusive, notion of potentiality has driven analysts to use indirect measures of power and often prompted them to ask large questions about the relation between social factors, like class stratification, bureaucratization, or industrial development, and power. Others, like political scientist Robert Dahl, have conceived of power as "actual": "A has power over B to the extent

[3] Richard Hofstadter, "History and the Social Sciences," in Fritz Stern, ed., *The Varieties of History: From Voltaire to the Present* (New York: The World Publishing Company, 1956), p. 364.

[4] Herbert Kaufman and Victor Jones, "The Mystery of Power," *Public Administration Review*, XIV (Summer 1954), p. 205.

[5] Max Weber, "Class, Status, Party," in Hans Gerth and C. Wright Mills, eds., *From Max Weber: Essays in Sociology* (New York: Oxford University Press, 1946), p. 180.

that he can get B to do something that B would not otherwise do."[6] This narrower definition has enabled those who accept it to focus on the political process
and to ask empirical questions about specific decisions. This division over the
meaning of power seems frequently to coincide with disciplinary lines, for most
sociologists accept notions of potential, whereas political scientists usually view
power as actual. Further, there has been some tendency for sociologists, who
begin with society and ask how it affects the state, to locate power elites and
ruling classes. Political scientists, who begin with the state and ask how it affects
society, have tended, conversely, to discover pluralistic distributions of power.

Yet scholars also have differed sharply in their evaluative conceptualization of
power, and the resulting polarization has cut across all disciplinary lines. Some
accept a "scarcity" or "zero-sum" model: there is only a given amount of power in
any political system, such theorists contend, and an increase in the power of one
group can therefore occur only at the expense of another. According to this
interpretation, conflict, coercion, or domination necessarily follows from inequalities in power. Other academic investigators champion a "resource" model, stressing
consensus and the part necessarily played by power in any successful achievement
of common social goals. Frequently, proponents of class and power elite theories,
either overtly or covertly, assume a scarcity model and stress undemocratic components of the power structure. Those of pluralist persuasion seem a bit more
likely to accept power as a resource and to emphasize its benevolence. There
tends, in effect, to be a strong political as well as theoretical element in these
differences, since a resource interpretation of power is often, if not always, used
to defend existing political arrangements, and a scarcity model is most frequently
employed to attack them.

Beyond this, the student must avoid confusing power with related concepts
like "authority," and "prestige" or "status." Authority is often understood as
legitimate power, such as that held by an elected official whose right to rule is
generally accepted. In this sense, authority is a special case of power; all authority
involves power, but not all power is authority. Status or prestige involves the
subjective evaluation of an individual or group by others; terms like "honor,"
"esteem," and "respect" are synonyms. Power and status often exist in symbiotic
union, yet the two are not identical. One may have prestige but little power, like
the retired elder statesman; or one may have power but little prestige, like some
mobsters. Further, care should be taken to understand the peculiarities of important terms like "class" and "elite," which various scholars may define
differently.

Students can ask still other questions about the various interpretations of
power to be found in this volume. What, for example, is actually being studied?
Some researchers simply examine *reputations* for power, even though reputations
may reflect prestige or status rather than power itself. Other analysts assume that
group interests control human behavior; hence, they concentrate on the *composition* of power groups and examine the social backgrounds or career lines of
those who come to power. Some scholars, as we have seen, examine only decisions

[6]Robert A. Dahl, "The Concept of Power," *Behavioral Science*, 2 (July 1957), pp. 202–
203.

made within the rather narrow limits of the formal political process; yet this may, in fact, confuse authority and power. Do these various approaches fully explore the *source* of power, the *means* of exercising it, the *amount* held, and the *limits* to which it may be subject?[7]

For the sake of clarity, these intricate and subtle problems may be translated into broader questions about American society. Ultimately, the value of pluralist, ruling class, and power elite theories must be measured by their ability to provide persuasive answers to questions like these: Do the rulers of society constitute a social group, and may this group be called a class or an elite? Is this group cohesive or divided, open or closed? How are its members selected? Is ruling group power based upon class advantage, institutional position, technical competence, popular mandate, or other factors? Is the power of rulers primarily economic, political, or social, and in what ways is this power restricted? Do rulers generally serve the interests of particular social groups and ignore those of others? How are decisions made? Does the character of ruling groups vary with time, and, if so, what are the dynamics of change? Such questions, though obviously not exhaustive, may help students to negotiate the formidable methodological and conceptual morass that blocks easy access to the mysteries of power.

Finally, the spirited debate between scholars with divergent points of view may pose an unhappy dilemma for those who demand an undisputed verdict. Many analyses of the American power structure, for example, are necessarily theoretical and often must rely as much on logical consistency as on empirical evidence. Thus, pluralist Robert Dahl has complained that some ruling group theories are virtually impossible to prove or to disprove.[8] If a pluralist finds that many groups have participated in a decision, his opponents can reply that dominant groups actually operated behind the scene, out of the public eye. In addition, class or elite theorists might claim that the truly powerful simply were not interested in the decision under examination and that the power potential of strategic classes or elites therefore remained inviolate. These analysts might add that the vital interests of the most powerful, established groups are consistently served by the existing political system, regardless of who participates in the decision-making process.

Even if empirical evidence could settle such disputes, we often do not have the necessary data about important decisions and the complex factors influencing them. This is especially true for the period since 1945, of primary interest here, because much documentation about domestic and foreign policy decisions is not open to public examination. Thus, it has been impossible for elite theorists fully to prove charges of overt elite coordination on specific decisions, whereas class analysts find it equally difficult to demonstrate conclusively that the concern for corporate interests has driven America's men of power to pursue certain opprobrious policies. Even pluralists, whose model of power is more easily verified empirically than those of class and elite theorists, cannot thoroughly document their case. Absolute confirmation would require pluralists adequately to define a

---

[7] Cf. *ibid.*, pp. 206 ff.

[8] Dahl's charges are made in his important article, "A Critique of the Ruling Elite Model," *American Political Science Review*, 52 (June 1958), pp. 463–469.

"major" decision and to consider each of these decisions as it related to every significant group and to every individual in American society. Much of the evidence necessary to such an undertaking is not available; and, even if it were, scholarly energies might not be equal to the formidable task of analysis.

It is unlikely, moreover, that even the fullest data could confirm the divergent assumptions about class consciousness, interest, and motive used by all interpreters of power to link the objective, empirical world with subjective imponderables of the human mind. Further, those who view power as potential are necessarily limited to indirect studies requiring many inferences to which devoted skeptics may always take exception. Facing such difficulties, it seems safe to conclude only that these disjunctions between theory and evidence will fuel the impassioned conflict between contending scholars for some time to come.

Since I have prefaced each essay in this volume with a short critical introduction, I shall here merely outline the general format and mention a few major themes. The first two selections deal primarily, if not exclusively, with community rather than national power and represent two divergent schools of community analysis. Floyd Hunter locates a "pyramid" of concentrated power, whereas Robert Dahl finds a pluralism of competing groups. These essays do not, of course, deal with every issue of fact and interpretation raised by the hundreds of other community studies published since World War II. Notably, the selections touch only indirectly upon the contemporary polemic over decentralization — a debate that, indeed, has not yet been examined in a scholarly and systematic fashion. The essays by Hunter and Dahl do, however, provide challenging introductions to the general problem of community power. In addition, they demonstrate some of the methodological and conceptual sophistications dividing scholars of different intellectual convictions.

Yet triumphs of theoretical synthesis do not readily follow from such studies involving single communities of different sizes, regional locations, ethnic compositions, economic structures, and historical backgrounds. Further, it is virtually impossible to generalize from the local to the national level of power. Even if elites or ruling classes do control the majority of American communities, for example, pluralism might still inform the distribution of national power. By the same token, local pluralism might coexist with elite or class rule at the national level. It may be, as C. Wright Mills has argued, that the local societies studied by community power theorists are simply "satellites of status and class and power systems that extend beyond their local horizon." Perhaps no community, whether controlled by classes, elites, or pluralistic groups, is truly autonomous; perhaps the "kinds of relations that exist between the countryside and the town, the town and the big city, and between the various big cities, form a structure that is now national in scope."[9] The authors of the essays and documents in the section on national power examine these possibilities.

The studies by David Riesman, Paul Sweezy, and C. Wright Mills establish the general form of the debate among pluralists, class theorists, and elitists. Ries-

[9] C. Wright Mills, *The Power Elite* (New York: Oxford University Press, 1956), pp. 45–46.

man ties his belief in a changed American character to the contention that power in America has moved, accordingly, from a ruling class to a plethora of veto groups, which are the handmaidens of pluralist democracy. Marxist Sweezy's simple, yet lucid theory of the ruling class is remarkably free of the vulgar economic determinism often associated with American Marxism. Mills' concept of the power elite requires little further comment; it is one of the most vital and provocative theories of the postwar period and has profoundly affected intellectuals, both in this country and abroad.

The following three essays either criticize or modify these primary theories. Talcott Parsons mounts a sustained, often effective attack upon Mills' book *The Power Elite*. He presents the case for a resource view of power and assails many specific interpretations resulting from the zero-sum model allegedly implicit in Mills' work. Psychologist G. William Domhoff, on the contrary, concludes that there is a power elite, but that it is grounded in an upper class. In the next essay, sociologist Arnold Rose contends that his "multi-influence hypothesis" is more realistic than the interpretations of scholars like Mills and Hunter.

The next several selections relate to the problem of corporate power. The first document is taken from testimony delivered in 1964 before the Subcommittee on Antitrust and Monopoly of the Senate Judiciary Committee. The data presented by government expert Willard F. Mueller, accompanied by Stanley E. Boyle (both of the Bureau of Economics, Federal Trade Commission) indicates that concentration in American manufacturing has substantially increased since World War II. In the subsequent essay, economist Walter Adams raises many questions about the concept of countervailing power. Finally, Morton Baratz suggests that we may have entered a period of "super-oligopoly" when the very existence of giant firms subtly influences many public decisions.

During recent years, few pronouncements by a public figure have received the attention accorded President Dwight D. Eisenhower's warning about the military-industrial complex. This cautionary proclamation is reprinted from Eisenhower's Farewell Address, delivered on January 17, 1961. The following analysis of defense contractors by Senator William Proxmire comes from the *Congressional Record*, March 24, 1969. The senator's data suggest that retired military officers are substantially involved in defense industry and that this involvement greatly increased during the sixties. In a bold challenge to prevailing orthodoxy, historian Gabriel Kolko next argues that the military may have lost rather than gained influence since World War II. In Kolko's eyes, business and not the military itself is "both a fount and magnet for the Military Establishment."

In the concluding essay, philosopher Robert Paul Wolff considers some ideological implications of pluralist theory. He demonstrates in his analysis that ideology can, indeed, be an effective agent of social control and, hence, of power. This is an appropriate closing selection, for it reminds us that the enduring warfare between scholars of elitist, class, and pluralist persuasions is in part an ideological conflict that, itself, is associated with the struggle for power.

Community Power

PYRAMID OF POWER
OR LOCAL PLURALISM?

Sociologist *Floyd Hunter's Book,* Community Power Structure: A Study of Decision Makers, *the source of the following selection, is among the most influential recent interpretations of community power. Even today, many scholars are concerned with proving or disproving the general conclusions set forth in Hunter's study of "Regional City" (Atlanta, Georgia).*

In his introduction, not reprinted here, Hunter makes a number of important assumptions about the nature of power, and these profoundly affect his subsequent analysis. He suggests, for example, that power is basically a social phenomenon involving relationships between individuals and groups. Effective power always assumes "associational, clique, or institutional patterns." Hunter implies, moreover, that a power structure exists in all communities and that it can always be located by the diligent researcher.

Like class analysts, Hunter generally emphasizes the economic origins of power. Like elitists, however, he uses terms like "cliques" and "crowds" to define powerful groups and neglects further to develop any articulate theory of economic causation. Still, Hunter does find that those who are economically powerful tend also to be politically powerful, thus indicating that pluralistic mechanisms of balance and equilibrium are relatively ineffective in Regional City. Hunter goes beyond even some advocates of class and elite theory by stressing that influential coteries intentionally use their power to initiate specific policies. In this sense, he explores the actual rather than the potential dimensions of community power and at times suggests the existence of powerful "conspiracies" detrimental to the public interest.

13

Hunter's reputational method enabled him to locate power simply by polling members of a presumably neutral panel of judges who selected the forty most powerful men in Regional City. This methodological breakthrough allowed researchers to probe the intricacies of community power without resort to the costly and time-consuming field work previously done in cities like "Middletown" and "Yankee City." Although this simplified method inspired a cavalcade of emulators, it also called forth its share of critics. Indeed, those dissatisfied with Hunter's findings have tended to attack his conclusions by way of his methodology.

Political scientists — led by Robert Dahl and his students Raymond Wolfinger and Nelson Polsby — have been especially vocal dissenters. They observe that Hunter, in fact, did not study power but merely reputations for power and that such reputations might actually be a better index of status than of power. Many scholars also charged that Hunter was guilty of other intellectual infelicities. By selecting only forty men as his leadership group and by asking leading questions about the structure of power, Hunter may have assumed what he set out to prove — that a definable group of leaders made the most important decisions in Regional City. Critics also asked if Hunter was justified in assuming that a power structure had to exist in all communities. A better assumption, concluded pluralists like Nelson Polsby, was "that at bottom nobody dominates in a town." ("How to Study Community Power: The Pluralist Alternative," Journal of Politics, 22 [August 1960], p. 476.) Raymond Wolfinger, in his essay, "Reputation and Reality in the Study of 'Community Power'," American Sociological Review, 25 (October 1960), pp. 636–644, has raised similar objections to Hunter's work.

Many of these critics believe that Community Power Structure unjustly focuses on only one of many powerful elites. Pluralists also disagree with Hunter's discovery of substantial overlap between political and economic power. On the contrary, they argue, different issues are usually decided by different elites. Polsby, for example, notes that in New Haven there was no significant overlap between economic and status elites. ("Three Problems in the Analysis of Community Power," American Journal of Sociology, 24 [December 1959], pp. 796–803.) Finally, Hunter may simply assert rather than prove that economic interest always unifies the elite and gives predictable content to their political decisions. If he had examined differences of opinion within the elite, critics contend, Hunter would have found that interest divides as well as unifies. It is possible, then, that Hunter imposes coherence on an economic elite where little exists and, hence, that his notion of cliques or crowds is not very helpful or meaningful.

Despite such compelling criticisms, Hunter's work cannot be lightly dismissed. Many distinguished scholars still defend his conclusions, and few would dispute Hunter's right to be called the father of modern community power analysis. In assessing this important analysis, the student may wish to consult another study by Hunter, Top Leadership, U.S.A. (Chapel Hill: University of North Carolina Press, 1959) and a more recent study of

Atlanta by *M. Kent Jennings*, Community Influentials: The Elites of Atlanta (New York: The Free Press of Glencoe, 1964).

FLOYD HUNTER
The Structure of Power
in Regional City

The personnel with which the current discussion is concerned represents but a minute fraction of the community in which it moves and functions. It does represent a definite group, however, and a very important one in Regional City. No pretense is made that the group to be discussed represents the totality of power leaders of the community, but it is felt that a representative case sample is presented, and that the men described come well within the range of the center of power in the community. . . .

. . . The leaders selected for study were secured from lists of leading civic, professional, and fraternal organizations, governmental personnel, business leaders, and "society" and "wealth" personnel suggested by various sources. These lists of more than 175 persons were rated by "judges" who selected by mutual choice the top forty persons in the total listings. These forty were the object of study and investigation in Regional City. Some data were collected about the total number. Twenty-seven members of the group were interviewed on the basis of a prepared schedule plus additional questions as the investigation proceeded. Any figures used in the study will need to be tied fairly rigidly to the twenty-seven members on whom there are comparable data. . . .

The system of power groups which is being examined may not be called a closed system. The groups are links in a total pattern, which may offer suggestive clues to total power patterns in the operating system of Regional City. There are gaps in the power arc which investigation may not be able to close. Actually the discussion here is primarily concerned with the structuring of power on a policy-making level. Only a rudimentary "power pyramid" of Regional City will be presented. One may be content to do this because I doubt seriously that power forms a single pyramid with any nicety in a community the size of Regional City. There are *pyramids* of power in this community which seem more important to the present discussion than *a* pyramid. . . .

. . . The "men of independent decision" are a relatively small group. The

From Floyd Hunter, *Community Power Structure: A Study of Decision Makers* (Chapel Hill, N.C.: University of North Carolina Press, 1953), pp. 61–113 (with deletions) by permission of the University of North Carolina Press.

"executors of policy" may run into the hundreds. This pattern of a relatively small decision-making group working through a larger under-structure is a reality, and if data were available, the total personnel involved in a major community project might possibly form a pyramid of power, but the constituency of the pyramid would change according to the project being acted upon.

In other words, the personnel of the pyramid would change depending upon what needs to be done at a particular time. Ten men might, for example, decide to bring a new industry into the community. Getting the industry physically established and operating might take the disciplined and coordinated action of a few more men or several hundred men, depending on the size of the project. Some of the same decision men in another instance might be involved in starting a program for some local governmental change, but another group of men would be involved in carrying out the decisions reached. Both projects are power orientated, but each requires different personnel in the execution. The men in the under-structure may have a multiplicity of individual roles within the totality of the community structure which can be set in motion by the men of decision.

As I became familiar with the list of forty names through the interviewing process, it became evident that certain men, even within the relatively narrow range of decision leaders with whom I was dealing, represented a top layer of personnel. Certain men were chosen more frequently than others, not only in relation to who should be chosen to decide on a project, as has already been indicated, but the same men interacted together on committees and were on the whole better known to each other than to those outside this group. . . . There is an *esprit de corps* among certain top leaders, and some of them may be said to operate on a very high level of decision in the community; but this will not necessarily mean that one of the top leaders can be considered subordinate to any other in the community as a whole. On specific projects one leader may allow another to carry the ball, as a leader is said to do when he is "out front" on a project which interests him. On the next community-wide project another may carry the ball. Each may subordinate himself to another on a temporary basis, but such a structure of subordination is quite fluid, and it is voluntary. . . .

. . . Power has been defined in terms of policy leadership, and the data given in the present chapter make a beginning at defining structural power relations. A group of men have been isolated who are among the most powerful in Regional City. It has been shown that they interact among themselves on community projects and select one another as leaders. Their relations with one another are not encompassed in a true pyramid of power, but some degree of ranking, even in the top-level policy leadership group, has been indicated. Let us now look at policy personnel patterns in another way.

In sizing up any individual one often asks, "What do you do for a living?" The reply to this question allows one rather quickly to rank another in a rough scale of social values. The men under discussion hold commercial, industrial, financial, and professional positions in Regional City that tend to classify them in the minds of any observer. In order to make a beginning at seeing the relations among the men of power in more personal terms than statistics will allow, let us examine a list of positions held by some of the leaders of the policy-determining group in Regional City (Table 1).

TABLE 1

Policy-making leaders in Regional City, by occupational position

Type of Occupation	Name of Leader	Name of organizational affiliation	Position
Banking, finance, insurance	Hardy	Investment Company of Old State	President
	Mines	Producer's Investments	President
	Schmidt	First Bank	President
	Simpson	Second Bank	Vice-President
	Spade	Growers Bank	President
	Tarbell	Commercial Bank	Executive Vice-President
	Trable	Regional City Life	President
Commercial	Aiken	Livestock Company	Chairman, Board
	Black	Realty Company of Regional City	President
	Delbert	Allied Utilities	President
	Dunham	Regional Gas Heat Company	General Manager
	Graves	Refrigeration, Incorporated	President
	Parker	Mercantile Company	Executive Manager
	Parks	Paper Box Company	Chairman, Board
	Smith	Cotton Cloth Company	Manager
	C. Stokes	Oil Pipe Line Company	President
	Webster	Regional City Publishing Company	Managing Editor
	Williams	Mercantile Company	Chairman, Board
Government	Barner	City Government	Mayor
	Gordon	City Schools	Superintendent
	Rake	County Schools	Superintendent
	Worth	County Government	Treasurer
Labor	Gregory	Local Union	President
	Stone	Local Union	President
Leisure	Fairly	None	Social Leader
	Howe	None	Social Leader
	Mills	None	Social Leader
	Moore	None	Social Leader
	Stevens	None	Social Leader
Manufacture and industry	Farris	Steel Spool Company	Chairman, Board
	Homer	Homer Chemical Company	Chairman, Board
	Spear	Homer Chemical Company	President
	E. Stokes	Stokes Gear Company	Chairman, Board
	Treat	Southern Yarn Company	President
Professional[a]	Farmer	Law Firm	Attorney
	Gould	Law Firm	Attorney
	Latham	Private Office	Dentist
	Moster	Law Firm	Attorney
	Street	Law Firm	Attorney
	Tidwell	Law Firm	Attorney

[a] *Attorneys' affiliations not given. Without exception they are corporation lawyers.*

It can be seen at a glance that most of the leaders hold positions as presidents of companies, chairmen of boards, or professional positions of some prestige. Generally speaking, the companies represented in the listing are of major enterprise proportions. More than half the men may be said to be businessmen, if the term is used broadly. The major economic interests of the community are overwhelmingly represented in the listing. The pattern of business dominance of civic affairs in Regional City is a fact. No other institution is as dominant in community life as the economic institution. . . .

Figure 1 represents those leaders who are related to one another as directors on boards of corporate enterprises in Regional City. The figure is intended to show that the economic interests of the leaders are in some measure coordinate. Again, one cannot rely too heavily upon a schematic diagram to understand the interrelations of leadership patterns, but such configurations as have been shown cumulatively tend to lend credence to the fact that there are structural relations among the members of the leadership group. All interviews with leaders helped to fill in some of the structural gaps. The sources of data for this figure give only

FIGURE 1

Interlocking Directorates of Corporate
Leaders in Regional City · · ·

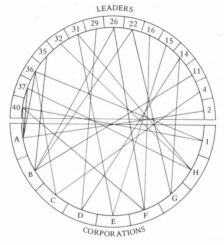

Code numbers used in analyzing data and corresponding to fictional
names of leaders are as follows:

1. Latham	14. Delbert	28. Mills
2. Graves	15. Farris	29. Spade
3. Dunham	16. Stevens	30. Gregory
4. Mines	17. Trable	31. Parker
5. Smith	18. Schmidt	32. Williams
6. Fairly	19. Moore	33. Black
7. Webster	20. Farmer	34. Tidwell
8. Worth	21. Barner	35. Tarbell
9. C. Strokes	22. Parks	36. Moster
10. Stone	23. Gould	37. Treat
11. Simpson	24. E. Stokes	38. Street
12. Aiken	25. Gordon	39. Rake
13. Howe	26. Spear	40. Homer
	27. Hardy	

a partial sample of existing corporate board relationships. Comparable data could be obtained only from fifteen out of the total leadership group of forty.

One of the first interviews had in Regional City was with James Treat of the Southern Yarn Company. He gave a great deal of information concerning power relations in the community. Among other things, he supplied a clue to certain existing clique relationships and considerable information about them which was later verified. Several times in his conversation he had used the term "crowds" in describing how certain men acted in relation to each other on community projects, and he was asked to explain the term. His reply ran in this vein:

"I simply mean that there are 'crowds' in Regional City — several of them — that pretty well make the big decisions. There is the crowd I belong to (the Homer Chemical crowd); then there is the First State Bank crowd — the Regional Gas Heat crowd — the Mercantile crowd — the Growers Bank crowd — and the like."

Mr. Treat was asked to give the names of some of the men who were active in each crowd, and he said:

"Sure! The biggest man in our crowd is Charles Homer. I belong to his crowd along with John Webster, Bert Tidwell, Ray Moster, Harold Jones, James Finer, Larry Stroup, and Harold Farmer. There are others, but they would be on the edges of this crowd. These would be the ones to be brought in on anything.

"In the State Bank crowd there would be Herman Schmidt, Harvey Aiken, Mark Parks, and Joseph Hardy. Schmidt used to be the biggest man in that crowd, but young Hardy is coming up fast over there.

"In the Regional Gas Heat crowd there is Fargo Dunham, Elsworth Mines, Gilbert Smith, and Percy Latham maybe. George Delbert might be said to belong to that crowd, but he is a pretty independent fellow. He moves around [from crowd to crowd] quite a bit.

"The Mercantile crowd is made up of Harry Parker, Jack Williams, Luke Street, Adam Graves, Cary Stokes, and Epworth Simpson.

"The Growers Bank crowd would be Ralph Spade, Arthur Tarbell, and Edward Stokes. They are kind of a weak outfit, but they come in on a lot of things. Spade is probably the most aggressive of the lot, but he's not too much at that!"

With this information given, Mr. Treat was asked to tell how these crowds would operate in relation to one another on a community-wide project, and he outlined the procedure very clearly. This type of action will be given in fuller detail in connection with the techniques of power wielding, but it may be said here that representatives from each crowd are drawn into any discussion relative to a major community decision. Each man mentioned as belonging to a crowd also belongs to a major business enterprise within the community — at least the clique leader does. His position within the bureaucratic structure of his business almost automatically makes him a community leader, if he wishes to become one. The test for admission to this circle of decision-makers is almost wholly a man's position in the business community in Regional City. The larger business enterprises represent pyramids of power in their own right, as work units within the community, and the leaders within these concerns gather around them some of the top personnel within their own organization. They then augment this nucleus of leadership by a coterie of selected friends from other establishments to form knots of interest called "crowds" by Mr. Treat. The outer edges of any crowd may pick up such men as Percy Latham, the dentist, who in turn picks up others in relation to any specific activity in which the crowd may be interested. The top men in any crowd tend to act together, and they depend upon men below them to serve as intermediaries in relation to the general community. . . .

.   .   .

The point made at this turn of the discussion is not a new one. Businessmen are the community leaders in Regional City as they are in other cities. Wealth, social prestige, and political machinery are functional to the wielding of power by the business leaders in the community. William E. Henry puts the matter this way:

> The business executive is the central figure in the economic and social life of the United States. His direction of business enterprise and his participation in informal social groupings give him a significant place in community life. In both its economic and its social aspects the role of the business executive is sociologically a highly visible one.[1]

The "visibility" suggested by Henry is a highly applicable concept in connection with an analysis of Regional City leadership. One need not labor the point. This study has already shown that business leaders take a prominent position in Regional City civic affairs.

In the general social structure of community life social scientists are prone to look upon the institutions and formal associations as powerful forces, and it is easy to be in basic agreement with this view. Most institutions and associations are subordinate, however, to the interests of the policy-makers who operate in the economic sphere of community life in Regional City. The institutions of the family, church, state, education, and the like draw sustenance from economic institutional sources and are thereby subordinate to this particular institution more than any other. The associations stand in the same relationship to the economic interests as do the institutions. We see both the institutions and the formal associations playing a vital role in the execution of determined policy, but the formulation of policy often takes place outside these formalized groupings. Within the policy-forming groups the economic interests are dominant. . . .

.   .   .

If a project of major proportions were before the community for consideration — let us say a project aimed at building a new municipal auditorium — a policy committee would be formed. This may be called Project Committee A. Such a policy committee would more than likely grow out of a series of informal meetings, and it might be related to a project that has been on the discussion agenda of many associations for months or even years. But the time has arrived for action. Money must be raised through private subscription or taxation, a site selected, and contracts let. The time for a policy committee is propitious. The selection of the policy committee will fall largely to the men of power in

---

[1] "The Business Executive: The Psycho-Dynamics of a Social Role," *American Journal of Sociology*, LIV (January 1949), 286.

the community. They will likely be businessmen in one or more of the larger business establishments. Mutual choices will be agreed upon for committee membership. In the early stages of policy formulation there will be a few men who make the basic decisions. As the project is trimmed, pared, and shaped into manageable proportions there will be a recognition that the committee should be enlarged. Top-ranking organization and institutional personnel will then be selected by the original members to augment their numbers, i.e., the committee will be expanded. The civic associations and the formalized institutions will next be drawn into certain phases of planning and initiation of the project on a community-wide basis. The newspapers will finally carry stories of the proposals, the ministers will preach sermons, and the associational members will hear speeches regarding plans. This rather simply is the process, familiar to many, that goes on in getting any community project under way.

Project B might be related to changing the tax structure of the community. Much the same organizational procedure will be repeated, but different associations may be drawn into the planning and execution stages. The policy-making personnel will tend to be much the same as in Project A and this is an important point in the present discussion. There will be a hard core of policy leadership on Policy Committee B that was also present on Project Committee A. This relative stability of the top policy-making group is a pattern quite apparent in Regional City civic affairs. A similar pattern of stable committee membership exists in the under-structure of the associational and corporate bureaucracies in the community which interact in a chain of command with the top power leaders on given projects.

It must be stressed that the same policy leaders do not interact repeatedly with the same under-structure personnel in getting projects put over. The interaction is based entirely upon a given project that is under consideration at a given time. The under-structure personnel may be likened to a keyboard over which the top structure personnel play, and the particular keys struck may vary from project to project. The players remain the same or nearly so, however.

A variation in the pattern of structuring a top-decision committee may be found in those policy committees in which the decision is made by individuals who are not to be out front on the project. In other words, the men of policy may wish to remain anonymous in relation to the action phases of the program in question. In such cases, the policy group remains informally intact, and "second-rate" or "third-rate" men are advertised as the sponsors of the particular project. This pattern may occur when a project is somewhat questionable as to its success. The policy-forming group is just as real, however, as if it were named publicly. The men upon whom falls the burden of carrying the project into its action stages are well aware of the persons who chose them.

Projects that are not originated in the policy-determining group are often allowed to proceed with a tentative blessing of a few of the men of decision if their interests and dominant values are not threatened by the proposed activity. If such a project goes sour, the men of decision cannot be blamed. This is another variation of structure and represents a real behavioral pattern in civic affairs in Regional City. . . .

.   .   .

In one of our postulates it is stated that, "Power is structured socially, in the United States, into a dual relationship between governmental and economic authorities on national, state, and local levels." In the light of the present analysis, there is less of a "dual" relationship than had been assumed. This is particularly true in Regional City, where the dominant factor in political life is the personnel of the economic interests. It is true that there is no formal tie between the economic interests and government, but the structure of policy-determining committees and their tie-in with the other powerful institutions and organizations of the community make government subservient to the interests of these combined groups. The governmental departments and their personnel are acutely aware of the power of key individuals and combinations of citizens' groups in the policy-making realm, and they are loathe to act before consulting and "clearing" with these interests.

[Robert] Brady is enlightening on this point when he says that the same interests tend to dominate politics and business, particularly in the realm of policy. "The same individuals, the same groups and cliques, [and] the same interests dominate each sphere [of property and politics]," he says.[2] One is compelled to agree with him from observations of the two groups in Regional City. There is evidence, too, that the local economic interests tie into larger groupings of like interests on the state and national levels which tend to overshadow the policymaking machinery of government at all levels. The structure is that of a dominant policy-making group using the machinery of government as a bureaucracy for the attainment of certain goals coordinate with the interests of the policy-forming group. . . .

. . . The leaders of Regional City tend to protect themselves from too many demands by channeling policy execution through an under-structure on matters of policy. This under-structure is not a rigid bureaucracy, as has been pointed out, but is a flexible system. It has elements of stability and tends to operate by levels. The men at each level are spoken of as first, second, third and fourth rate by the power leaders, who operate primarily in conjunction with individuals of the first two ratings. The types of personnel which may be found in each rating by a sample classification are as follows:

> *Example of Personnel from First*
> *to Fourth Rate in Regional City*

First rate: Industrial, commercial, financial owners and top executives of large enterprises.

Second rate: Operations officials, bank vice-presidents, public-relations men, small businessmen (owners), top-ranking public officials, corporation attorneys, contractors.

Third rate: Civic organization personnel, civic agency board personnel, newspaper columnists, radio commentators, petty public officials, selected organization executives.

Fourth rate: Professionals such as ministers, teachers, social workers, personnel

[2] R. A. Brady, *Business as a System of Power* (New York: Columbia University Press, 1938), p. 314.

directors, and such persons as small business managers, higher paid accountants, and the like.

These ratings might be expanded. They are given simply to indicate a suggested ranking of selected personnel who operate below the policy-making leaders in Regional City. The first two ratings are personnel who are said to "set the line of policy," while the latter two groups "hold the line." The ratings are very real to the under-structure professional personnel. One of these men said: "I know that the top boys get together on things. This community is divided into tiers. You can't get the first-tier men to work on anything originating in the second- and third-tier level. The top ones may put their names on second- and third-tier projects, but you cannot get them to work with you. They will not attend your meetings, but you know they are attending their own meetings all the time." The top leaders are conserving their time and energies for the primary role they play — policy-determination. They are also interested in holding a balance of power in the community. . . .

.   .   .

The top group of the power hierarchy has been isolated and defined as comprised of policy-makers. These men are drawn largely from the businessmen's class in Regional City. They form cliques or crowds, as the term is more often used in the community, which formulate policy. Committees for formulation of policy are commonplace, and on community-wide issues policy is channeled by a "fluid committee structure" down to institutional, associational groupings through a lower-level bureaucracy which executes policy.

Many of Floyd Hunter's early critics, as one social scientist has sardonically observed, were "apparently uninhibited by experience in systematic community power structure research." Recently, however, dissenting scholars finally began to base their critique of Hunter upon such systematic, empirical study. Robert Dahl's impressive work on New Haven, Connecticut, Who Governs? Democracy and Power in An American City (New Haven: Yale University Press, 1961), has been the most influential of these revisionist studies, and today his conclusions seem to command allegiance from most American community analysts.

In this essay, based primarily on the case of New Haven, Dahl develops a pluralist theory of "dispersed inequalities" in an effort to reconcile the unequal distribution of power with equalitarian, democratic ideals. Dahl concludes, unlike Floyd Hunter, that different groups or elites are active in different areas and that influence, therefore, is widely dispersed. In addition, he argues that groups with few power resources can compensate for this disability in several different ways. Many of these interpretive divergences between Dahl and Hunter follow from more basic differences in methodology and ideology, which the student must carefully assess.

Hunter, for example, studies reputations for power, whereas Dahl is concerned with specific decisions. Hunter believes that power structures are present in all communities; Dahl, like Nelson Polsby, rejects this notion. Hunter concentrates on social and economic power, but Dahl emphasizes political power. Hunter describes only the contemporary power structure of Regional City; Dahl studies the historical development of New Haven, and demonstrates the shift from cumulative to dispersed inequalities. Hunter measures the structure of power in Regional City against the ideal standards of participatory democracy. Dahl uses the more pragmatic and elitist standards of theorists like Locke and Tocqueville, contending that elite "competition" prevents domination by an oligarchic minority.

Dahl's conclusions about New Haven perhaps balance those of Hunter about Regional City, yet the pluralist alternative may itself be challenged on a number of grounds. Dahl, for example, focuses primarily upon the governmental process. This emphasis tends to confuse authority, which is legitimately and openly exercised, with the larger phenomenon of power, which may be illegitimate and covert. Dahl also overlooks what E. E. Schattschneider has called "the mobilization of bias," the fact that "all forms of political organizations have a bias in favor of the exploitation of some kinds of conflict and the suppression of others. . . ." (E. E. Schattschneider, The Semi-Sovereign People [New York: Holt, Rinehart, Winston, 1960].) In addition, Dahl studies power only when it surfaces in open conflict between groups disputing specific issues. He does not consider instances when power is absolute and there is no open conflict; nor does he consider "nondecisions," the process of exercising power by confining the scope of decision-making to "safe" issues. (These inadequacies are discussed by Peter Bachrach and Morton Baratz in two perceptive articles: "Two Faces of Power," The American Political Science Review, LVI [December, 1962], pp. 947–952, and "Decisions and Nondecisions: An Analytical Framework," ibid., LVII [September 1963], pp. 632–642.) Dahl's theory also neglects those powerless citizens not belonging to legitimate pluralist groups. Further, factors like bureaucratization and non-responsible elite leadership may block the political consciousness of those who do belong to legitimate pluralist groups, leading to apathy and despair.

Significantly, Dahl's work is distinguished by attention to the leaders rather than the led. As a result, he may not give adequate attention to the discontents seething within the body politic. The five-day outbreak of civil disorder that swept New Haven's Negro community in August 1967, for example, suggests misjudgments in Dahl's optimistic discussion of that community's black citizens. The current increase in such demonstrations of popular frustration may, in fact, give us less reason for sanguineness today than existed during the fifties when Dahl first studied New Haven.

ROBERT A. DAHL

Power in New Haven:

The Pluralist Thesis

Now consider the charge that power rests with a small inner circle of leaders who operate *outside* of the official governing bodies. Fear, pessimism, and silence, it is said, dominate the community's social climate; this is certainly not true of any community that I ever lived in. Many critics of the American community expect that there *must* be a monolithic structure of some kind, a monolithic structure run either by "good guys" or by "bad guys." Consequently, when one discovers that the local community is in pretty bad shape, which it is, then the only inference that one can make is that it is run by the evil elements. Now if you look for a monolithic structure in any community, or in any human organization, and if you look only at the evidence that suggests a monolith, then you will almost certainly find a monolith. Yet despite countless variations, I don't think that the typical American community *is* a monolithic but rather a pluralistic system. We need to learn how to recognize, how to analyze, and how to work with pluralistic systems. I would contend that in most American communities there isn't a single center of power. There is even a sense in which *nobody* runs the community. In fact, perhaps this is the most distressing discovery of all: typically a community is run by many different people, in many different ways, at many different times.

Next, I doubt very much whether businessmen "dominate" community policies, except perhaps by definition. What policies? Fund-raising? If one means fund-raising, then this is so. New Haven, like most communities, has a community fund drive that is carried on mainly by young businessmen who are looking for a chance to make a mark as go-getters and to pick up some recognition and prestige. But what about public schools? Have these been dominated by businessmen? In New Haven they are "dominated" by other groups. What about police? What about the welfare programs themselves, that is, the decisions about what's done with the money raised by the businessmen or by taxes? In my community these welfare groups are dominated by the professionals, who make decisions mainly by lobbying with one another on a council of social agencies. What can be said about charter reform? There have been businessmen in communities all over the United States, who year after year have tried to change the

From "Equality and Power in American Society," in *Power and Democracy in America*, William V. D'Antonio and Howard J. Ehrlich, eds. Reprinted by permission of University of Notre Dame Press. Copyright 1961.

city charter; one would suppose that if they were a dominant elite, by now they would have achieved the kind of charter they want. But for the most part, I think, cities tend to have the kinds of charters that politicians want. What of urban redevelopment? If there is anything in the community in which business-men are involved it is urban redevelopment. Yet by and large the businessmen do not even "dominate" urban redevelopment. It is the strong executive, Mayor Dilworth or Mayor Lee, who provides the leadership on redevelopment. . . . [Further,] a *reputation* for power is not necessarily a valid index of power. An alternative way to determine who "runs things" is to study a series of concrete decisions in order to find out who specifically dominates those decisions. If this is done, you may or may not find a correlation with reputations. In talking with a good many businessmen in New Haven I have found that even with respect to decisions in which they have participated, often they are extremely vague as to what actually transpired.

Moreover, no proposition about power or influence has much meaning unless one specifies power or influence with respect to something: power over public schools, over fund-raising, over redevelopment, over the local police, in the courts, or what? If these different sectors are specified, probably in many communities people who are influential with respect to one sector are not terribly influential with respect to another; and individuals influential in one sector may come out of different socioeconomic strata from those who are influential in another. Fi-nally, I should like to suggest a simple test. We know from public opinion polls and other research that large businessmen, in the main, are Republicans and that they are very anxious for Republican candidates to win. Now if they are the *dominant* power in a community, it should follow, I should think, that they would be able to win elections. If they can't, then I don't know what the word *dominant* means. Therefore, one test is to see what happens in the presidential elections. Which candidate will carry the cities — that is, the communities where businessmen are said to be "dominant"? I should think that if business-men are "the dominant power institution in the United States" then the election is already foreclosed. Yet we know that the 106 cities with populations over 100,000 have been the stronghold of the Democratic Party. In 1936, Franklin Roosevelt carried 104 out of these 106 cities — in 1940, 97. . . . Did business-men *want* Roosevelt to win? If not, and if they *dominate* these communities, why can't they win in a really critical trial of strength such as the elections of 1936 and 1940 surely were? Do candidates backed by business regularly win elections for mayor? Do business proposals regularly win on referenda? If not, how can we conclude that businessmen "dominate"? . . .

. . . Let me turn now to another interpretation of certain problems of Ameri-can communities — problems created by their failure to measure up to the exacting demands of democratic ideals.

My emphasis, however, will be on *appraisal* rather than on description or ex-planation. What I want to evaluate are the distribution and patterns of influence over political decisions in American life. I shall lean heavily on New Haven for information on the distribution and patterns of influence, but I do so in the belief that New Haven is similar to many other communities and strikingly similar in many ways to the United States as a whole. Where there are differences, I shall try to take these into account.

To appraise, one needs standards of appraisal, criteria of performance, values. Many different criteria are relevant to the task of arriving at an appraisal of the distribution and patterns of influence. I propose, however, to concern myself with only one, the criterion of political equality. Obviously, other criteria might also be invoked. I will not attempt here to justify my choice of equality, except to say that it is a value that has always been a salient aspect of democratic beliefs.

When one examines a political decision — that is, a decision determining the policies enforced by governmental officials — or what persons become officials — one usually finds that for any particular sector of policy only a small number of persons ever initiate alternatives or veto the proposals of others. These individuals are leaders or policy-makers. One may say that they have the greatest *direct* influence on decisions. A larger number of persons, subleaders, generally have moderate influence. But most citizens usually have little or no *direct* influence in this sense: they never initiate or veto any alternatives.

One is also likely to find, however, that some leaders are extremely sensitive to the attitudes and preferences of individuals and groups who do not directly initiate or veto alternatives. Often this indirect influence is *anticipatory*: a leader initiates or vetoes a particular alternative because he anticipates rewards for choosing from one set of alternatives, or sanctions if he chooses from a different set. In this way, persons or groups who are not leaders may exert great indirect influence on the choice of alternatives even though they never directly initiate or veto.

In New Haven, for example, the present mayor has not until this present year ever advocated an increase in taxes, although he has done almost everything else to raise money. Why has he not tried to increase taxes? It was not, I think, because someone said, "Mayor Lee, don't you dare raise taxes!" For the mayor grew up in New Haven; he knows enough about the city to know that raising taxes is politically risky. He *anticipated* what might happen to him in the next election if he should raise taxes. If the decision to take the risk is made, at least it is a fact that the risk involved has been anticipated.

Indirect influence, which is often anticipatory in character, is very important for some kinds of leaders, particularly those who have to win elections. Yet even when indirect influence of this sort is taken into account, the distribution of influence in most sectors of policy is very far indeed from the perfect equality that some democratic theorists would regard as ideal.

One of the main reasons why the system does not very closely approximate political equality is the unequal distribution of access to political resources — that is, to inducements of all kinds. One's influence is partly a function of the political resources to which one has access — labor time, money and credit, jobs, information, popularity, wealth, social standing, legality, and the like. An examination of any one of these political resources will show that some persons have much greater access to it than others. So long as this is the case, political equality is not likely to be approximated. This is hardly a novel conclusion, for a great many writers on politics have said in one way or another that a high

degree of equality in the distribution of political resources is a necessary —
though by no means a sufficient — condition for a high degree of equality of
control over political decisions. This was, for example, one of Tocqueville's key
propositions in his analysis of democracy in America.

In appraising inequality in political resources, it is important not to make
the mistake of assuming that what we are trying to judge is a ruling elite
masquerading in the name of democracy. For if citizens do not rule the system
as political equals neither does a unified elite control decisions, at least not in
New Haven. There may be exceptions in specific communities, but I am inclined to think that most cities and states, and certainly the national government, are in this respect rather like New Haven.

To condemn our political system for inequality is one thing; to condemn
it for being dominated by a ruling elite is another. In my view, appraisal is
infinitely more complicated, precisely because the political system is neither a
democracy in which citizens share equally in all important decisions nor an
oligarchy ruled by an elite. Rather, it combines elements of both.

In the American system (insofar as New Haven is a fair prototype), though
political equality is certainly not attained and political resources are unequally
distributed, democracy is not wholly subverted into oligarchy because the growth
of oligarchy is inhibited both by the *patterns* according to which political resources are allocated and by the ways in which resources are actually *used*.

Let me try to make my point clearer first by some abstract considerations on
the nature of power and influence. Abstractly, there is no reason to assume that
the relative influence different individuals or groups exert on the decisions of
one another is simply and solely a funtion of the "size" of their resources, that
is, of the inducements they have at their disposal.

In the first place, an individual need not *use* his political resources to gain
direct or indirect influence over officials of government. To be sure, the extent
to which one is willing to use his political resources for political ends, depends
in part on the magnitude of his resources; for example a millionaire who con-
tributed $100 to a political campaign gives up fewer alternative opportunities
than a poor man. But the extent to which a person uses his political resources
will depend on other factors as well, including his confidence in the success of
his effort, the extent to which he has alternative ways of gaining his ends other
than through politics, and the extent to which he expects he will be benefited
or injured by government policies. In New Haven, we have found variations
attributable to each of these factors.

For example, Negroes in New Haven, a minority of probably 10 or 12 per
cent of the population, operate at a much higher level of political participation
than any other single isolated group in the community. What is the reason for
this? The political arena is one area where Negroes are not thwarted and blocked
by substantial discrimination. They can get jobs, patronage, and city contracts;
they have their votes; their votes are legitimate, and they are counted; and so
it has been for a century. This isn't true in the other sectors of community life;
so Negroes work harder in the political arena to compensate for their disadvantages.

In the second place, one individual may use his political resources more *skill-*

fully than another — a variation known to students of politics for several centuries. By a skillful use of limited resources, in fact, a political entrepreneur — Machiavelli's Prince — can increase his resources and thus his influence.

In the third place, the relative influence of different potential coalitions will depend in part on the extent to which individuals and groups actually *combine* their resources. The combined political resources of a very numerous group of individuals who are not very well off may easily exceed the combined political resources of a small elite, each member of which is, individually, very well off. The extent to which people in a group actually combine their resources depends, of course, on the degree of political unity among them. There is no a priori reason for supposing that the rich will display more unity than the poor; and even if they do, it does not follow that the combined resources of the well-off strata will inevitably exceed the combined resources of the badly-off strata of a society.

Now, when we turn from these abstract considerations to the way in which different kinds of inducements — political resources — are actually distributed in New Haven we discover that a most significant change seems to have taken place during the last century and a half. In 1800, the citizens of New Haven were not only very unequal in access to political resources of all kinds but their inequalities were *cumulative*. That is, the same tiny elite possessed the highest social standing, wealth, dominance in economic affairs, superior education, control over educational and religious institutions, a monopoly of public offices, evidently a large measure of legitimacy, and perhaps (though this is more doubtful) even popularity. Today, however, inequalities that exist with respect to all these resources tend to be noncumulative or *dispersed*. I can find no single elite at the top of the heap; instead there are many different varieties of political resources, with a somewhat different elite at the top of each. I am inclined to think that this pattern is not peculiar to New Haven but is common throughout the United States, though one would doubtless find exceptions to it here and there.

Moreover, I am tempted toward the hypothesis that the pattern of dispersed inequalities is a likely product of an advanced industrial society, at least if it operates with the kinds of political institutions that most of us would call democratic. The impact of Marx and Weber on habits of thought about industrial society has been very great, even among non-Marxists and non-Weberians, and both men lead us to expect that an advanced industrial society will be rather neatly and consistently stratified along lines shaped by economic class or bureaucratic position. I believe we should entertain the hypothesis that any industrial society in an advanced stage enters on a profound change that can be held back, if at all, only by a most vigorous and oppressive centralized regime. In a moderately free political system, at this stage, increasing affluence, widespread education, impersonal standards of recruitment, incredible specialization of functions and skills, the varieties of popularity, prestige, and achievement, standardization of consumer goods, social and geographical mobility, and probably many other factors, all tend to produce a pattern of dispersed rather than cumulative inequalities. The advance of industrial society may somewhat reduce inequalities in political resources; it does not, however, erase them. Nonetheless, in New Haven, and I think in American society generally, these inequalities are no longer cumulative.

To the extent that inequalities persist, tendencies toward oligarchy also exist in advanced industrial societies. But to the extent that inequalities are dispersed rather than cumulative — as I am suggesting they are in the United States — the growth of a unified oligarchy is inhibited. For the pattern of dispersed inequalities means that an individual or a group at a disadvantage with respect to one resource may compensate for his handicap by exploiting his superior access to a different resource. In New Haven, for example, for the past half century men whose main political resources were popularity and ethnic solidarity have been able to win elections. Very few individuals or groups in New Haven, and I believe this to be true in the United States, are totally lacking in political resources *of some kind*.

The possibility of turning to alternative kinds of resources would be less significant if one kind of resource — say wealth or social standing — dominated all the others, in the sense that a person or group superior in the one resource would invariably exert superior influence in a conflict with persons who drew on other political resources. Yet — and this is the second great limit on the growth of oligarchy — this is simply not the case, despite a tradition of economic determinism that runs in a straight line from Madison to Veblen, Beard, the Lynds, and C. Wright Mills. Surely if the New Deal demonstrated anything, it proved that leaders with popularity and votes can — even if they do not always do so — carry out their policies despite the opposition of leaders supported by men of wealth and social standing. This is a point that was perfectly obvious to both Aristole and Tocqueville, who considered the problem in the light of observations made on radically different sorts of political systems.

In the third place, individuals or groups who are at a disadvantage in their access to resources can sometimes compensate by using their resources at a relatively high level. In New Haven, Negroes who, as I said before, are more active politically than any other identifiable ethnic group in the city, have overcome some of the disadvantages imposed by their incomes, status, and occupations.

Fourth, an individual or group at a disadvantage in resources may compensate by developing a high level of political skill. Fortunately the skills required in electioneering and party politics are by no means a monopoly of any stratum in the community; one might even conclude that leaders drawn from the well-to-do tend to be somewhat less likely to develop these skills to a high peak of proficiency than leaders drawn from the less-well-off strata of the community. In fact, many sorts of politicking run more sharply counter to the norms of the upper strata than of the lower or lower-middle strata.

Fifth, a group of citizens each of whom is weak in political resources may compensate by combining resources so that in the aggregate these are formidable. One resource that can be most easily aggregated by the less-well-off strata is the ballot. In New Haven, historically the least well-off citizens in the community have been Negroes and members of various immigrant groups whose circumstances produce a unity at the polls that declines as assimilation progresses. This unity among the poor has enabled them — or more accurately, perhaps, their leaders — to influence nominations, elections, and policies (often, to be sure, covert rather than overt policies) despite their lowly status, their low incomes, and their poverty in many other political resources.

Sixth, competitive elections insure that elected officials attempt to shape their covert and overt policies so as to win elections, hence to maximize votes, or at any rate to gain more votes than any rival. Consequently, whenever the many are believed to hold views on government policies at odds with the views held among the few, there exists one set of persons, elected politicians, who are strongly impelled to win votes by shaping or seeming to shape governmental policies according to the views of the many. . . .

There can be no doubt . . . that our political system falls far short of the high standards of performance indicated by the criterion of political equality. No one who places a high value on political equality can afford to be complacent about the achievements of the American political system.

Nonetheless, it is misleading in the extreme to interpret the inequalities of power that mark our political life as signs of oligarchy. For in our system of dispersed inequalities, almost every group, as said before, has access to some resources that it can exploit to gain influence. Consequently, any group that feels itself badly abused is likely to possess both the resources it needs to halt the abuse and the incentive to use these resources at a high enough level to bring about changes. Nearly every group has enough potential influence to mitigate harsh injustice to its members, though not necessarily enough influence to attain a full measure of justice. The system thus tends to be self-corrective, at least in a limited fashion. If equality and justice are rarely attained, harsh and persistent oppression is almost always avoided. To this extent, the system attains one of the important ends of political equality without the means.

National Power

VETO GROUPS, RULING CLASS, OR POWER ELITE?

The Debate in Brief

David Riesman's challenging work, The Lonely Crowd: A Study of the Changing American Character (written with the aid of Nathan Glazer and Reuel Denney), has been among the most widely read and discussed scholarly books of the postwar era. In the selection reprinted here, Riesman ties his idea of an altered American character to changes in the national system of power.

Riesman believes there have been four major stages in the growth of America's power structure. From the founding of the Republic to the Jacksonian era, there was a discrete ruling group composed of the "landed-gentry and mercantilist-money leadership." Between the Age of Jackson and the Civil War, yeoman farmers and artisans checked the growth of oligarchy and gained a veto over what was done. After the war, however, popular power declined and the captains of industry emerged as a new ruling class. Finally, after the death of President McKinley power was again diffused among a variety of veto groups.

According to Riesman, a transformation in the national psyche accompanied these changes. Americans originally possessed an inner-directed character distinguished by self-reliance and dedication to the Protestant Ethic. The inner-directed man in politics was a "moralizer" motivated by self-interest and the concern for personal or group aggrandizement, and this character type prevailed during earlier periods of class rule. Today, however, "other-direction" has replaced "inner-direction" as the dominant orientation in the American character. Other-directed members of the new middle classes are now more concerned with the expectations of others than with personal conviction and, therefore, tend to avoid strong political commitments. In contemporary America, the prevalence of other-direction reduces the possibility of divisive social conflict, born of impassioned self-interest, and instead encourages tolerance and consensus. Political apathy, springing from other-direction, has also helped to create and to maintain the amorphous American power structure.

Since The Lonely Crowd relates national character to power structure, the student must critically assess Riesman's suggestion that the American character has metamorphosed from inner- to other-direction. A number of scholars have sharply challenged this interpretation. Historian Carl Degler, for example — "The Sociologist as Historian: Riesman's The Lonely Crowd," American Quarterly, XV (Winter 1963), pp. 483–497 — believes that Riesman overemphasizes the changes in our national character. Similarly, sociologist Seymour Martin Lipset — The First New Nation: The United States in Historical and Comparative Perspective (New York: Basic Books, 1963) — argues that basic national values, such as equality and achievement, have remained constant and have informed an unchanging American character. If such critics are correct, then Riesman has failed adequately to explain historical changes in the American system of power. Perhaps he misinterprets the changing dynamic of personality and power by incorrectly assuming that power "is founded, in large measure, on interpersonal expectations and values."

We may also doubt that veto groups are always in the ideal equilibrium or balance described by Riesman. In his preface to the 1961 edition of The Lonely Crowd, Riesman himself admits that he previously underestimated the power of business and "the climate of a business culture." It seems possible, then, that he also misjudged the power of political, military, and other elites. Further, Riesman is vague about how veto groups supposedly check the exercise of power at the national level. In what way, for example, do they influence foreign policy decisions made privately rather than publicly? Are they able to control the amount of military spending or prevent giant corporations from raising prices? Does not apathy limit the effectiveness of veto groups and, hence, increase the power of those in a position to make major public decisions? In a later essay, written with Michael Maccoby, Riesman evidences many such doubts of his own and calls for greater participation in the political arena ("The American Crisis" in James Roosevelt, ed. The Liberal Papers [Garden City, N.Y.: Doubleday, 1962]).

Finally, it is instructive to differentiate Riesman's views from those of many other pluralists. Unlike some of his ideological brethren, who view power in positive terms, Riesman clearly fears power and emphasizes its exploitative and coercive potential. Riesman does, of course, conclude that public apathy, the decline in the importance of politics, and the mutual impotence of veto groups have reduced the danger of power. Nevertheless, he at times seems to lament the rise of veto groups, the decline of strong leadership, and to be less content than many pluralists with the new amorphousness of power. Riesman also violates the pluralist orthodoxy by suggesting that small communities, as contrasted with the nation, may in fact be controlled by ruling groups. For such reasons, The Lonely Crowd has been assailed almost as frequently by pluralist scholars as by those of elite or ruling class convictions. Despite such criticisms, however, Riesman's analysis remains an original and provocative contribution to our understanding of power in postwar America.

DAVID RIESMAN
The Theory of Veto Groups

WHO HAS THE POWER?

The Veto Groups. The shifting nature of the lobby provides us with an important clue as to the difference between the present American political scene and that of the age of McKinley. The ruling class of businessmen could relatively easily (though perhaps mistakenly) decide where their interests lay and what editors, lawyers, and legislators might be paid to advance them. The lobby ministered to the clear leadership, privilege, and imperative of the business ruling class.

Today we have substituted for that leadership a series of groups, each of which has struggled for and finally attained a power to stop things conceivably inimical to its interests and, within far narrower limits, to start things. The various business groups, large and small, the movie-censoring groups, the farm groups and the labor and professional groups, the major ethnic groups and major regional groups, have in many instances succeeded in maneuvering themselves into a position in which they are able to neutralize those who might attack them. The very increase in the number of these groups, and in the kinds of interests "practical" and "fictional" they are protecting, marks, therefore, a decisive change from the lobbies of an earlier day. There is a change in method, too, in the way the groups are organized, the way they handle each other, and the way they handle the public, that is, the unorganized.

These veto groups are neither leader-groups nor led-groups. The only leaders of national scope left in the United States today are those who can placate the veto groups. The only followers left in the United States today are those un-

From David Riesman, with Nathan Glazer and Reuel Denney, *The Lonely Crowd: A Study of the Changing American Character.* Copyright © 1950, 1961 by Yale University Press. Reprinted by permission.

organized and sometimes disorganized unfortunates who have not yet invented their group.

Within the veto groups, there is, of course, the same struggle for top places that goes on in other bureaucratic setups. Among the veto groups competition is monopolistic; rules of fairness and fellowship dictate how far one can go. Despite the rules there are, of course, occasional "price wars," like the jurisdictional disputes of labor unions or Jewish defense groups; these are ended by negotiation, the division of territory, and the formation of a roof organization for the previously split constituency. These big monopolies, taken as a single group, are in devastating competition with the not yet grouped, much as the fair-trade economy competes against the free-trade economy. These latter scattered followers find what protection they can in the interstices around the group-minded.[1]

Each of the veto groups in this pattern is capable of an aggressive move, but the move is sharply limited in its range by the way in which the various groups have already cut up the sphere of politics and arrayed certain massive expectations behind each cut. Both within the groups and in the situation created by their presence, the political mood tends to become one of other-directed tolerance. The vetoes so bind action that it is hard for the moralizers to conceive of a program that might in any large way alter the relations between political and personal life or between political and economic life. In the amorphous power structure created by the veto groups it is hard to distinguish rulers from the ruled, those to be aided from those to be opposed, those on your side from those on the other side. This very pattern encourages the inside-dopester who can unravel the personal linkages, and discourages the enthusiast or indignant who wants to install the good or fend off the bad. Probably, most of all it encourages the new-style indifferent who feels and is often told that his and everyone else's affairs are in the hands of the experts and that laymen, though they should "participate," should not really be too inquisitive or aroused.

By their very nature the veto groups exist as defense groups, not as leadership groups. If it is true that they do "have the power," they have it by virtue of a necessary mutual tolerance. More and more they mirror each other in their style of political action, including their interest in public relations and their emphasis on internal harmony of feelings. There is a tendency for organizations as differently oriented as, say, the Young Socialists and the 4-H Club, to adopt similar psychological methods of salesmanship to obtain and solidify their recruits.

This does not mean, however, that the veto groups are formed along the

---

[1] It should be clear that monopolistic competition, both in business and politics, *is* competition. People are very much aware of their rivals, within and without the organization. They know who they are, but by the very nature of monopolistic competition they are seldom able to eliminate them entirely. While we have been talking of fair trade and tolerance, this should not obscure the fact that for the participants the feeling of being in a rivalrous setup is very strong. Indeed, they face the problem of so many other-directed people: how to combine the appearance of friendly, personalized, "sincere" behavior with the ruthless, sometimes almost paranoid, envies of their occupational life.

lines of character structure. As in a business corporation there is room for extreme inner-directed and other-directed types, and all mixtures between, so in
a veto group there can exist complex symbiotic relationships among people of
different political styles. Thus a team of lobbyists may include both moralizers
and inside-dopesters, sometimes working in harness, sometimes in conflict; and
the constituency of the team may be composed mainly of new-style political
indifferents who have enough literacy and organizational experience to throw
weight around when called upon. Despite these complications I think it fair to
say that the veto groups, even when they are set up to protect a clear-cut
moralizing interest, are generally forced to adopt the political manners of the
other-directed.

In saying this I am talking about the national scene. The smaller the constituency, of course, the smaller the number of veto groups involved and the
greater the chance that some one of them will be dominant. Thus, in local
politics there is more indignation and less tolerance, just as even the *Chicago
Tribune* is a tolerant paper in comparison with the community throwaways in
many Chicago neighborhoods.

The same problem may be considered from another perspective. Various
groups have discovered that they can go quite far in the amorphous power
situation in America without being stopped. Our society is behaviorally open
enough to permit a considerable community of gangsters a comfortable living
under a variety of partisan political regimes. In their lack of concern for public
relations these men are belated businessmen. So are some labor leaders who
have discovered their power to hold up the economy, though in most situations
what is surprising is the moderation of labor demands — a moderation based
more on psychological restraints than on any power that could effectively be
interposed. Likewise, it is sometimes possible for an aggressive group, while not
belonging to the entrenched veto-power teams, to push a bill through a legis-
lature. Thus, the original Social Security Act went through Congress, so far as I
can discover, because it was pushed by a devoted but tiny cohort; the large veto
groups including organized labor were neither very much for it nor very much
against it.

For similar reasons those veto groups are in many political situations strongest
whose own memberships are composed of veto groups, especially veto groups of
one. The best example of this is the individual farmer who, after one of the farm
lobbies has made a deal for him, can still hold out for more. The farm lobby's
concern for the reaction of other veto groups, such as labor unions, cuts little
ice with the individual farmer. This fact may strengthen the lobby in a negotiation: it can use its internal public relations problems as a counter in bargaining,
very much as does a diplomat who tells a foreign minister that he must consider
how Senator so-and-so will react. For, no matter what the other-directedness of
the lobby's leaders, they cannot bind their membership to carry out a public
relations approach. Many labor unions have a similar power because they cannot
control their memberships who, if not satisfied with a deal made by the union,
can walk off or otherwise sabotage a job.

In contrast, those veto groups are often weaker whose other-directed orientation can dominate their memberships. Large corporations are vulnerable to a call from the White House because, save for a residual indignant like Sewell Avery, their officials are themselves other-directed and because, once the word from the chief goes out, the factory superintendents, no matter how boiling mad, have to fall into line with the new policy by the very nature of the centralized organization for which they work: they can sabotage top management on minor matters but not, say, on wage rates or tax accounting. As against this, the American Catholic Church possesses immense veto-group power because it combines a certain amount of centralized command — and a public picture of a still greater amount — with a highly decentralized priesthood (each priest is in a sense his own trade association secretary) and a membership organization of wide-ranging ethnic, social, and political loyalties; this structure permits great flexibility in bargaining.

These qualifications, however, do not change the fact that the veto groups, taken together, constitute a new buffer region between the old, altered, and thinning extremes of those who were once leaders and led. It is both the attenuation of leaders and led, and the other-oriented doings of these buffers, that help to give many moralizers a sense of vacuum in American political life.

The veto groups, by the conditions their presence creates and by the requirements they set for leadership in politics, foster the tolerant mood of other-direction and hasten the retreat of the inner-directed indignants.

IS THERE A RULING CLASS LEFT?

Nevertheless, people go on acting as if there still were a decisive ruling class in contemporary America. In the postwar years, businessmen thought labor leaders and politicians ran the country, while labor and the left thought that "Wall Street" ran it, or the "sixty families." Wall Street, confused perhaps by its dethronement as a telling barometer of capital-formation weather, may have thought that the midwestern industrial barons, cushioned on plant expansion money in the form of heavy depreciation reserves and undivided profits, ran the country. They might have had some evidence for this in the fact that the New Deal was much tougher with finance capital — e.g., the SEC and the Holding Company Act — than with industrial capital and that when, in the undistributed profits tax, it tried to subject the latter to a stockholder and money-market control, the tax was quickly repealed.

But these barons of Pittsburgh, Weirton, Akron, and Detroit, though certainly a tougher crowd than the Wall Streeters, are, as we saw earlier, coming more and more to think of themselves as trustees for their beneficiaries. And whereas, from the point of view of labor and the left, these men ran the War Production Board in the interest of their respective companies, one could argue just as easily that the WPB experience was one of the congeries of factors that have tamed the barons. It put them in a situation where they had to view their company from the point of view of "the others."

Despite the absence of intensive studies of business power and of what happens in a business negotiation, one can readily get an impressionistic sense of the change in business behavior in the last generation. In the pages of *Fortune*, that excellent chronicler of business, one can see that there are few survivals of the kinds of dealings — with other businessmen, with labor, with the government — that were standard operating practice for the pre-World War I tycoons. Moreover, in its twenty-year history, *Fortune* itself has shown, and perhaps it may be considered not too unrepresentative of its audience, a steady decline of interest in business as such and a growing interest in once peripheral matters, such as international relations, social science, and other accoutrements of the modern executive.

But it is of course more difficult to know whether character has changed as well as behavior — whether, as some contend, businessmen simply rule today in a more subtle, more "managerial" way. In "Manager Meets Union" Joseph M. Goldsen and Lillian Low have depicted the psychological dependence of a contemporary sales manager on the approval of the men under him, his willingness to go to great lengths, in terms of concessions, to maintain interpersonal warmth in his relations with them, and his fierce resentment of the union as a barrier to this emotional exchange.[2] As against this, one must set the attitude of some of the auto-supply companies whose leadership still seems much more craft-oriented than people-oriented and therefore unwilling to make concessions and none too concerned with the emotional atmosphere of negotiations. Likewise, the General Motors-UAW negotiations of 1946, as reported in print, sound more like a cockfight than a Platonic symposium, although in Peter Drucker's *Concept of the Corporation*, a study of General Motors published in the same year, there is much evidence of management eagerness to build a big, happy family.

Power, indeed, is founded, in a large measure, on interpersonal expectations and attitudes. If businessmen feel weak and dependent, they do in actuality become weaker and more dependent, no matter what material resources may be ascribed to them. My impression, based mainly on experiences of my own in business and law practice, is that businessmen from large manufacturing companies, though they often talk big, are easily frightened by the threat of others' hostility; they may pound the table, but they look to others for leadership and do not care to get out of line with their peer-groupers. Possibly, attitudes toward such an irascible businessman as Sewell Avery might mark a good dividing line between the older and the newer attitudes. Those businessmen who admire Avery, though they might not dare to imitate him, are becoming increasingly an elderly minority, while the younger men generally are shocked by Avery's "highhandedness," his rebuff of the glad hand.

The desire of businessmen to be well thought of has led to the irony that each time a professor writes a book attacking business, even if almost nobody reads it, he creates jobs in industry for his students in public relations, trade association work, and market research! While the Black Horse Cavalry of an earlier era held up businessmen by threatening to let pass crippling legislation desired by anti-business moralizers, today many honest intellectuals who would not think of taking a bribe hold business or trade association jobs because their

[2] "Manager Meets Union: a Case Study of Personal Immaturity," *Human Factors in Management*, ed. S. D. Hoslett (Parkville, Missouri: Park College Press, 1946), p. 77.

clients have been scared, perhaps by these very men, into taking cognizance of some actual or imaginary veto group. Since a large structure is built up to woo the group, no test of power is made to see whether the group has real existence or real strength. Understandably, ideologies about who has power in America are relied upon to support these amiable fictions which serve . . . to provide the modern businessman with an endless shopping list, an endless task of glad-handing. This is a far cry, I suggest, from the opportunistic glad-handing of the wealthy on which Tocqueville comments . . . ; very likely, what was mere practice in his day has become embedded in character in ours.

Businessmen, moreover, are not the only people who fail to exploit the power position they are supposed, in the eyes of many observers, to have. Army officers are also astonishingly timid about exercising their leadership. During the war one would have thought that the army would be relatively impervious to criticism. But frequently the generals went to great lengths to refrain from doing something about which a congressman might make an unfriendly speech. They did so even at times when they might have brushed the congressman off like an angry fly. When dealing with businessmen or labor leaders, army officers were, it seemed to me, astonishingly deferential; and this was as true of the West Pointers as of the reservists. Of course, there were exceptions, but in many of the situations where the armed services made concessions to propitiate some veto group, they rationalized the concessions in terms of morale or of postwar public relations or, frequently, simply were not aware of their power.

To be sure, some came to the same result by the route of a democratic tradition of civilian dominance. Very likely, it was a good thing for the country that the services were so self-restrained. I do not here deal with the matter on the merits but use it as an illustration of changing character and changing social structure.

All this may lead to the question: well, who really runs things? What people fail to see is that, while it may take leadership to start things running, or to stop them, very little leadership is needed once things are under way — that, indeed, things can get terribly snarled up and still go on running. If one studies a factory, an army group, or other large organization, one wonders how things get done at all, with the lack of leadership and with all the featherbedding. Perhaps they get done because we are still trading on our reserves of inner-direction, especially in the lower ranks. At any rate, the fact they do get done is no proof that there is someone in charge.

There are, of course, still some veto groups that have more power than others and some individuals who have more power than others. But the determination of who these are has to be made all over again for our time: we cannot be satisfied with the answers given by Marx, Mosca, Michels, Pareto, Weber, Veblen, or Burnham, though we can learn from all of them. . . .

. . . Power on the national scene must be viewed in terms of issues. It is possible that, where an issue involves only two or three veto groups, themselves tiny minorities, the official or unofficial broker among the groups can be quite powerful — but only on that issue. However, where the issue involves the country as a whole, no individual or group leadership is likely to be very effective,

because the entrenched veto groups cannot be budged: unlike a party that may
be defeated at the polls, or a class that may be replaced by another class, the
veto groups are always "in."

One might ask whether one would not find, over a long period of time, that
decisions in America favored one group or class — thereby, by definition, the
ruling group or class — over others. Does not wealth exert its pull in the long
run? In the past this has been so; for the future I doubt it. The future seems
to be in the hands of the small business and professional men who control Congress, such as realtors, lawyers, car salesmen, undertakers, and so on; of the military men who control defense and, in part, foreign policy; of the big business
managers and their lawyers, finance-committee men, and other counselors who
decide on plant investment and influence the rate of technological change; of
the labor leaders who control worker productivity and worker votes; of the black
belt whites who have the greatest stake in southern politics; of the Poles, Italians,
Jews, and Irishmen who have stakes in foreign policy, city jobs, and ethnic, religious and cultural organizations; of the editorializers and storytellers who help
socialize the young, tease and train the adult, and amuse and annoy the aged;
of the farmers — themselves a warring congeries of cattlemen, corn men, dairy-
men, cotton men, and so on — who control key departments and committees
and who, as the living representatives of our inner-directed past, control many
of our memories; of the Russians and, to a lesser degree, other foreign powers
who control much of our agenda of attention; and so on. The reader can complete the list. Power in America seems to me situational and mercurial; it resists
attempts to locate it the way a molecule, under the Heisenberg principle, resists attempts simultaneously to locate it and time its velocity.

But people are afraid of this indeterminacy and amorphousness in the cos-
mology of power. Even those intellectuals, for instance, who feel themselves very
much out of power and who are frightened of those who they think have the
power, prefer to be scared by the power structures they conjure up than to face
the possibility that the power structure they believe exists has largely evaporated.
Most people prefer to suffer with interpretations that give their world meaning
than to relax in the cave without an Ariadne's thread.

Paul M. Sweezy, editor of the Monthly Review, *author of* The Theory of
Capitalist Development *(New York: Monthly Review Press, 1964, 1942)
and, with Paul Baran, of* Monopoly Capital *(New York: Monthly Review
Press, 1966), has long been one of American Marxism's most articulate
and energetic spokesmen. In his essay on "The American Ruling Class,"
first published in 1951, Sweezy briefly outlines a general theory of social
classes.*

*In a short introduction, not included here, Sweezy suggests that a social
class "is made up of freely intermarrying families." The property system
generally defines the character of class structure: "The upper classes are the*

property-owning classes; the lower classes are the propertyless classes." Further, no class is perfectly homogeneous, but instead is "made up of a core surrounded by fringes which are in varying degrees attached to the core." Also, since no class system is completely closed, there is always a certain amount of interclass mobility.

Representatives of the national upper class, in Sweezy's view, are individuals born to wealthy families and bound together by common personal experience, education, "a massive network of institutional relations," and a common ideology transmitted through the family and the school. Members of this class "rule" the economy either by making basic decisions themselves, or by controlling the jobs of those who do make the decisions. In much the same way, the class "rules" the government because its members hold key positions themselves or finance candidates and parties who do control the governmental process.

Many critics of class analysis, however, argue that property no longer determines access to power. (See, for example, Daniel Bell's provocative essay, "The Breakup of Family Capitalism," in The End of Ideology [New York: The Free Press, 1960].) Many scholars accept the related idea of a "managerial revolution" and suggest that technical personnel now have replaced the capitalist at the helm of corporations and other large bureaucratic institutions. Unlike advocates of class analysis, these critics believe that managerial personnel have today become indispensable and, accordingly, that power has passed from the economically privileged to these other, more qualified managerial elites. This argument is sophisticated and often convincing, yet many theorists have responded effectively to such criticisms. Managers, they argue, may actually be assimilated into the upper class and, hence, act as would any other member of the property-holding group. Next, it is not clear that the functional indispensability of technical or managerial experts automatically brings them more power than is held by the very rich. "If 'indispensability' were decisive," Max Weber argued, "then where slave labor prevailed . . . the 'indispensable' slaves ought to have held the positions of power," for they were certainly as indispensable as today's managers. These and other major objections to the thesis of a managerial revolution are raised by Hans Gerth and C. Wright Mills in their penetrating article, "A Marx for the Managers," Ethics, 52 (January 1942), pp. 200–215, although Gerth and Mills also dispute the Marxian theory of power.

In addition to a supposed managerial revolution, critics have suggested that still another factor may upset the framework of class analysis. Great social mobility, they claim, has been a characteristic of American society, and the resulting ferment has blurred class lines, undermining class consciousness. Further, many scholars argue that the American social structure is becoming less, rather than more rigid and, therefore, that the probability of control by a ruling class is decreasing. Yet there is no great agreement on these points. A large number of social scientists still contend that mobility into the upper class remains low and that the class is essentially self-perpetuating. Ruling class theorists often claim, too, that mobility rates have no bearing at all on the question of social class. Thus, social origins do not always control class affiliation because individuals will tend to adopt the values and attitudes of any class into which they move. Workers who become members of the upper class will behave no differently from those who are born into it.

This brings us to another problem regarding class analysis. The utility of Sweezy's framework depends, in large part, upon the existence of a common ruling class ideology. Critics contend that the heterogeneity and conflict within the ruling class belies the presence of such a definable ideology. Class analysts reply that intraclass disagreement ceases when important questions affecting class interest are at issue. If class ideology is to be a useful concept, however, it must more clearly define the nature of this interest and of those important issues upon which the ruling class will unite. Will the ruling class, for example, take a unified stand on questions of foreign and domestic policy? Do ruling class decisions always violate the interest of the lower classes? What will be the content of ruling class policies? In fact, only a more comprehensive examination of such questions can adequately test the class theory that Sweezy outlines below.

PAUL M. SWEEZY
The American Ruling Class

THE AMERICAN CLASS SYSTEM

The United States is a capitalist society, the purest capitalist society that ever existed. It has no feudal hangovers to complicate the class system. Independent producers (working with their own means of production but without hired labor) there are, but both economically and socially they constitute a relatively unimportant feature of the American system. What do we expect the class structure of such a pure capitalist society to be?

Clearly, the two decisive classes are defined by the very nature of capitalism: the owners of the means of production (the capitalist class), and the wage laborers who set the means of production in motion (the working class). There is no doubt about the existence or importance of these two classes in America. Taken together they can be said to constitute the foundation of the American class system.

The foundation of a building, however, is not the whole building; nor does

From Paul M. Sweezy, "The American Ruling Class," *The Monthly Review*, Vol. 3, No. 1 (May 1951), pp. 14–17, and Vol. 3, No. 2 (June 1951), pp. 58–64. Reprinted by permission of Monthly Review Press, Inc.

the American economic system contain only capitalists and workers. For one thing, as we have already noted, there are independent producers (artisans and small farmers), and to these we should add small shopkeepers and providers of services (for example, the proprietors of local gas stations). These people make up the lower-middle class, or *petite bourgeoisie*, in the original sense of the term. For another thing, there are a variety of types which stand somewhere between the capitalists and the workers and cannot easily be classified with either: government and business bureaucrats, professionals, teachers, journalists, advertising men, and so on. These are often, and not inappropriately, called the new middle classes — "new" because of their spectacular growth, both absolutely and relatively to other classes, in the last 75 years or so. Finally, there are what are usually called declassed elements — bums, gamblers, thugs, prostitutes, and the like — who are not recognized in the official statistics but who nevertheless play an important role in capitalist society, especially in its political life.

Viewing the matter from a primarily economic angle, then, we could say that the American class structure consists of capitalists, lower-middle class in the classical sense, new middle classes, workers, and declassed elements. There is no doubt, however, that this is not a strictly accurate description of the actual living social classes which we observe about us. If we apply the criterion of inter-marriageability as a test of social class membership, we shall often find that people who from an economic standpoint belong to the new middle classes are actually on the same social level as the larger captalists; that smaller capitalists are socially indistinguishable from a large proportion of the new middle classes; and that the working class includes without very much social distinction those who perform certain generally comparable kinds of labor, whether it be with their own means of production or with means of production belonging to others.

These considerations lead us to the following conclusion: The social classes which we observe about us are not *identical* with the economic classes of capitalist society. They are rather *modifications* of the latter. This is, I believe, an important principle. If we keep it firmly in mind we shall be able to appreciate the decisive role of the economic factor in the structure and behavior of social classes while at the same time avoiding an overmechanical (and hence false) economic determinism.

How shall we describe the actual social-class structure of America? This is partly a matter of fact and partly a matter of convention, and on neither score is there anything that could be called general agreement among students of American society. Warner and associates, for example, say that in a typical American community there are exactly six classes to which they give the names upper-upper, lower-upper, upper-middle, lower-middle, upper-lower, and lower-lower. There are a number of objections to this scheme, however. It is based on studies of small cities; the dividing lines are largely arbitrary; and the labels suggest that the only important thing about classes is their position in relation to other classes. Warner and associates admit that there are some communities which lack one or more of the six classes they believe they found in "Jonesville" and "Yankee City"; and one hesitates to speculate on how many classes they might plausibly claim to find, by using essentially the same methods, in a really big city. Their scheme, in other words, while representing a serious attempt to cope with the problem, is unsatisfactory. Its inadequacy is particularly obvious when we attempt to pass beyond the individual community and deal with social classes on a national scale.

What we need is a scheme which both highlights the fundamental economic conditioning of the social-class system and at the same time is flexible enough to encompass the anomalies and irregularities which actually characterize it.

The starting point must surely be the recognition that two social classes, at bottom shaped by the very nature of capitalism, determine the form and content of the system as a whole. I prefer to call these classes the ruling class and the working class. The core of the ruling class is made up of big capitalists (or, more generally, big property-owners, though the distinction is not very important since most large aggregates of property have the form of capital in this country today). There are numerous fringes to the ruling class, including smaller property-owners, government and business executives (insofar as they are not big owners in their own right), professionals, and so on: we shall have more to say on this subject later. The core of the working class is made up of wage laborers who have no productive property of their own. Here again there are fringes, including especially, independent craftsmen and petty traders.

The fringes of the ruling class do not reach to the fringes of the working class. Between the two there is a wide social space which is occupied by what we can hardly avoid calling the middle class. We should not forget, however, that the middle class is much more heterogeneous than either the ruling class or the working class. It has no solid core, and it shades off irregularly (and differently in different localities) into the fringes of the class above it and the class below it. Indeed we might say that the middle class consists of a collection of fringes, and that its social cohesion is largely due to the existence in all of its elements of a desire to be in the ruling class above it and to avoid being in the working class below it.

This generalized description of the social-class structure seems to me to have many merits and no fatal defects. The terminology calls attention to the chief functions of the basic classes and indicates clearly enough the relative positions of the three classes in the social hierarchy. More important, the use of the fringe concept enables us to face frankly the *fact* that the dividing lines in American society are not sharply drawn, and that even the borderlands are irregular and unstable. This fact is often seized upon to "prove" that there are *no* classes in America. It cannot be banished or hidden by the use of an elaborate multi-class scheme like that of Warner and associates, for the simple reason that such a scheme, however well it may seem to apply to some situations, breaks down when applied to others. What we must have is a scheme which takes full account of the fact in question without at the same time obscuring the fundamental outlines and character of the class system itself.

I shall next try to show that, at least, as concerns the ruling class, the scheme proposed above does satisfy these requirements.

Every community study shows clearly the existence of an upper social crust which is based on wealth. The nucleus is always the "old families" which have transmitted and usually augmented their fortunes from one generation to the next. Around this nucleus are grouped the *nouveaux riches*, the solidly estab-

lished lawyers and doctors, the more successful of the social climbers and syco-
phants, and people whose family connections are better than their bank accounts.
Taken all together, these are the people who comprise what is called "society."
Except in very large cities, the whole community is aware of their existence and
knows that they constitute a more or less well-defined "upper class."

So much is obvious. Certain other things, however, are not so obvious. It is
not obvious, for example, that these local "upper classes" are in fact merely
sections of a national upper class, nor that this national upper class is in fact
the national ruling class. What we shall have to concentrate on therefore are
two points: first, the structure of the national ruling class; and second, how the
ruling class rules.

THE STRUCTURE OF THE NATIONAL RULING CLASS

That the local upper crusts are merely sections of a national class (also of an
international class, but that is beyond the scope of the present article) follows
from the way they freely mix and intermarry. The facts in this regard are well
known to any reasonably attentive observer of American life, and no attempt at
documentation is called for here. I merely suggest that those sociologists who
believe that only field work can yield reliable data, could provide valuable light
on the mixing of the local upper crusts by a careful field study of a typical summer or winter resort.

The national ruling class, however, is not merely a collection of interrelated
local upper crusts, all on a par with each other. It is rather a hierarchy of upper
crusts which has a fairly definite organizational structure, including lines of authority from leaders to followers. It is here that serious study of the ruling class
is most obviously lacking and also most urgently needed. I shall confine myself
to a few hints and suggestions, some of which may turn out on closer investigation to be mistaken or at any rate out of proportion.

Generally speaking, the sections of the national ruling class are hierarchically
organized with hundreds of towns at the bottom of the pyramid and a handful
of very large cities at the top. Very small communities can be counted out:
normally the wealth and standing of their leading citizens is no more than
enough to gain them entry into the middle class when they go to the city. Even
towns as large as five or ten thousand may have only a few representatives in
good standing in the national ruling class. You can always tell such a representative. Typically, he is a man "of independent means"; he went to a good college;
he has connections and spends considerable time in the state capital and/or the
nearest big city; he takes his family for part of the year to a resort where it can
enjoy the company of its social equals. And, most important of all, he is a person of unquestioned prestige and authority in his own community: he is, so to
speak, a local lieutenant of the ruling class.

Cities, of course, have more — I should also judge proportionately more —
national ruling-class members. And as a rule those who live in smaller cities
look up to and seek guidance from and actually follow those who live in large
cities. Certain of these larger cities have in turn acquired the position of what
we might call regional capitals (San Francisco, Chicago, Cleveland, Boston, and

so on): the lines of authority in the given region run to and end in the capital. The relation which exists among these regional capitals is a very important subject which deserves careful study. There was a time in our national history when it would probably have been true to say that the sections of the ruling class in the regional capitals looked up to and sought guidance from and actually followed the New York section, and to a considerable extent this may still be the case. At any rate this is the kernel of truth in the Wall Street theory. My own guess, for what it is worth, is that economic and political changes in the last thirty years (especially changes in the structure and functions of the banking system and the expansion of the economic role of the state) have reduced the relative importance of New York to a marked degree, and that today it is more accurate to describe New York as *primus inter pares* rather than as the undisputed leader of all the rest.

The ruling-class hierarchy is not based solely on personal or family relations among the members of the ruling class. On the contrary, it is bulwarked and buttressed by a massive network of institutional relations. Of paramount importance in this connection are the corporate giants with divisions, branches, and subsidiaries reaching out to all corners of the country. The American Telephone and Telegraph Company, with headquarters in New York and regional subsidiaries covering all 48 states, is in itself a powerful force welding the unity of the American ruling class; and it is merely the best-developed example of its kind. Formerly, a very large proportion of these business empires were centered in New York, and it was this more than anything else that gave that city a unique position. Today that proportion is much reduced, and cities like Pittsburgh, Cleveland, Detroit, Chicago, and San Francisco play a relatively more prominent part than they used to. In addition to corporations, an integrating role in the ruling class is performed by businessmen's organizations like the National Association of Manufacturers, the Chambers of Commerce, the Rotary and other so-called service clubs; by colleges and their alumni associations; by churches and women's clubs; by scores of fashionable winter and summer resorts (not all located in this country); and by a myriad other institutions too numerous even to attempt to list. (It will be noted that I have not mentioned the two great political parties in this connection. The reason is not that they don't to some extent play the part of an integrator of the ruling class: they do, and in a variety of ways. But their main function is quite different, namely, to provide the channels through which the ruling class manipulates and controls the lower classes. Compared to this function, their role *within* the ruling class is of quite secondary significance.)

Finally, we should note the key part played by the press in unifying and organizing the ruling class. To be sure, not all organs of the press figure here: the great majority, like the political parties, are instruments for controlling the lower classes. But the solider kind of newspaper (of which *The New York Times* is, of course, the prototype), the so-called quality magazines, the business and technical journals, the high-priced newsletters and dopesheets — all of these are designed primarily for the ruling class and are tremendously important in guiding and shaping its thinking. This does not mean that they in some way make up or determine the *content* of ruling-class ideas — this content is basically determined by what I may call the class situation (about which more will be said presently) — but it does mean that they standardize and propagate the ideas in such a way that the entire ruling class lives on a nearly uniform intellectual diet.

All of the formal and informal, the personal and institutional, ties that bind the ruling class together have a twofold character: on the one hand they are transmission belts and channels of communication; and on the other hand they are themselves molders of ideas and values and behavior norms — let us say for short, of ruling-class ideology. And here we have to note another mechanism of the greatest importance, the mechanism by which the class passes its ideology on from one generation to the next. The key parts of this mechanism are the family and the educational system. Ruling-class families are jealous protectors and indoctrinators of ruling-class ideology; the public school system faithfully reflects it and even, contrary to popular beliefs, fosters class distinctions; and private preparatory schools and colleges finish the job of dividing the ruling-class young from their compatriots. (In this connection, we must not be confused by the fact that a considerable number of lower-class families succeed in getting their sons and daughters into the private preparatory schools and colleges. This is merely a method by which the ruling class recruits the ablest elements of the lower classes into its service and often into its ranks. It is probably the most important such method in the United States today, having replaced the older method by which the abler lower-class young people worked their way directly up in the business world.)

HOW THE RULING CLASS RULES

Let us now turn, very briefly, to the question of how or in what sense the ruling class can be said to rule. This is a question which can easily lead to much mystification, but I think it can also be dealt with in a perfectly simple, straightforward way.

The question has two aspects, economic and political. The ruling class rules the economy in the sense that its members either directly occupy the positions in the economy where the key decisions are made or, if they don't occupy these positions themselves, they hire and fire those who do. The ruling class rules the government (using the term as a shorthand expression for all levels of government) in the sense that its members either directly occupy the key positions (largely true in the higher judiciary and the more honorific legislative jobs, increasingly true in the higher administrative jobs), or they finance and thus indirectly control the political parties which are responsible for staffing and managing the routine business of government. In short, the ruling class rules through its members who (1) do the job themselves, (2) hire and fire those who do, or (3) pay for the upkeep of political machines to do the job for them. That this rule through the members of the class is in fact *class rule* does not require to be separately demonstrated: it follows from the nature and structure of the class as we have already analyzed them.

This analysis of the way the ruling class rules is, of course, sketchy and oversimplified. I think nevertheless that it will stand up provided we can meet one objection, namely, that if the ruling class really ruled it would not put up with New Deals and Fair Deals and trade unions and John L. Lewises and Sidney Hillmans and all sorts of other outrages — *you* may not think them outrages, but the important thing from our present point of view is that the upper class *does* think them outrages. I have found in lectures and conversations about the ruling class that this is by far the most important and frequent objection to this analysis.

A full answer, I think, would require a careful examination of the nature and limits of political power, something which obviously cannot be undertaken here. But the main point is clearly indicated in the following passage from Lincoln Steffens's *Autobiography*. The passage concludes a chapter entitled "Wall Street Again":

> It is a very common error to think of sovereignty as absolute. Rasputin, a sovereign in Russia, made that mistake; many kings have made it and so lost their power to premiers and ministers who represented the "vested interests" of powerful classes, groups, and individuals. A dictator is never absolute. Nothing is absolute. A political boss concentrates in himself and personifies a very "wise" adjustment of the grafts upon which his throne is established. He must know these, reckon their power, and bring them all to the support of his power, which is, therefore, representative and limited. Mussolini, in our day, had to "deal with" the Church of Rome. A business boss has to yield to the powerful men who support him. The Southern Pacific Railroad had to "let the city grafters get theirs." The big bankers had to let the life insurance officers and employees get theirs. J. P. Morgan should have known what he soon found out, that he could not lick Diamond Jim Brady. Under a dictatorship nobody is free, not even the dictator; sovereign power is as representative as a democracy. It's all a matter of what is represented by His Majesty on the throne. In short, what I got out of my second period in Wall Street was this perception that everything I looked into in organized society was really a dictatorship, in this sense, that it was an organization of the privileged for the control of privileges, of the sources of privilege and of the thoughts and acts of the unprivileged; and that neither the privileged nor the unprivileged, neither the bosses nor the bossed, understood this or meant it.

There is, I think, more sound political science packed into that one paragraph than you will find in the whole of an average textbook. And it clearly contains the fundamental answer to the contention that the upper class doesn't rule because it has to put up with many things it doesn't like. Obviously the ruling class has to make concessions and compromises to keep the people, and especially the working class, in a condition of sufficient ignorance and contentment to accept the system as a whole. In other words, the ruling class operates within a definite framework, more or less restricted according to circumstances, which it can ignore only at the peril of losing its power altogether — and, along with its power, its wealth and privileges.

We must next consider the problem of "class position," which determines the basic content of ruling-class ideology. Here I can do no more than indicate what is meant by the expression. This, however, is not so serious a deficiency as at first sight it might appear to be; for once the nature of class position is understood it will be seen to be the very stuff of contemporary history, the constant preoccupation of any one who attempts to interpret the world from a socialist standpoint.

Class position has two aspects: the relation of the class to its own national social system, and the relation of the national social system to the world at large. For purposes of analyzing the position of the American ruling class we can identify it with the body of American capitalists: in respect to basic ideology, the fringes of the ruling class have no independence whatever. The problem therefore can be reduced to the state of American capitalism on the one hand, and the place of American capitalism in the world on the other. As I have tried to show in more detail in an earlier article ("The American Economy and the Threat of War," *Monthly Review*, November 1950), American capitalism has now reached the stage in which it is dominated by a strong tendency to chronic depression; while world capitalism, of which America is by far the most important component, is faced by a young, vigorous, and rapidly expanding international socialist system. These are the conditions and trends which determine the basic content of ruling-class ideology.

One final problem remains, that of divisions and conflicts within the ruling class. We are now in a position to see this problem in its proper setting and proportions. Aside from more or less accidental rivalries and feuds, the divisions within the ruling class are of several kinds: regional (based on economic differences and buttressed by historical traditions, and memories — the North-South division is the clearest example of this kind); industrial (for example, coal capitalists vs. oil capitalists); corporate (for example, General Motors vs. Ford); dynastic (for example, Du Ponts vs. Mellons); political (Republicans vs. Democrats); and idelogical (reactionaries vs. liberals). These divisions cut across and mutually condition one another, and the dividing lines are irregular and shifting. These factors introduce elements of indeterminacy and instability into the behavior of the ruling class and make of capitalist politics something more than a mere puppet show staged for the benefit (and obfuscation) of the man in the street. But we must not exaggerate the depth of the divisions inside the ruling class: capitalists can and do fight among themselves to further individual or group interests, and they differ over the best way of coping with the problems which arise from the class position; but overshadowing all these divisions is their common interest in preserving and strengthening a system which guarantees their wealth and privileges. In the event of a real threat to the system, there are no longer class differences — only class traitors, and they are few and far between. . . .

The late C. Wright Mills was among the most important social critics of the postwar decade, and his collected works may prove to be one of the most enduring monuments left by any American intellectual in recent memory.

In several books — The New Men of Power: America's Labor Leaders (New York: Harcourt, Brace, 1948), White Collar: The American Middle Classes (New York: Oxford University Press, 1951), The Power Elite (New York: Oxford University Press, 1956), and The Cultural Apparatus (unfinished) — Mills attempted systematically to survey and to explain the various levels of America's power structure. In the essay reprinted here, Mills summarizes his theory of power, displaying the characteristic sense of moral indignation, the gift for apt aphorism, and the polemical intensity that differentiated him from so many of his fellow academics.

Mills' major attack is upon pluralists who argue that power is widely distributed and equally available to all. The idea of balance or equilibrium underwriting such theory, he argues, is both atavistic and conservative. For, as Mills suggests in The Power Elite, "to say that various interests are 'balanced' is generally to evaluate the status quo as satisfactory or even good; the hopeful ideal of balance often masquerades as a description of fact." The independent middle class, in fact, has given way to the "new middle classes" of a modern "mass society." Congress has declined as an independent power, and the two major parties no longer offer real political choices. Unlike many pluralists, then, Mills believes that the fourth era of power relations (described by Riesman in The Lonely Crowd) has been superseded by a fifth period which can no longer be understood within the framework of liberal political theory.

In addition to pluralism, however, Mills also rejects many radical analyses. "Ruling Class," he contends in The Power Elite, "is a badly loaded phrase. 'Class' is an economic term; 'rule' a political one. The phrase 'ruling class' thus contains the theory that an economic class rules politically." Mills suggests, instead, that economic determinism should be supplemented by "political determinism" and by "military determinism." In this manner, he arrives at the theory, presented in the following essay, that economic, military, and political elites have today combined into a dominant "power elite." This conclusion has helped to create an intellectual schism in the American left between ruling class and power elite analysis. Mills generally stresses institutional power, domination, and consensus, whereas those of a more Marxian or Populist bent emphasize economic power and raise the possibility of class conflict or of popular uprisings. Unlike many class analysts, moreover, Mills tends to neglect the theory of imperialism (although he does use the concept in some of his short books, such as The Causes of World War Three [New York: Simon and Schuster, 1958]).

Pluralists, too, have assailed Mills' concept of the power elite. This theory, they charge, ignores the heterogeneity of rulers: business, political, and military elites differ from one another on many questions, and, further, each elite is itself internally divided. In addition, pluralists charge that the notion of intentional coordination between elites derives from an untenable "conspiracy" interpretation of history (even though Mills denies that the power elite emerged "as the realization of a plot"). Some critics, like Robert Dahl, argue that the power elite hypothesis cannot be proved or disproved and, hence, that it is meaningless. ("A Critique of the Ruling

Elite Model," American Political Science Review, 52 [June 1958], pp. 463–469.) Several observers — Dahl, Daniel Bell, Richard Rovere — sharply attack Mills for not closely examining any of the "key" or "big" decisions supposedly made by the power elite. Rovere — "The Interlocking Overlappers . . . " in The American Establishment: And Other Reports, Opinions, and Speculations (New York: Harcourt, Brace & World, 1962) — contends that a number of illustrative big decisions cited in The Power Elite were not made by irresponsible elites. Rovere argues, for instance, that the decision not to intervene in Indochina during the siege of Dienbienphu was profoundly influenced by public opinion. (Melvin Gurtov's recent study — The First Vietnam Crisis [New York: Columbia University Press, 1968] — suggests, on the contrary, that public opinion was not a major influence in this decision.) Mills, pluralist critics believe, overstates the case for a mass society and underestimates the continued vitality of "publics." They argue, in addition, that Mills often draws generalizations about the power elite from circumstances perhaps unique to the Eisenhower years, such as the growth of military power and the influence of big business on public policy.

We may also question whether Mills gives proper consideration to ruling class analyses. By charging Marxists with economic determinism, for instance, he greatly oversimplifies the sophisticated notion of social class informing many ruling class theories. Radicals themselves often wonder if Mills has not superimposed his power elite on a reality more congenial to class interpretations. See, for example, Robert Lynd's review essay, "Power in the United States," The Nation, 182 (May 12, 1956), pp. 408–411, and Paul Sweezy's, "Power Elite or Ruling Class?" Monthly Review, 8 (September 1956), pp. 138–150. These, and other critical reviews of The Power Elite have been collected by G. William Domhoff and Hoyt B. Ballard, eds., C. Wright Mills and The Power Elite (Boston: Beacon Press, 1968).

Despite criticism, Mills' work still commands respect. His analysis of the power elite breathed new life into a debate previously dominated by pluralists and gave expression to many disquieting public reservations about power in postwar America. If some of his insights have succumbed to critical attack, many others have survived and continue to invigorate contemporary social thought. The extent of Mills' contemporary relevance is in part suggested by Ralph Milibaud's excellent comparative study, The State in Capitalist Society (New York: Basic Books, 1969), which draws judiciously on both the Millsian and the Marxian traditions of social analysis.

C. WRIGHT MILLS
The Structure of Power
in American Society

Power has to do with whatever decisions men make about the arrangements under which they live, and about the events which make up the history of their times. Events that are beyond human decision do happen; social arrangements do change without benefit of explicit decision. But in so far as such decisions are made, the probem of who is involved in making them is the basic problem of power. In so far as they could be made but are not, the problem becomes who fails to make them?

We cannot today merely assume that in the last resort men must always be governed by their own consent. For among the means of power which now prevail is the power to manage and to manipulate the consent of men. That we do not know the limits of such power, and that we hope it does have limits, does not remove the fact that much power today is successfully employed without the sanction of the reason or the conscience of the obedient.

Surely nowadays we need not argue that, in the last resort, coercion is the "final" form of power. But then, we are by no means constantly at the last resort. Authority (power that is justified by the beliefs of the voluntarily obedient) and manipulation (power that is wielded unbeknown to the powerless) — must also be considered, along with coercion. In fact, the three types must be sorted out whenever we think about power.

In the modern world, we must bear in mind, power is often not so authoritative as it seemed to be in the medieval epoch: ideas which justify rulers no longer seem so necessary to their exercise of power. At least for many of the great decisions of our time — especially those of an international sort — mass "persuasion" has not been "necessary"; the fact is simply accomplished. Furthermore, such ideas as are available to the powerful are often neither taken up nor used by them. Such ideologies usually arise as a response to an effective debunking of power; in the United States such opposition has not been effective enough recently to create the felt need for new ideologies of rule.

There has, in fact, come about a situation in which many who have lost faith in prevailing loyalties have not acquired new ones, and so pay no attention to politics of any kind. They are not radical, not liberal, not conservative, not

From "The Structure of Power in American Society," by C. Wright Mills, *The British Journal of Sociology*, Vol. IX, No. 1, March 1958. Copyright Routledge & Kegan Paul, Ltd., 1958. Reprinted by permission of Brandt and Brandt.

reactionary. They are inactionary. They are out of it. If we accept the Greek's definition of the idiot as an altogether private man, then we must conclude that many American citizens are now idiots. And I should not be surprised, although I do not know, if there were not some such idiots even in Germany. This — and I use the word with care — this spiritual condition seems to me the key to many modern troubles of political intellectuals, as well as the key to much political bewilderment in modern society. Intellectual "conviction" and moral "belief" are not necessary, in either the rulers or the ruled, for a ruling power to persist and even to flourish. So far as the role of ideologies is concerned, their frequent absences and the prevalence of mass indifference are surely two of the major political facts about the western societies today.

How large a role any explicit decisions do play in the making of history is itself an historical problem. For how large that role may be depends very much upon the means of power that are available at any given time in any given society. In some societies, the innumerable actions of innumerable men modify their milieux, and so gradually modify the structure itself. These modifications — the course of history — go on behind the backs of men. History is drift, although in total "men make it." Thus, innumerable entrepreneurs and innumerable consumers by ten-thousand decisions per minute may shape and re-shape the free-market economy. Perhaps this was the chief kind of limitation Marx had in mind when he wrote, in *The 18th Brumaire:* that "Men make their own history, but they do not make it just as they please; they do not make it under circumstances chosen by themselves. . . ."

But in other societies — certainly in the United States and in the Soviet Union today — a few men may be so placed within the structure that by their decisions they modify the milieux of many other men, and in fact nowadays the structural conditions under which most men live. Such elites of power also make history under circumstances not chosen altogether by themselves, yet compared with other men, and compared with other periods of world history, these circumstances do indeed seem less limiting.

I should contend that "men are free to make history," but that some men are indeed much freer than others. For such freedom requires access to the means of decision and of power by which history can now be made. It has not always been so made; but in the later phases of the modern epoch it is. It is with reference to this epoch that I am contending that if men do not make history, they tend increasingly to become the utensils of history-makers as well as the mere objects of history.

The history of modern society may readily be understood as the story of the enlargement and the centralization of the means of power — in economic, in political, and in military institutions. The rise of industrial society has involved these developments in the means of economic production. The rise of the nation-state has involved similar developments in the means of violence and in those of political administration.

In the western societies, such transformations have generally occurred gradually, and many cultural traditions have restrained and shaped them. In most of the Soviet societies, they are happening very rapidly indeed and without the great discourse of western civilization, without the Renaissance and without the Reformation, which so greatly strengthened and gave political focus to the idea of freedom. In those societies, the enlargement and the co-ordination of all the means of power has occurred more brutally, and from the beginning under tightly centralized authority. But in both types, the means of power have now become international in scope and similar in form. To be sure, each of them has its own ups and downs; neither is as yet absolute; how they are run differs quite sharply.

Yet so great is the reach of the means of violence, and so great the economy required to produce and support them, that we have in the immediate past witnessed the consolidation of these two world centres, either of which dwarfs the power of Ancient Rome. As we pay attention to the awesome means of power now available to quite small groups of men we come to realize that Caesar could do less with Rome than Napoleon with France; Napoleon less with France than Lenin with Russia. But what was Caesar's power at its height compared with the power of the changing inner circles of Soviet Russia and the temporary administrations of the United States? We come to realize — indeed they continually remind us — how a few men have access to the means by which in a few days continents can be turned into thermonuclear wastelands. That the facilities of power are so enormously enlarged and so decisively centralized surely means that the powers of quite small groups of men, which we may call elites, are now of literally inhuman consequence.

My concern here is not with the international scene but with the United States in the middle of the twentieth century. I must emphasize "in the middle of the twentieth century" because in our attempt to understand any society we come upon images which have been drawn from its past and which often confuse our attempt to confront its present reality. That is one minor reason why history is the shank of any social science: we must study it if only to rid ourselves of it. In the United States, there are indeed many such images and usually they have to do with the first half of the nineteenth century. At that time the economic facilities of the United States were very widely dispersed and subject to little or to no central authority.

The state watched in the night but was without decisive voice in the day.

One man meant one rifle and the militia were without centralized orders.

Any American as old-fashioned as I can only agree with R. H. Tawney that "Whatever the future may contain, the past has shown no more excellent social order than that in which the mass of the people were the masters of the holdings which they ploughed and the tools with which they worked, and could boast . . . 'It is a quietness to a man's mind to live upon his own and to know his heir certain.' "

But then we must immediately add: all that is of the past and of little relevance to our understanding of the United States today. Within this society three broad levels of power may now be distinguished. I shall begin at the top and move downward.

The power to make decisions of national and international consequence is now so clearly seated in political, military, and economic institutions that other areas of society seem off to the side and, on occasion, readily subordinated to these. The scattered institutions of religion, education and family are increasingly shaped by the big three, in which history-making decisions now regularly occur. Behind this fact there is all the push and drive of a fabulous technology; for these three institutional orders have incorporated this technology and now guide it, even as it shapes and paces their development.

As each has assumed its modern shape, its effects upon the other two have become greater, and the traffic between the three has increased. There is no longer, on the one hand, an economy, and, on the other, a political order, containing a military establishment unimportant to politics and to money-making. There is a political economy numerously linked with military order and decision. This triangle of power is now a structural fact, and it is the key to any understanding of the higher circles in America today. For as each of these domains has coincided with the others, as decisions in each have become broader, the leading men of each — the high military, the corporation executives, the political directorate — have tended to come together to form the power elite of America.

The political order, once composed of several dozen states with a weak federal-centre, has become an executive apparatus which has taken up into itself many powers previously scattered, legislative as well as administrative, and which now reaches into all parts of the social structure. The long-time tendency of business and government to become more closely connected has since World War II reached a new point of explicitness. Neither can now be seen clearly as a distinct world. The growth of executive government does not mean merely the 'enlargement of government' as some kind of autonomous bureaucracy: under American conditions, it has meant the ascendancy of the corporation man into political eminence. Already during the New Deal, such men had joined the political directorate; as of World War II they came to dominate it. Long involved with government, now they have moved into quite full direction of the economy of the war effort and of the post-war era.

The economy, once a great scatter of small productive units in somewhat automatic balance, has become internally dominated by a few hundred corporations, administratively and politically interrelated, which together hold the keys to economic decision. This economy is at once a permanent-war economy and a private-corporation economy. The most important relations of the corporation to the state now rest on the coincidence between military and corporate interests, as defined by the military and the corporate rich, and accepted by politicians and public. Within the elite as a whole, this coincidence of military domain and corporate realm strengthens both of them and further subordinates the merely political man. Not the party politician, but the corporation executive, is now more likely to sit with the military to answer the question: what is to be done?

The military order, once a slim establishment in a context of civilian distrust, has become the largest and most expensive feature of government; behind smiling public relations, it has all the grim and clumsy efficiency of a great and sprawling bureaucracy. The high military have gained decisive political and economic relevance. The seemingly permanent military threat places a premium upon them and virtually all political and economic actions are now judged in terms of military definitions of reality: the higher military have ascended to a firm position within the power elite of our time.

In part at least this is a result of an historical fact, pivotal for the years since

1939: the attention of the elite has shifted from domestic problems — centered in the 'thirties around slump — to international problems — centered in the 'forties and 'fifties around war. By long historical usage, the government of the United States has been shaped by domestic clash and balance; it does not have suitable agencies and traditions for the democratic handling of international affairs. In considerable part, it is in this vacuum that the power elite has grown.

(i) To understand the unity of this power elite, we must pay attention to the psychology of its several members in their respective milieux. In so far as the power elite is composed of men of similar origin and education, of similar career and style of life, their unity may be said to rest upon the fact that they are of similar social type, and to lead to the fact of their easy intermingling. This kind of unity reaches its frothier apex in the sharing of that prestige which is to be had in the world of the celebrity. It achieves a more solid culmination in the fact of the interchangeability of positions between the three dominant institutional orders. It is revealed by considerable traffic of personnel within and between these three, as well as by the rise of specialized go-betweens as in the new style high-level lobbying.

(ii) Behind such psychological and social unity are the structure and the mechanics of those institutional hierarchies over which the political directorate, the corporate rich, and the high military now preside. How each of these hierarchies is shaped and what relations it has with the others determine in large part the relations of their rulers. Were these hierarchies scattered and disjointed, then their respective elites might tend to be scattered and disjointed; but if they have many interconnections and points of coinciding interest, then their elites tend to form a coherent kind of grouping. The unity of the elite is not a simple reflection of the unity of institutions, but men and institutions are always related; that is why we must understand the elite today in connection with such institutional trends as the development of a permanent-war establishment, alongside a privately incorporated economy, inside a virtual political vacuum. For the men at the top have been selected and formed by such institutional trends.

(iii) Their unity, however, does not rest solely upon psychological similarity and social intermingling, nor entirely upon the structural blending of commanding positions and common interests. At times it is the unity of a more explicit co-ordination.

To say that these higher circles are increasingly co-ordinated, that this is one basis of their unity, and that at times — as during open war — such co-ordination is quite wilful, is not to say that the co-ordination is total or continuous, or even that it is very surefooted. Much less is it to say that the power elite has emerged as the realization of a plot. Its rise cannot be adequately explained in any psychological terms.

Yet we must remember that institutional trends may be defined as opportunities by those who occupy the command posts. Once such opportunities are recognized, men may avail themselves of them. Certain types of men from each of these three areas, more far-sighted than others, have actively promoted the liaison even before it took its truly modern shape. Now more have come to see that their several interests can more easily be realized if they work together, in informal as well as in formal ways, and accordingly they have done so.

The idea of the power elite is of course an interpretation. It rests upon and it enables us to make sense of major institutional trends, the social similarities and psychological affinities of the men at the top. But the idea is also based upon what has been happening on the middle and lower levels of power, to which I now turn.

There are of course other interpretations of the American system of power. The most usual is that it is a moving balance of many competing interests. The image of balance, at least in America, is derived from the idea of the economic market: in the nineteenth century, the balance was thought to occur between a great scatter of individuals and enterprises; in the twentieth century, it is thought to occur between great interest blocs. In both views, the politician is the key man of power because he is the broker of many conflicting powers.

I believe that the balance and the compromise in American society — the "countervailing powers" and the "veto groups," of parties and associations, of strata and unions — must now be seen as having mainly to do with the middle levels of power. It is these middle levels that the political journalist and the scholar of politics are most likely to understand and to write about — if only because, being mainly middle class themselves, they are closer to them. Moreover these levels provide the noisy content of most "political" news and gossip; the images of these levels are more or less in accord with the folklore of how democracy works; and, if the master-image of balance is accepted, many intellectuals, especially in their current patrioteering, are readily able to satisfy such political optimism as they wish to feel. Accordingly, liberal interpretations of what is happening in the United States are now virtually the only interpretations that are widely distributed.

But to believe that the power system reflects a balancing society is, I think, to confuse the present era with earlier times, and to confuse its top and bottom with its middle levels.

By the top levels, as distinguished from the midde, I intend to refer, first of all, to the scope of the decisions that are made. At the top today, these decisions have to do with all the issues of war and peace. They have also to do with slump and poverty which are now so very much problems of international scope. I intend also to refer to whether or not the groups that struggle politically have a chance to gain the positions from which such top decisions are made, and indeed whether their members do usually hope for such top national command. Most of the competing interests which make up the clang and clash of American politics are strictly concerned with their slice of the existing pie. Labour unions, for example, certainly have no policies of an international sort other than those which given unions adopt for the strict economic protection of their members. Neither do farm organizations. The actions of such middle-level powers may indeed have consequence for top-level policy; certainly at times they hamper these policies. But they are not truly concerned with them, which means of course that their influence tends to be quite irresponsible.

The facts of the middle levels may in part be understood in terms of the rise of the power elite. The expanded and centralized and interlocked hierarchies over which the power elite preside have encroached upon the old balance and relegated it to the middle level. But there are also independent developments of the middle levels. These, it seems to me, are better understood as an affair of intrenched and provincial demands than as a centre of national decision. As such, the middle level often seems much more of a stalemate than a moving balance.

(i) The middle level of politics is not a forum in which there are debated the big decisions of national and international life. Such debate is not carried on by nationally responsible parties representing and clarifying alternative policies. There are no such parties in the United States. More and more, fundamental issues never come to any point or decision before the Congress, much less before the electorate in party campaigns. In the case of Formosa, in the spring of 1955, the Congress abdicated all debate concerning events and decisions which surely bordered on war. The same is largely true of the 1957 crisis in the Middle East. Such decisions now regularly by-pass the Congress, and are never clearly focused issues for public decision.

The American political campaign distracts attention from national and international issues, but that is not to say that there are no issues in these campaigns. In each district and state, issues are set up and watched by organized interests of sovereign local importance. The professional politician is of course a party politician, and the two parties are semi-feudal organizations: they trade patronage and other favours for votes and for protection. The differences between them, so far as national issues are concerned, are very narrow and very mixed up. Often each seems to be forty-eight parties, one to each state; and accordingly, the politician as campaigner and as Congressman is not concerned with national party lines, if any are discernible. Often he is not subject to any effective national party discipline. He speaks for the interests of his own constituency, and he is concerned with national issues only in so far as they affect the interests effectively organized there, and hence his chances of re-election. That is why, when he does speak of national matters, the result is so often such an empty rhetoric. Seated in his sovereign locality, the politician is not at the national summit. He is on and of the middle levels of power.

(ii) Politics is not an arena in which free and independent organizations truly connect the lower and middle levels of society with the top levels of decision. Such organizations are not an effective and major part of American life today. As more people are drawn into the political arena, their associations become mass in scale, and the power of the individual becomes dependent upon them; to the extent that they are effective, they have become larger, and to that extent they have become less accessible to the influence of the individual. This is a central fact about associations in any mass society: it is of most consequence for political parties and for trade unions.

In the 'thirties, it often seemed that labour would become an insurgent power independent of corporation and state. Organized labour was then emerging for the first time on an American scale, and the only political sense of direction it needed was the slogan, "organize the unorganized." Now without the mandate of the slump, labour remains without political direction. Instead of economic and political struggles it has become deeply entangled in administrative routines with both corporation and state. One of its major functions, as a vested interest of the new society, is the regulation of such irregular tendencies as may occur among the rank and file.

There is nothing, it seems to me, in the make-up of the current labour leadership to allow us to expect that it can or that it will lead, rather than merely react. In so far as it fights at all it fights over a share of the goods of a single way of life and not over that way of life itself. The typical labour leader in the U.S.A. today is better understood as an adaptive creature of the main business drift than as an independent actor in a truly national context.

(iii) The idea that this society is a balance of powers requires us to assume that the units in balance are of more or less equal power and that they are truly independent of one another. These assumptions have rested, it seems clear, upon the historical importance of a large and independent middle class. In the latter nineteenth century and during the Progressive Era, such a class of farmers and small businessmen fought politically — and lost — their last struggle for a paramount role in national decision. Even then, their aspirations seemed bound to their own imagined past.

This old, independent middle class has of course declined. On the most generous count, it is now 40 per cent of the total middle class (at most 20 per cent of the total labour force). Moreover, it has become politically as well as economically dependent upon the state, most notably in the case of the subsidized farmer.

The *new* middle class of white-collar employees is certainly not the political pivot of any balancing society. It is in no way politically unified. Its unions, such as they are, often serve merely to incorporate it as hanger-on of the labour interest. For a considerable period, the old middle class *was* an independent base of power; the new middle class cannot be. Political freedom and economic security *were* anchored in small and independent properties; they are not anchored in the worlds of the white-collar job. Scattered property holders were economically united by more or less free markets; the jobs of the new middle class are integrated by corporate authority. Economically, the white-collar classes are in the same condition as wage workers; politically, they are in a worse condition, for they are not organized. They are no vanguard of historic change; they are at best a rearguard of the welfare state.

The agrarian revolt of the nineties, the small-business revolt that has been more or less continuous since the eighties, the labour revolt of the thirties — each of these has failed as an independent movement which could countervail against the powers that be; they have failed as politically autonomous third parties. But they have succeeded, in varying degree, as interests vested in the expanded corporation and state; they have succeeded as parochial interests seated in particular districts, in local divisions of the two parties, and in the Congress. What they would become, in short, are well-established features of the *middle* levels of balancing power, on which we may now observe all those strata and interests which in the course of American history have been defeated in their bids for top power or which have never made such bids.

Fifty years ago many observers thought of the American state as a mask behind which an invisible government operated. But nowadays, much of what was called the old lobby, visible or invisible, is part of the quite visible government. The "governmentalization of the lobby" has proceeded in both the legislative and the executive domain, as well as between them. The executive bureaucracy becomes not only the centre of decision but also the arena within which major conflicts of power are resolved or denied resolution. "Administration" replaces electoral politics; the manœuvring of cliques (which include leading Senators as well as civil servants) replaces the open clash of parties.

The shift of corporation men into the political directorate has accelerated the decline of the politicians in the Congress to the middle levels of power; the formation of the power elite rests in part upon this relegation. It rests also upon the semi-organized stalemate of the interests of sovereign localities, into which the legislative function has so largely fallen; upon the virtually complete absence of a civil service that is a politically neutral but politically relevant, depository of brain-power and executive skill; and it rests upon the increased official secrecy behind which great decisions are made without benefit of public or even of Congressional debate.

There is one last belief upon which liberal observers everywhere base their interpretations and rest their hopes. That is the idea of the public and the associated idea of public opinion. Conservative thinkers, since the French Revolution, have of course Viewed With Alarm the rise of the public, which they have usually called the masses, or something to that effect. "The populace is sovereign," wrote Gustave Le Bon, "and the tide of barbarism mounts." But surely those who have supposed the masses to be well on their way to triumph are mistaken. In our time, the influence of publics or of masses within political life is in fact decreasing, and such influence as on occasion they do have tends, to an unknown but increasing degree, to be guided by the means of mass communication.

In a society of publics, discussion is the ascendant means of communication, and the mass media, if they exist, simply enlarge and animate this discussion, linking one face-to-face public with the discussions of another. In a mass society, the dominant type of communication is the formal media, and publics become mere markets for these media: the "public" of a radio programme consists of all those exposed to it. When we try to look upon the United States today as a society of publics, we realize that it has moved a considerable distance along the road to the mass society.

In official circles, the very term, "the public," has come to have a phantom meaning, which dramatically reveals its eclipse. The deciding elite can identify some of those who clamour publicly as "Labour," others as "Business," still others as "Farmer." But these are not the public. "The public" consists of the unidentified and the non-partisan in a world of defined and partisan interests. In this faint echo of the classic notion, the public is composed of these remnants of the old and new middle classes whose interests are not explicitly defined, organized, or clamorous. In a curious adaptation, "the public" often becomes, in administrative fact, "the disengaged expert," who, although ever so well informed, has never taken a clear-cut and public stand on controversial issues. He is the "public" member of the board, the commission, the committee. What "the public" stands for, accordingly, is often a vagueness of policy (called "open-mindedness"), a lack of involvement in public affairs (know as "reasonableness"), and a professional disinterest (known as "tolerance").

All this is indeed far removed from the eighteenth-century idea of the public of public opinion. That idea parallels the economic idea of the magical market. Here is the market composed of freely competing entrepreneurs; there is the public composed of circles of people in discussion. As price is the result of anonymous, equally weighted, bargaining indivduals, so public opinion is the result of each man's having thought things out for himself and then contributing his voice to the great chorus. To be sure, some may have more influence on the state of opinion than others, but no one group monopolizes the discussion, or by itself determines the opinions that prevail.

In this classic image, the people are presented with problems. They discuss them. They formulate viewpoints. These viewpoints are organized, and they compete. One viewpoint "wins out." Then the people act on this view, or their representatives are instructed to act it out, and this they promptly do.

Such are the images of democracy which are still used as working justifications of power in America. We must now recognize this description as more a fairy tale than a useful approximation. The issues that now shape man's fate are neither raised nor decided by any public at large. The idea of a society that is at bottom composed of publics is not a matter of fact; it is the proclamation of an ideal, and as well the assertion of a legitimation masquerading as fact.

I cannot here describe the several great forces within American society as well as elsewhere which have been at work in the debilitation of the public. I want only to remind you that publics, like free associations, can be deliberately and suddenly smashed, or they can more slowly wither away. But whether smashed in a week or withered in a generation, the demise of the public must be seen in connection with the rise of centralized organizations, with all their new means of power, including those of the mass media of distraction. These, we now know, often seem to expropriate the rationality and the will of the terrorized or — as the case may be — the voluntarily indifferent society of masses. In the more democratic process of indifference the remnants of such publics as remain may only occasionally be intimidated by fanatics in search of "disloyalty." But regardless of that, they lose their will for decision because they do not possess the instruments for decision; they lose their sense of political belonging because they do not belong; they lose their political will because they see no way to realize it.

The political structure of a modern democratic state requires that such a public as is projected by democratic theorists not only exist but that it be the very forum within which a politics of real issues is enacted.

It requires a civil service that is firmly linked with the world of knowledge and sensibility, and which is composed of skilled men who, in their careers and in their aspirations, are truly independent of any private, which is to say, corporation, interests.

It requires nationally responsible parties which debate openly and clearly the issues which the nation, and indeed the world, now so rigidly confronts.

It requires an intelligentsia, inside as well as outside the universities, who carry on the big discourse of the western world, and whose work is relevant to and influential among parties and movements and publics.

And it certainly requires, as a fact of power, that there be free associations standing between families and smaller communities and publics, on the one hand, and the state, the military, the corporation, on the other. For unless these do exist, there are no vehicles for reasoned opinion, no instruments for the rational exertion of public will.

Such democratic formations are not now ascendant in the power structure of the United States, and accordingly the men of decision are not men selected and formed by careers within such associations and by their performance before such publics. The top of modern American society is increasingly unified, and often seems wilfully co-ordinated: at the top there has emerged an elite whose power probably exceeds that of any small group of men in world history. The middle levels are often a drifting set of stalemated forces: the middle does not link the bottom with the top. The bottom of this society is politically fragmented, and even as a passive fact, increasingly powerless: at the bottom there is emerging a mass society.

These developments, I believe, can be correctly understood neither in terms of the liberal nor the marxian interpretation of politics and history. Both these ways of thought arose as guidelines to reflection about a type of society which does not now exist in the United States. We confront there a new kind of social structure, which embodies elements and tendencies of all modern society, but in which they have assumed a more naked and flamboyant prominence.

That does not mean that we must give up the ideals of these classic political expectations. I believe that both have been concerned with the problem of rationality and of freedom: liberalism, with freedom and rationality as supreme facts about the indivdual; marxism, as supreme facts about man's role in the political making of history. What I have said here, I suppose, may be taken as an attempt to make evident why the ideas of freedom and of rationality now so often seem so ambiguous in the new society of the United States of America.

Revisionist Interpretations

Harvard sociologist Talcott Parsons has long been an influential advocate of "functional" sociology and a strong champion of liberal pluralism. His work is marked by a recurrent emphasis upon factors creating integration, co-

hesion, and consensus within a social system, and he touches continually on questions of equilibrium, order, and "systems maintenance." Parsons and Mills have a common interest in large social questions and in theoretical sociology, yet they diverge sharply in their stress on different facets of the social equation. Parsons looks to elements of consensus and community, whereas Mills centers upon coercion and manipulation. In the article reprinted below, Parsons details his disagreement with the concept of a power elite and summarizes the major pluralist objections to Mills' theory.

Parsons admits that the American economy is no longer one of small units, but he suggests, unlike Mills, that it has reached "some kind of equilibrium condition with respect to the degree of concentration in the system as a whole." Like Berle and Means, Parsons believes that a managerial revolution now makes it impossible to speak of the very rich and the corporate rich as a single class. Economic advantage is no longer cumulative and ascriptive but increasingly depends upon achievement; competence rather than property characterizes those who control large American corporations. Further, Parsons accepts the liberal view that "in a complex society the primary locus of power lies in the political system." He denies that politics has been controlled by any class or elite and contends that government, in fact, has effectively restrained business power in the public interest. Parsons also questions Mills' analysis of political parties, disputes his idea of a mass society, and disagrees with his assessment of military power.

Parsons' most intriguing theoretical contribution is his distinction between "zero-sum" and "resource" interpretations of power. In essence, Parsons charges that Mills, "like a nostalgic Jeffersonian," falsely associates power with the exploitative relationship between groups competing for scarce resources. Parsons believes, on the contrary, that power is necessary to the functional integration of society. Power is consensual and constructive rather than divisive and oppressive, for it may be used positively to mobilize society in the pursuit of collective social goals. This interpretation of power not only challenges radical analyses emphasizing exploitation and manipulation, but also takes issue with the liberal individualism of certain pluralists.

Yet Parsons' critique may be criticized in several particulars. He equates the distribution of power with the distribution of wealth, for example, and in so doing may rely upon an inappropriate analogy. There is always a continuum of wealth, and hence it can never be viewed as a zero-sum phenomenon. Power, on the other hand, may more properly be defined in terms of those who participate in its exercise and those who are subject to it; in this regard, see sociologist Ralf Dahrendorf's zero-sum definition of power in Class and Class Conflict in Industrial Society (Stanford: Stanford University Press, 1959). It is no doubt true, as Parsons claims, that power may be used as a resource to increase the unity and integration of a society. Yet this does not mean that power is always exercised for such commendable purposes, nor does it demonstrate that power is never the servant of special interests. If Parsons detects the bias of some radical critics, in short, his own analysis errs equally in the other direction, giving inadequate attention

to the deleterious uses of power. Some commentators further suggest that
Parsons misreads The Power Elite and that Mills, in fact, does not develop a zero-sum model of power. (See Jeffrey M. Schevitz, "The Incor-
poration of Pluralism into Parsons' Theory of the Polity," American Behavioral Scientist, 12 [November–December 1968], pp. 21–27.) Other
ideas vital to Parsons' analysis, such as the managerial revolution and the
effective regulation of business by government, are discussed elsewhere in
this volume.

TALCOTT PARSONS
The Distribution of Power
in American Society

It has been remarked that it is relatively rare, in the United States at least, for
social scientists to attempt interpretive analyses of major aspects of the total
society in which they live. This is particularly true of sociologists,[1] unlike economists, who have made notable attempts in recent years to interpret their societies
— for example, Schumpeter's *Capitalism, Socialism and Democracy* and Galbraith's *American Capitalism*. If for this reason alone, the present book of
Professor Mills, which must be understood as one of a series as yet far from
complete, would be worthy of serious attention.

In the nature of the case, to produce such a study is a very difficult enterprise.
However operationally useful precise data may be — and Mr. Mills makes
copious and, with some exceptions, relatively good use of them — they cannot
suffice for a full empirical grounding of interpretive conclusions, not only because on their own level they are fragmentary and incomplete, but because
many of the crucial empirical questions arise on a level at which available operational procedures are not of much or any use. This is not in the least to say
that observation is not feasible, but rather that it cannot be precise observation
in the usual operational sense.

I am referring to questions of the type which are central to Mr. Mills' argument, as to whether and in what sense a relatively small group of the occupants
of "command posts" in the society has acquired a paramount position of power,

From Talcott Parsons, "The Distribution of Power in American Society," *World Politics*,
Vol. X, No. 1, October 1957. Reprinted by permission of *World Politics*.
    [1] The main exception here is Robin M. Williams' excellent *American Society* (New
York: 1951), which has received far less general attention than it deserves, perhaps because
of its somewhat textbookish orientation.

as to whether the relative power of such a group has greatly increased in the last twenty years, as to how unified such a group is, and the like.

There are technical ways of reducing the element of arbitrariness in such judgments and protecting them against at least the grosser sorts of ideological distortion. Checking against all the available precise data is one such method; viewing the problem from the perspective given by wide and deep knowledge, not only of our own society but of others, is another. But I think the most important is exercising control through the use of a relatively well-integrated and technical theoretical scheme. Undertaking as a professional sociologist to review Mr. Mills' book, I am motivated largely by the opportunity to test some of his main conclusions against expectations derived from a type of technical theory that is at best only partially shared by the author of the book. In these terms I wish to take serious issue with Mr. Mills' position on a number of very important points and to outline an alternative interpretation of what I take to be the salient facts of the situation. There are some points at which I differ from Mills on simple questions of fact, but for the most part my criticisms will deal with empirical generalizations and their theoretical background.[2] These generalizations concern not only the facts he chooses to state and emphasize but others he omits or treats as unimportant.

What is the gist of Mills' argument? I am able here to give only a very brief summary. The reader should not depend on this review alone for his information about the contents of the book itself, but should go directly to Mills' own statement of his case.

Mills' central theme is the contention — in contrast to what he refers to as the traditional view of the political pluralism of American society — that there has developed to an unprecedented degree in the last generation or so a concentration of power in the hands of a small, relatively tightly integrated group of people. These are defined as the people occupying the institutional "command posts" of the society, the places where the decisions are made that have the greatest immediate and direct influence on the course of events in the society and on the shaping of its future and that of the rest of the world, so far as that future is dependent on what happens in the United States. Mills argues that the power of this group has grown disproportionately to the growth in size and power of the society as a whole.

The "command posts" in question are centered in large-scale organizations, which are certainly a prominent feature of American society. The power elite are in general those who occupy the decision-making positions in these large organizations. Mills identifies these in only two basic areas, business and government — although for his purposes the field of government is subdivided into the military and the political sectors; indeed, he almost tends to treat the military as independent of the rest of government. He clearly is thinking of the centralized type of organization where a few "top executives" exercise the main

---

[2] Mr. Mills is clearly writing only partly for an audience of technical social scientists. Though my own argument will be largely based on considerations of technical theory, I shall not introduce explicit justification of my theoretical judgment into this review, but will try to state my case in relatively non-technical terms.

immediate decision-making power, in contrast to the democratic association with a somewhat more decentralized structure of authority and influence. It seems to be largely on this ground that he contends that the executive branch of the federal government has gained a pronounced ascendancy over the legislative. He relegates Congress — even the most influential group of Senators — to what he calls the "middle level" of the power structure; such people do not belong to the "power elite."

Mills broadly identifies the power elite with the "upper class." But he does not agree with Lloyd Warner and his group that the primary element of this upper class is a hereditary group of families or lineages; its position clearly depends on occupational status, though there is also emphasis on the importance within it of the "very rich," the majority of whom have inherited their wealth. Contrary to most sociological usage, Mills restricts the term "class" to an economic meaning, so that by "upper class" he means, essentially, the rich. But this still leaves open the question of the substantive relations between inherited and newly acquired wealth, family status relatively independent of at least very large wealth, occupational status within various income ranges, and similar problems.

Generally, Mills is rather vague on the relations between the power elite and other elements which in some sense enjoy rather high prestige. He emphasizes the prominence of lawyers among the "political directorate," but there is no clear analysis of the role of professional groups in the occupational structure generally; one presumes that except for a few lawyers who are successful in politics or business, and perhaps some engineers, professional people do not belong to the power elite. Similarly he emphasizes that members of the power elite have more than the average amount of education, and in particular he stresses the proportion who have been to select private schools and to "Ivy League" colleges. In general, he is greatly concerned about the fact that the power elite are not "representative" of the population as a whole in the sense of constituting a random sample by socio-economic origin, by education, by ethnic group, etc. This is a point to which I shall return.

Neither the "higher circles" generally nor the component of the "very rich" (Mills' term) are a leisure class in Veblen's sense; many, if not most of them, "work" in various fields of business and financial management. Furthermore, the processes of recruitment are about what social scientists have come to expect. Mills does not give any exact criteria for what he considers to be "upper class" as a category of social origin, but I have the impression that he puts the line somewhat lower than most sociologists would. But, however that may be, it is clear that there is a considerable element of stability from generation to generation in the higher-status groups in American society. Thus if, to employ a pattern used by Mills, we take a group of prominent persons, the family origin of from two-thirds to three-fourths of them will be the upper third of the American status structure. It is not these essential facts but the interpretation placed upon them which raises questions for us. The only point of fact I would question is whether the recruitment of the very rich has shown a sharper increase through the process of inheritance than through self-earning. It is possible that this is so, but I am inclined to doubt it, and in any case their position does not depend only on the process which Mills calls "cumulative advantage."

Mills radically denies that the group he calls the "very rich" and the "corporate rich" are distinct "classes," in his sense. He explictly lumps them together and on the whole gives the very rich a greater position of influence than they are usually accorded or than, I think, they actually enjoy. This is in line with his thesis that there is a single, unified power elite. Clearly, it is his contention that the base of the (business) group as a whole lies in command of the very large business enterprises — somewhat erroneously, or at least ambiguously, he puts the primary emphasis on control of property in accounting for this power.

Of the three main subgroups, Mills treats the "political directorate" as by far the weakest. It has, according to him, been greatly infiltrated by the business element, so that it can scarcely be treated as independent. Hence virtually the only element independent of what might be called the business oligarchy is the military — and this, he holds, is coming increasingly to fuse with the business group, or at least to form a close community of interest with it.

The pluralistic components of our older political traditions, Mills feels, are rooted primarily in local groupings — partly, of course, through the constitutional provisions which establish federalism and make Congressional representation dependent on local constituencies. But the operations of the big organizations have become national in scope, and often international. Hence structures rooted in localism have simply been pushed into a secondary position.

But at the same time Mills contends that the structural base of authentic localism has been progressively atrophied through the development of what he calls the "mass society." The most conspicuous phenomena of the mass society are the prevalence and characteristics of the media of mass communication, which tend to serve as instruments of the power elite out of the reach of locally based "publics" and influential elements in them. The theory of the mass society is only very sketchily presented in one chapter near the end of the book, but is clearly meant to provide one of the main components of the total picture of American society which Mills is presenting.

In terms of recent history, one of Mills' main contentions is that the New Deal period did not represent a turning point in social development, but rather a superficial flurry which only momentarily disturbed the process of emergence of the power elite and the dominance of the business contingent within it. Thus Mills speaks of the economic elite as in due course coming "to control and to use for their own purposes the New Deal institutions whose creation they had so bitterly denounced" (pp. 272–73).

Mills repeatedly disavows any intention of presenting a "conspiratorial" interpretation of American social and political development. He stresses the institutional positions occupied by his elite rather than their personalities and conspiratorial activities. Nevertheless he often comes very close to this implication because of his special theory that a peculiar irresponsibility attaches to the elite and their actions. By this he seems to mean the absence or relative ineffectiveness of formal legal restraints or of a system of "checks and balances" of the sort which has traditionally been associated with our political system. His contention thus is that the power elite has been freed from the historic restraints of our society and uses its power in terms of what he calls a "higher immorality" — a conception which is not very clearly explained.

Finally, it should be mentioned that in this, as in some of his previous writings, Mills' general tone toward both men and institutions is sharply caustic. *The Power Elite* certainly purports to be an exposition and an explanation of what has been happening in American society, but it is equally an indictment. There is no pretense of even trying to maintain a scientific neutrality; the book is a fiery and sarcastic attack on the pretensions of the "higher circles" in America either to competence in exercise of their responsibilities or to moral legitimation of their position. In such a case, the critic must ascertain the moral position from which the indictment is formulated; I shall have something to say about this later. In his combination of often insightful exposition and analysis, empirical one-sidedness and distortion, and moral indictment and sarcasm, Mills reminds one more of Veblen than of any other figure; that he has attained the stature of Veblen I question, but the role he is cutting out for himself is similar.

As I have said, the Mills analysis presents what, to me, is a subtle and complex combination of acceptable and unacceptable elements. Let me now attempt, at some of the most important points, to unravel these elements from each other. I want to try this first on the level of empirical generalization and then to raise one or two more strictly theoretical problems. I shall do so more in my own terms than in those employed by Mills.

In my opinion, two salient sets of processes have been going on in American society during the past half-century, the combination of which encompasses the main facts which are essential to our problem. The first of these is the dynamic of a maturing industrial society, including not only the highly industrialized economy itself but its setting in the society as a whole — notably, its political system and class structure (in a wider sense of the term "class" than Mills') — and the repercussions of the industrial development on the rest of the society. The second concerns the altered position of the United States in world society, which is a consequence in part of our own economic growth, in part of a variety of exogenous changes, including the relative decline of the Western European powers, the rise of Soviet Russia, and the break-up of the "colonial" organization of much of the non-white world. The enormous enhancement of American power and responsibility in the world has taken place in a relatively short time and was bound to have profound repercussions on the characteristics of our own society. Our old political isolation has disappeared and given way to the deepest of involvements.

My first thesis is that these two processes *both* work in the direction of increasing the relative importance of government in our society and, with it, of political power. But their impact has been all the greater because of the extent to which the United States has been an almost specifically non-political society. This has been evidenced above all in the institutions and tradition of political decentralization already mentioned, one aspect of which is the localism which Mills discusses. A second, however, has been a cultural tradition which has emphasized economic values — an emphasis on enterprise and production in an activist sense, not a merely passive hedonistic valuation of the enjoyment of material well-being. Moreover, the virtually unimpeded process of settlement of a continent in political isolation from the main system of world powers has favored maintenance of this emphasis to a greater extent than would otherwise have readily been possible.

At some points in his discussion, Mills seems to look back to the Jeffersonian picture of a system of economic production consisting mainly of small farmers and artisans, with presumably a small mercantile class mediating between them and consumers. Clearly this is not a situation compatible with high industrial development, in either of two respects. First, the order of decentralization of production where the standard unit is a family-size one is incompatible with either the organization or the technology necessary for high industrialism. Second, the "Jeffersonian" economy is not one in which economic production is differentiated from other social functions in specialized organizations; instead, the typical productive unit is at the same time a kinship unit and a unit of citizenship in the community.[3]

In all salient respects, the modern economy has moved very far from the Jeffersonian ideal. The pace-setting units have become both large and specialized. Their development has been part of a general process of structural differentiation in the society which has led to greater specialization in many fields. An essential aspect of the process of development of the economy as a system in *both* these senses is greater specialization on at least three levels: first, the specialization of organizations in the functions of economic production as distinguished from other functions; second, the specialization of functions within the economy; and third, the specialization of the roles of classes of individuals within the organization.

Leadership is an essential function in all social systems, which with their increase of scale and their functional differentiation tend to become more specialized. I think we can, within considerable limits, regard the emergence of the large firm with operations on a nation-wide basis as a "normal" outcome of the process of growth and differentiation of the economy. Similarly, the rise to prominence within the firm of specialized executive functions is also a normal outcome of a process of growth in size and in structural differentiation. The question then arises whether the process of concentration of firms, and of executive power within firms, has "gone too far" because it has been greatly influenced by factors extraneous to the process of economic development itself.

Mills makes the assertion that the size of the large firm has exceeded the limits of economic efficiency. He presents no evidence, and I think most competent persons would regard this as an exceedingly difficult question. There is, however, one line of evidence not cited by Mills which has a bearing on it. It is true that the absolute size of firms has steadily increased — General Motors

[3] How far this "Jeffersonianism" thus represents the moral position from which Mills launches his indictment is a question I will discuss at the end of the article. It provides a convenient reference point in terms of contrast both for Mills' characterization of the current society and for my own very different one.

today is larger than any firm of the 1920's. But the *relative* share of the largest firms in the production of the economy has remained essentially stable for more than a generation, a fact which points to some kind of equilibrium condition with respect to the degree of concentration in the system as a whole.

A cognate question is whether the power of the executive or managerial class within industry, and particularly within the large firms, has increased inordinately, which if true would indicate that factors other than the functional needs of the productive process were operating to skew the internal power structure of firms in favor of the executive groups.

Generally speaking, Mills' argument is that the power of the very rich and the corporate rich *within* the economy is inordinately great and, by virtue of the factor of cumulative advantage, is becoming continually greater. At the very least, I think it can be said that his case is not proved and that there is equally good, if not better, evidence for an alternative view, particularly with reference to the trend.

First, I am not able to accept Mills' close identification of the very rich (i.e., the holders of "great fortunes") with the "corporate rich" (the primary holders of executive power in business organizations) as a single class in any very useful sense. Certainly, in the "heroic age" of American capitalism, from the Civil War to just after the turn of the century, the dominant figures were the entrepreneurs who, mainly as the founders of great enterprises and as the bankers and promoters concerned with mergers and reorganizations and the like, came to control these great organizations. But the dominant sociological fact of the outcome of that era was that these owning groups did not, as a group, succeed in consolidating their position precisely *within* their own enterprises and in the economy. It is a notorious fact that the *very* large enterprise still largely under family control through property holdings is much more the exception than the rule. Instead, the control has passed — by no means fully, but for the most part — to professional career executives, who have not reached their positions through the exercise of *property* rights but through some sort of process of appointment and promotion.

Mills concedes the main facts of this situation but fails, in my opinion, to evaluate them properly. It seems to be clear that the original "captains of industry," the makers of the great fortunes, *failed* to achieve or to exercise sufficient cumulative advantages to consolidate control of the enterprises in their families and their class ("class" in a sociological, not an economic, sense). This came about essentially because there were factors operating contrary to that of cumulative advantage, which Mills stresses so heavily. The main factor was the pressure to link executive responsibility with competence in such a way that the ascriptive rights of property ownership have tended to give way to the occupational functions of "professionals."

There are, above all, two ways in which Mills' treatment obscures the importance and nature of this shift. First, he continues to speak of power *within* the economy as based on property. To a considerable degree, of course, this is legally true, since the legal control of enterprise rests with stockholders. But, as Berle and Means first made abundantly clear, very generally it is not substantively true. In the old-style family enterprise, still predominant in the small-business sector of the economy, the functions of management and ownership are fused in the same people. In the larger enterprise they have by and large become differentiated. The fact that executives receive large salaries and bonuses is not to be twisted into an assumption that they control, so far as they do, through their property rights. Paradoxical as it may seem, a relatively backward industrial economy like that of France is far more *property*-based than is the case with the United States. In general, property holdings have not, of course, been expropriated, except for their diminution through inheritance and income taxes, which are not as negligible as Mills maintains. What has happened is that their relation to the *power* structure of the economy has been greatly altered. Mills almost entirely passes over this change.

The second problem concerns the process of recruitment in the higher occupational reaches of the economy. It is entirely clear that the process operates in the higher reaches overwhelmingly by appointment, i.e., the decisions of superiors as individuals or in small groups as to who should occupy certain positions. It is also true that the process is relatively unformalized — e.g., there are no competitive examinations and few, if any, formal qualifications of training. But from these facts Mills concludes, and again and again reiterates, that executive competence has very little, if anything, to do with the selection, that it is an overwhelmingly arbitrary process of choosing those who are congenial to the selectors, presumably because they can be counted upon to be "yes men." At the very least this contention is unproved, and I seriously doubt its correctness. There are certainly many difficulties and imperfections in the selection process. But I think it almost certain that higher levels of competence are selected than would on the average be the case through kinship ascription, and that, as such processes go, the levels selected are relatively high.

One final point in this field. It does seem probable that the factor of cumulative advantage has a good deal to do with the high levels of financial remuneration of the higher executive groups and with the discrepancies between their incomes and those of governmental and professional people on comparable levels of competence and responsibility. But this is very far from the great fortune level of the founding entrepreneur type, and the evidence seems to be that the discrepancy has not been cumulatively increasing to an appreciable degree, particularly relative to wages at the labor levels; cases like that of the academic profession are somewhat special.

So far I have been speaking about the nature and power position of the elite *within* the economy. The general tenor of my argument has been that, given the nature of an industrial society, a relatively well-defined elite or leadership group *should be expected to develop* in the business world; it is out of the question that power should be diffused equally among an indefinite number of very small units, as the ideal of pure competition and a good deal of the ideology of business itself would have it. But first I question whether the position of power of the business leadership groups is such that a heavy operation of the factor of cumulative advantage must be invoked to account for it. Secondly, I must stress that the business elite is no longer primarily an elite of *property*-owners, but that its center of gravity has shifted to occupationally professional executives or managers. Differential advantages of family origin, etc., are about the same for admission to this group as to other groups requiring educational and other qualifications. Again the evidence is that the proportion of its members recruited from the upper economic and social groups is and remains relatively high, but it has not, in recent times, been increasing, as the theory of cumulative advantage would lead us to expect.

The problem of an elite within the economy must, however, be clearly distinguished from that of an elite in the society as a whole and the power position occupied by such an elite. There are two main orders of questions bearing on the transition from one to the other. Though a thorough consideration of this transition would lead into very far-reaching questions, for present purposes one can be treated rather briefly. Mills gives us the impression that "eliteness" in any society, including our own, is overwhelmingly a question of the power that an individual or a group can command. By this, he means (I shall further discuss his concept of power presently) influence on the "big" decisions directly affecting what happens in the society in the short run. But there are many elements in the society which are relatively powerless in this sense, but nevertheless of the greatest functional importance. Our society has almost divested kinship units as such of important power in this sense. But this does not mean at all that the family has ceased to be important. Closely linked with this is the question of the feminine role. Women qua women by and large do not have a position of power comparable to that of men; but this is not to say that they are unimportant — otherwise how can we account for the extent of our national preoccupations with questions of sexuality? Finally, there is a *distinct* difference between the rank-order of occupations — which, relative to other role-types, are closely involved with decision-making in a society like ours — by power and by prestige. The most striking case is the relatively high position of the professions relative to executive roles in business, as revealed by the famous North-Hatt data. Physicians as a group do not exercise great power, but there is no reason to question their very high prestige, which has been demonstrated in study after study.

The second main context, however, directly concerns the question of power. In a complex society the primary locus of power lies in the political system. There are many subtle analytical problems involved in the delineation of this system and its functions in the society which cannot be gone into here; this formula will have to suffice. Two questions are, however, primary for our purposes: the degree of differentiation of the political system from other systems; and its own internal structure. These two problems, it will be noted, parallel those raised with reference to the economy.

For historical reasons it seems clear that the development of the American political system, since the breakdown of the first synthesis associated with the "founders of the Republic," has lagged behind that of the economy. This is a function primarily of the two factors already noted — the economic emphasis inherent in our system of values, and the relative lack of urgency of certain political problems because of our especially protected and favored national position. Relative to the economic structure, which had by that time grown enormously, the political was at its weakest in the period from the Civil War to the end of the century; this situation is sketched by Mills in broadly correct terms. Since then, both internal exigencies and the exigencies of our international position have been stimuli for major changes.

Internally, beyond the more elementary provisions for law and order and essential minimum services — much of this, of course, on a local basis — the main focus of the development of our political system has been *control* of economic organization and processes, and coping with some of the social consequences of economic growth and industrialization. The process started well before the turn of the century with the Interstate Commerce legislation and the Anti-Trust Act and continued through the New Deal era, not steadily but with waves of new measures and levels of political control.

A major problem in relation to Mills' analysis is whether this is "genuine" control. His view seems to be that at times it has been, but that on balance it is the business power-holders who control government, not vice versa; the above quotation about the outcome of the New Deal puts it succinctly. In my opinion this is a misinterpretation. If genuine and in some sense effective controls had not been imposed, I find it impossible to understand the bitter and continuing opposition on the part of business to the measures which have been taken.[4] Even some of those most completely taken for granted now, like the Federal Reserve system, were bitterly fought at the time. It therefore seems to me to be the sounder interpretation that there has been a genuine growth of autonomous governmental power — apart from the military aspect, which will be discussed presently — and that one major aspect of this has been relatively effective control of the business system. This control and the growth of "big government" have been generally accepted in the society as a whole. The participation of big-business men in governmental processes is by no means to be interpreted as a simple index of their power to dominate government in their own interests, as Mills often seems to maintain.

To me, another indication of Mills' biased view of the governmental situation is his almost complete failure even to mention the political parties, or to analyze their differences. It seems to me broadly true that the Republican party, though a coalition, is more than any other single thing the party of the bigger sector of business. Four years of a Republican administration — two of them without control of Congress — is certainly not enough to indicate that big business through its favorite party organ controls the government on a long-run basis. So Mills is practically forced to the view that the alleged control operates above and beyond the party system. This seems to be connected with his relegation of the legislative branch to the "middle level" of power. I have strong reservations about this, but also it must not be forgotten that the presidency is the biggest prize of all in party politics, and it is its importance which forms the primary integrating focus of our particular type of party system. Surely the

---

[4] Cf. F. X. Sutton, *et al.*, *The American Business Creed* (Cambridge, Mass.: 1956), for an excellent analysis of the point of view of business toward its relations to government. The authors make it clear that the present state of affairs is far from being fully accepted in business circles even now.

presidency is not simply the football of an inner clique which manipulates the executive branch independently of the party.[5]

Mills, of course, recognizes that the aftermath of two world wars, the rise of Communist power, and the relative decline of the older Western Great Powers provide the occasion for the increasing prominence of the military group in our governmental system. Before these changes — and, indeed, to a remarkable extent, as late as the 1930's — the military played a far smaller role in this country than in any other society of comparable scale and organizational and technological development. Part of the change may be interpreted as simply the redressing of a balance. But it seems to me correct to say that for the last ten years there has been a special situation attributable to the extremely unsettled condition of the world at large and to the difficulties entailed for the American system given its background, in meeting the problem on its own terms. There is thus a sense in which it is true that the higher military officers have tended to fill a vacuum in the field of national decision-making. There are two main points to be made about Mills' treatment of the matter. First, more in this field than perhaps any other, Mills' discussion is marred by a hasty tendency to generalize from very recent short-run developments to the long-run prospects of the structure of the society. Even here he fails to mention that in certain crucial questions the recommendations of the military have been overruled by civilian authority, although the President is a former military man. Secondly, the tone of indictment, particularly evidenced by the quite unnecessary and, I think, inappropriate parading of the term "warlord," is stronger in his discussion of this area than in any other, except perhaps the "mass society."

Related to the position of the higher military officers is what Mills calls the "military metaphysic," meaning the definition of international problems in terms of the primacy of military force. That there has been such a tendency, and that it has gone beyond the objective requirements of the situation, seem to be unquestionable. But I very much doubt whether it is as absolute as many of Mills' statements make it appear, and a swing in another direction is discernible already.[6] This seems to be another case of Mills' tendency to make large generalizations about major trends from short-run experience.

Finally, let us say a word about what Mills calls the "political directorate" — that is, the non-military component in the groups most influential in the affairs of government and politics. Again I think there is a certain correctness in his contention that a definite weakness exists here, and that the high participation both of business and of military elements in the exercise of power is related to this. But a difficulty arises in terms of the perspective on American society

[5] Somewhat curiously, though tending to suggest that President Eisenhower's elevation to the presidency is symptomatic of the alliance between the "warlords" and the upper business group, Mills does not even mention Adlai Stevenson as a significant figure in the American political scene. To be sure, his book appeared before Stevenson's second nomination. But where does Stevenson fit?

[6] Whatever may be thought of it in other respects, Mr. Dulles' reluctance to join Britain and France in military measures against Egypt was hardly an expression of the "military metaphysic" now allegedly dominating the government.

which I have been emphasizing throughout. But the non-political stress in American social structure and values generally, and the recency and intensity of the pressures to build up this aspect of our structure, would lead one to predict that it would be a major focus of strain. American society has not developed a well-integrated political-government elite, in the sense that it has developed a relatively well-integrated business-executive group. For this reason responsibility has been carried — imperfectly, of course — by a very miscellaneous group which includes members of the business and military groups, as would be expected, but also "politicians," in the usual sense of people making an at least partial career out of elective office and the influencing of elections; professional people, particularly lawyers but also economists, political scientists, and even natural scientists (e.g., John von Neumann as Atomic Energy Commissioner); journalists; and, a very important element, upper-class people in more than the purely economic sense that Mills employs, of whom Franklin Roosevelt was one and Adlai Stevenson, though also a lawyer, is another. In my opinion, the structure of the American political leadership group is far from a settled thing. It certainly is not settled in terms of the long-run dominance of a business-military coalition.

Mills holds that the United States has no higher civil service at all, in the European sense, and seems to imply that we should have. There is relative truth in his empirical contention, though I think he tends to underestimate the real influence of "non-political" government officials on longer-run policy.[7] At least it seems highly probable that in the nature of the case the tendency will be toward a strengthening of the element of professional governmental officials who are essentially independent both of short-run "politics" and of elements extraneous to the structure of government and its responsibilities. In fact, the military officer is a special case of this type, and though his role is not stabilized, it presumably must come to be more important than it traditionally has been. However, it is questionable how far the specific models of civil service organization either of Britain or of Continental Europe — particularly, certain of their special connections with the class structure and the educational system — are appropriate to American conditions. Such connections in the American case would accentuate rather than mitigate the prominence of the Ivy League element to which Mills so seriously objects.[8]

Above all, I do not think that Mills has made a convincing case for his contention that the power structure impinging directly on American government is in process of crystallizing into a top business-military coalition with a much weaker political "junior partner" whose main function presumably is, by

[7] Good examples are the Department of Agriculture and the Reclamation Service of the Department of the Interior — and now, increasingly, the Public Health Service. I think that this is even true of the Foreign Service, and that Mills here, as in so many other connections, seriously exaggerates the probable long-run consequences of the McCarthyites' intervention in the affairs of the State Department.

[8] I think it correct to say that five years of Labour government in Britain, far from lessening the prominence of Oxford and Cambridge educations as qualifications for the civil service, in fact increased their relative importance, by increasing the national importance of the civil service itself.

manipulation of the mass media and the political process in the narrower sense, to keep the great majority of Americans from protesting too loudly or even from awakening to what allegedly is "really" going on. On a number of counts which have been reviewed, there is a case on a short-run basis for part of his interpretation. But I think that the kinds of factors brought out in the previous discussion make it extremely dubious that even the partial correctness of his interpretation of a current situation will prove to be a sound indicator of what is to be expected over such longer periods as a generation or more.

My conviction on this point is strengthened by a variety of other considerations which, for reasons of space, cannot be discussed here, but may be mentioned. First, I am extremely skeptical of Mills' interpretation of what he calls the "mass society," which includes the structural position of the great majority of the American population. In this he ignores both kinship and friendship, and the whole mass of associational activities and relationships. One example is the spread of church membership — which I suppose Mills would dismiss as simply an escape from the boredom of white-collar life, but in my opinion is of considerable positive significance.

Another very important complex which Mills either treats cavalierly or ignores completely involves education at the various levels, and with it the enormous development, over a century, of science and learning and the professions resting upon them. It is true that the people rooted in these areas of the social structure are not prominent in the power elite, and are even subject to some conflicts with it; but they would not be expected to be prominent in this way — their functions in the society are different. Nonetheless, they must be taken very seriously into account in a diagnosis of what has been happening to the society as a whole. One of the most important sets of facts concerns the ways in which the services of technical professional groups have come to penetrate the structures both of business and of government, a circumstance which over a period of time has greatly enhanced the role of the universities as custodians of learning and sources of trained personnel.

Finally, there is one special case of a professional group whose role Mills treats with serious inadequacy — namely, lawyers. First, he dismisses the judicial branch of government as just "trailing along," with the implication that with a slight lag it simply does the bidding of the "real" holders of power. This seems to be a most biased appraisal of the role of the courts. Not to speak of the longer-run record, the initiative taken by the courts in the matter of racial segregation and in the reassertion of civil liberties after the miasma of McCarthyism does not appear to me to be compatible with Mills' views. Similar considerations seem to apply to various aspects of the role of the private legal profession, notably with respect to the *control* of processes in the business world. Mills tends to assume that the relation between law and business is an overwhelmingly one-way relation; lawyers are there to serve the interests of businessmen and essentially have no independent influence. This, I think, is an illusion stemming largely from Mills' preoccupation with a certain kind of power. His implicit reasoning seems to be that since lawyers have less power than businessmen, they do not really "count."

The last problem I wish to raise, therefore, concerns Mills' conception of power and its use as a category of social analysis. Unfortunately, the concept of power is not a settled one in the social sciences, either in political science or in sociology. Mills, however, adopts one main version of the concept without attempting to justify it. This is what may be called the "zero-sum" concept; power, that is to say, is power *over* others. The power A has in a system is necessarily and by definition at the expense of B. This conception of power then is generalized to the whole conception of the political process when Mills says that "Politics is a struggle for power."

Within limits, every student of social affairs is free to define important concepts the way he prefers; there is no canonically "correct" definition. But choosing one alternative will have consequences which differ from those implied in another, and this is the case with Mills' conception of power. The essential point at present is that, to Mills, power is not a facility for the performance of function in and on behalf of the society as a system, but is interpreted exclusively as a facility for getting what one group, the holders of power, wants by preventing another group, the "outs," from getting what it wants.

What this conception does is to elevate a secondary and derived aspect of a total phenomenon into the central place. A comparison may help to make this clear. There is obviously a distributive aspect of wealth and it is in a sense true that the wealth of one person or group by definition cannot also be possessed by another group. Thus the *distribution* of wealth is, in the nature of the case, a focus of conflicts of interest in a society. But what of the positive functions of wealth and of the conditions of its production? It has become fully established that the wealth available for distribution can only come about through the processes of production, and that these processes require the "co-operation" or integration of a variety of different agencies — what economists call the "factors of production." Wealth in turn is a generalized class of facilities available to units of the society — individuals and various types and levels of collectivities — for whatever uses may be important to them. But even apart from the question of what share each gets, the fact that there should be wealth to divide, and how much, cannot be taken for granted as given except within a very limited context.

Very similar things can be said about power in a political sense. Power is a generalized facility or resource in the society. It has to be divided or allocated, but it also has to be produced and it has collective as well as distributive functions. It is the capacity to mobilize the resources of the society for the attainment of goals for which a general "public" commitment has been made, or may be made. It is mobilization, above all, of the action of persons and groups, which is *binding* on them by virtue of their position in the society. Thus within a much larger complex Mills concentrates almost exclusively on the distributive aspect of power. He is interested only in *who* has power and what *sectoral* interests he is serving with his power, not in how power comes to be generated or in what communal rather than sectoral interests are served.

The result is a highly selective treatment of the whole complex of the power problem. There is, in the first place, a tendency to exaggerate the empirical importance of power by alleging that it is only power which "really" determines what happens in a society. Against this, I would place the view that power is

only one of several cognate factors in the determination of social events. This
bias of Mills is particularly evident in his tendency to foreshorten social processes
and emphasize overwhelmingly short-run factors. There is, secondly, the tendency
to think of power as presumptively illegitimate; if people exercise considerable
power, it must be because they have somehow usurped it where they had no
right and they intend to use it to the detriment of others. This comes out most
conspicuously in Mills' imputation of irresponsibility to his "power elite" and
the allegation, vaguely conceived and presented with very little evidence, that
they are characterized by a "higher immorality." It is notable that as he approaches the climax indicated by the title of his final chapter the tone of indictment becomes shriller and shriller and the atmosphere of objective analysis
recedes.

Back of all this lies, I am sure, an only partly manifest "metaphysical" position which Mills shares with Veblen and a long line of indicters of modern
industrial society. I would call it a utopian conception of an ideal society in
which power does not play a part at all.

This is a philosophical and ethical background which is common both to
utopian liberalism and socialism in our society and to a good deal of "capitalist"
ideology. They have in common an underlying "individualism" of a certain type.
This is not primarily individualism in the sense that the welfare and rights of
the individual constitute fundamental moral values, but rather that *both* individual and collective rights are alleged to be promoted only by *minimizing* the
positive organization of social groups. Social organization as such is presumptively bad because, on a limited, short-run basis, it always and necessarily limits
the freedom of the individual to do exactly what he may happen to want. The
question of the deeper and longer-run dependence of the goals and capacities
of individuals themselves on social organization is simply shoved into the background. From this point of view, both power in the individual enterprise and
power in the larger society are presumptively evil in themselves, because they
represent the primary visible focus of the capacity of somebody to see to it that
somebody else acts or does not act in certain ways, whether at the moment he wants
to or not.

There are, in contemporary society, three main versions of this individualistic
utopianism, which may be called "liberal" and "capitalist" and "socialist" — I
place all three terms in quotation marks deliberately. The liberal version is mainly
"humanistically" oriented to the *total* welfare of the individual as a person, and
in American terms it is very likely to assume a Jeffersonian cast, to hold up the
vision of a simpler and hence almost by definition "better" society against the
inhumanities and impersonalities of large-scale modern industrialism and all its
concomitants.

The capitalist version is, with all the qualifications which such an assertion
must occasion, *primarily* production-oriented. Essentially it says that, whatever
the cost to individuals — including even businessmen themselves, or especially
so — production must be achieved, carried on, and so far as possible increased.
This is the focus of what has been called the "business creed."[9] Understandably

---

[9] Cf. Sutton, *et al.*, *op. cit.*

it has been highly sensitive to "interferences" on both fronts, from liberal sources which would sacrifice productivity to humanistic values, and from governmentalist sources which would "interfere" with the businessman's primary responsibility for production. Social organization beyond the level of the firm is thus presumptively a limitation of its freedom.

The socialist version has been a secondary theme in American ideology largely because of the apolitical character of American society, which, as I have noted, has been prominent historically. The opposition to capitalism has centered on two fronts, the control of the economy in the interests of preventing abuses of power and the steering of the benefits of productivity in the humanistic direction of "welfare." But the socialist questions whether *control* of the abuses of private enterprise is possible at all; to him, for the state to take over production directly is the only way. From this perspective, furthermore, the "Jeffersonian" version of romantic utopianism seems particularly unrealistic and unacceptable.

From one point of view, the socialist romanticizes the state and the political process. Whereas he distrusts private interests almost totally and feels that they cannot be entrusted with any responsibility, he romantically believes that if public authority alone is entrusted with all responsibilities, all will be well — because some mystical "popular will" or "public interest" controls it — forgetting that public authority, like other forms of social organization, is administered by human beings. And that he does not fundamentally trust even public authority is evidenced by his ultimate ideal that the state should "wither away" and the spontaneous co-operation of institutionally unorganized human beings should take over. The socialist has been put in a particularly difficult position in the contemporary world by the development of communism which, while still paying lip service to the eventual withering-away of the state, carries the enforcement of its predominance over all private interests, including the liberties of its citizens, to the totalitarian extreme.

Mills does not make his own position explicit in this book. As noted, at times he speaks like a nostalgic Jeffersonian liberal. I understand, however, that he professes to be a socialist — non-Communist, of course. But a basic strain of his thinking is consistent with both wings of the liberal-socialist dilemma on the basically *individualistic* premises that I have outlined: either that social organization beyond the level of the family and the local community is a bad thing *in toto*, or that it is instrumentally justified only to get society over a particular hump, the threat of the capitalist evil.

Mills seems to be suggesting that the development of the power elite is bringing that capitalist evil to a climax, to a situation which is intolerable to liberals and socialists alike. I suggest an alternative view: that, though of course accompanied by a whole range of "abuses," the main lines of social development in America are essentially acceptable to a humanistic ethic which in my case is closer to the liberal than to either of the other two outlined here. But it differs in not being in the older sense an individualistic liberalism. If the individualistic assumptions are modified in favor of a set which not only admit the necessity but assert the desirability of positive social organization, much of the ideological conflict between the three positions as total "systems" evaporates. Above all, it can be positively asserted that power, while of course subject to

abuses and in need of many controls, is an essential and desirable component
of a highly organized society. This position, in asserting and justifying the increased importance of government, thus grants that there is a grain of truth in
the "socialist" theme. There is, however, also some justification for the existence
of "capitalism," if by that is meant the institutionalization of responsibility for
the larger part of economic production in the hands of a variety of private, non-
governmental agencies. To my mind, there is no more reason why all important
economic production should be controlled by government than why all scientific
research should be.

Hence, in my opinion, many of the difficulties of Mills' analysis of a crucial
problem in American society arise from his failure to transcend the dilemmas
inherent in much of the individualistic tradition in American and, more broadly,
in Western thought. It seems to me that he is clearly and, in the degree to
which he pushes this position, unjustifiably anti-capitalist. He is partly pro-liberal
and probably even more pro-socialist. But in the American scene a choice between
these old alternatives of ideological orientation is no longer enough. It is necessary
not only to criticize existing conditions from the older philosophical or ideological
points of view, but to take serious stock of the ideological assumptions underlying
the bulk of American political discussion of such problems as power.

During recent years, ruling class and power elite analyses have gained
renewed favor, partly because they lend powerful insights into the tu-
multuous, often unhappy developments of the 1960's. Dissenting scholars
attempt, with increasing frequency, to resolve the inconsistencies of these
radical theories and to contend with articulate pluralist criticisms. Thus,
in the following selection taken from his recent book Who Rules America?, G. William Domhoff confronts many of the familiar objections
voiced by pluralist scholars, while fashioning a synthesis of class and elite
analysis.

Domhoff incorporates the idea of a power elite into a model of power
based primarily on class. There is, he believes, a national upper class "made
up of rich businessmen and their descendants, who interact at private
schools, exclusive social clubs, exclusive summer resorts, and similar institutions." This group, he further contends, is also a "governing class,"
defined as "a social upper class which receives a disproportionate amount
of a country's income, owns a disproportionate amount of a country's
wealth, and contributes a disproportionate number of its members to the
controlling institutions and key decision-making groups in that country."
Upper-class power is exercised through a power elite, which commands
the major institutional hierarchies and makes the major decisions in this
country. Unlike Mills, however, Domhoff argues that most members of
the power elite either come from the upper class or, in various ways, have
been co-opted by that class and therefore serve its interests.

To demonstrate upper-class hegemony, Domhoff relies on the sociology of leadership method and emphasizes the social backgrounds of individuals who control institutions and make major decisions. In large corporations he finds that members of the social upper class are disproportionately represented on boards of directors. Domhoff concludes, in essence, that these directors control the corporations, the corporations control the economy, and, therefore, that the upper class also must control the economy. He follows the same procedure regarding other important national institutions such as foundations, universities, mass media, and agencies of government, thereby confirming, to his satisfaction, that upper-class influence pervades the American power elite.

Yet many critics have challenged this analysis. Domhoff locates individuals in the upper class if they meet only one of several criteria, including listing in the Social Register (here he follows E. Digby Baltzell), membership in certain clubs, graduation from specific schools, and so on. Some critics — such as sociologist Vernon K. Dibble, "Our Elusive Upper Class," The Nation, CCVII (November 4, 1968), pp. 470–475 — charge that this definition of upper class is too arbitrary and inclusive. Frequently, Domhoff also generalizes directly from statistics on social origin to the fact of upper-class control or rule: if certain key institutional positions are occupied by individuals from the upper class, then Domhoff assumes that the upper class in fact controls that institution. Yet control thus becomes a curious variable which, at times, can change dramatically as different men of different social origins move in and out of a particular key position. We may well question the efficacy of such control if it varies so fortuitously with the social background of an individual or small groups of individuals. At a minimum, the proper assessment of upper-class power demands the additional investigation of class ideology and a close examination of specific decisions made by members of the governing class. Domhoff himself has taken up many of these unresolved issues in a provocative new book, The Higher Circles: The Governing Class in America (New York: Random House, 1970), which students may profitably consult.

Despite criticism of Who Rules America? however, Domhoff's study does clearly document some of the collective similarities evidenced by America's men of power. In the selection reprinted here, moreover, he also discusses the primary pluralist criticisms of class and elite theory. Domhoff comments on the managerial revolution, the role of expertise, class heterogeneity, restraints on power, and the antigovernment bias of business. This rebuttal to a number of venerable pluralist assumptions about American society deserves thoughtful consideration by students of power in postwar America.

G. WILLIAM DOMHOFF
Is the American Upper Class
a Governing Class?

SCOPE AND MAGNITUDE OF POWER

The first question to be asked of a study emphasizing the sociology-of-leadership methodology concerns the specific powers that go with the various institutional positions held by members or representatives of the American upper class. [Andrew] Hacker points out that several of Mills's critics raised such a question about *The Power Elite*.[1] [Robert] Dahl emphasizes that a study such as ours must, among other things, demonstrate the basis, technique, scope, and magnitude of the power of the hypothetical ruling group.[2] Our answer is as follows:

1. *The corporations.* The corporations are controlled by boards of directors. These boards have the final say-so on investment decisions. They can therefore influence the rate of national economic growth, the rise and fall of the stock market, and the number and type of jobs available. The corporate boards also choose the chief officers of the corporations, who in turn determine day-to-day operations and the advancement of lower-level managers.[3] Dahl, relying primarily upon a study by [Robert] Gordon, would dispute these statements.[4] He believes that managers control the corporations, telling the directors which officers to advance to the very highest positions. Gordon, in turn, makes his claim because (a) 35 of 155 corporations had more "inside" than "outside" directors; (b) directors hold very little stock; and (c) the importance of interest groups has waned. We do not agree with Gordon's analysis for a number of reasons. First, we are inclined to accept the testimony of observers such as Berle who are closer to the day-to-day functioning of the corporate world.[5] Second, the small amount

From G. William Domhoff, *Who Rules America?* © 1967. Reprinted by permission of Prentice-Hall, Inc., Englewood Cliffs, New Jersey.

[1] Andrew Hacker, "Power to Do What?" *The New Sociology*, edited by Irving Horowitz (New York: Oxford University Press, 1964).

[2] Robert Dahl, "Business and Politics: A Critical Appraisal of Political Science," *Social Science Research on Business: Product and Potential* (New York: Columbia University Press, 1959).

[3] See Hacker, 1964, for details and references.

[4] Dahl, 1959; Robert Gordon, *Business Leadership in the Large Corporation* (New York: The Brookings Institution, 1945).

[5] Berle is himself a corporate director.

of stock held by directors may be explained in other ways, such as its being held by one's wife or a bank trust. Third, the greater number of inside directors in some corporations is not necessarily significant. We have seen, for example, that many private school graduates go to work in the corporate world and on Wall Street. Also, inside directors are not necessarily indicative of management control. Family-owned companies, which are dominated by a few persons, often have many employees on the board. Fourth, where the evidence is available, as in the case of the Cleveland interest group, the Mellon interest group, and the du Pont interest group, there is no reason to believe that the power of interest groups has declined. Finally, we mean by "control" the power to change management if the operation of the corporation does not suit its owners. That managers make day-to-day business decisions on technical matters is really irrelevant. As corporate spokesman after corporate spokesman makes clear, the primary goal is to make a profit, and that is what most concerns members of the upper class when it comes to their corporations.

2. *The corporation lawyers.* Corporate lawyers derive their power from their relationship to the corporate economy they helped to construct. They have the power of expertise on legal matters. They also have the power of persons who have a broader perspective of the system and can thereby give advice to those who function in narrower channels.[6]

3. *The foundation boards.* The foundation boards have the power to accept or reject various scientific, educational, and cultural ventures. They therefore have the power to exert considerable influence over the noneconomic aspects of American life.

4. *The associations (CFR, FPA, BAC, CED, NAC, and NAM).** The leaders of these associations, through their publications, seminars, and advertisements, have the power to influence public opinion. They also serve to educate persons who are going to be decision-makers in a given issue-area, such as economic development or foreign policy.

5. *The boards of trustees of universities.* The boards of trustees make long-term policy, thus setting the tone and orientation of the university. They also have the power to hire and fire university presidents and other top-level personnel.[7]

6. *The Executive branch of the federal government.* The Executive branch takes the initiative in matters of legislation and federal spending. It includes departments such as State, Treasury, and Defense which control the crucial issue-areas of foreign policy, financial policy, and military policy. The Executive branch also has appointive powers over the Judicial branch and the independent regulatory agencies. It can use its prestige to influence public opinion and its expertise to influence Congress.

---

* The Council on Foreign Relations, Foreign Policy Association, Business Advisory Council, Committee for Economic Development, National Advertising Council, and National Association of Manufacturers. [Editor's note.]

6 See Erwin O. Smigal, *The Wall Street Lawyer* (New York: The Free Press, 1964), for details and references.

7 See Hubert Beck, *Men Who Control Our Universities*, (New York: King's Crown Press, 1947), for further details.

7. *The military.* The military has the power to carry out whatever activity is called for by the National Security Council and the Defense Department. It has the power of expertise in giving advice on whether or not to undertake a given operation, how various operations should be carried out, and which branches of the military should be utilized in defense planning and military operations. Once a plan has been set, the military has the power to decide on operational details and to select personnel to carry out the task. The military has the power to influence public opinion through its large public relations apparatus.

THE MANAGERIAL REVOLUTION

The second major objection likely to be raised has to do with the decline of family capitalism and the rise of the managers (the managerial revolution). It is often argued that the owners no longer control and that the managers are a separate social group from the social upper class of stockholders. Sometimes it is argued that the rich have been diminished by inheritance taxes. Contrary to these arguments, it has been shown that successful managers become owners themselves with the help of stock options and stock tips, and that they are assimilated socially into the upper class. It also has been shown that a considerable number of corporate executives are of the upper class originally even when they are not majority owners in a given corporation. Finally, it has been shown that stock ownership is not so dispersed that it is meaningless. The rich have *not* lost in wealth, and may even be gaining because of easily avoided taxes. On the basis of these findings, it has been argued that the dispersal of stock ownership within the upper class makes members of this class concerned with the success of the system as a whole rather than with their own given company, as was the case with family capitalism. It was further argued that the dispersal of stock and the death of family capitalism freed the hereditary rich to go into government service, the professions, and the arts, contributing further to their control of the system and to its stability.

THE ROLE OF EXPERTISE

A third major objection has to do with the importance of expertise in the modern world and the rise of the "meritocracy." This argument, which incorporates the rise of the corporate managers as one of its examples, claims that the upper-middle class of well-educated specialists, who are drawn before their training from all socioeconomic levels, has replaced the upper class of property owners as the wielders of power, as the makers of big decisions. There are several comments that can be made about this argument:

1. To advise a decision-maker is not to make a decision. As Mills was well aware, experts are often the "captains" of the power elite's higher thoughts, but as he also said of chief executives, "Theirs [is] the Judgment."[8] It is the function

[8] C. Wright Mills, *The Power Elite* (New York: Oxford University Press, 1956), p. 4, p. 134.

of the decision-maker to choose among the usually conflicting advice that he receives from his usually divided experts.

2. Final authority, or decision-making power, does not follow from the fact that one is necessary to the functioning of a system. Most parts of any system are necessary. It is perfectly possible for one part of a system to function for the benefit of another, which is the point we have argued by stressing the distribution of income and wealth.

3. We believe it is an *empirical* mistake to downgrade the amount of expertise located *within* the upper class. Too much is made of "café society," "the jet set," and the "functionless genteel" within the upper class. The fact is that most members of the upper class are hard-working and competent. We have demonstrated this in a number of ways:

a. Almost all graduates of private schools go on to college. Our study of one alumni bulletin showed that private school graduates go into a variety of activities that require a considerable amount of expertise.

b. Private school graduates go to the finest universities in the country, universities which are the major suppliers of American expertise.

c. Our study of the 1965 *Social Register Locater* showed that 8 per cent of a sample of 182 adult males have the title "doctor" before their names. Whether the degree is medical or academic, this percentage suggests a considerable amount of expertise within the upper class. [E. Digby] Baltzell's study of Philadelphia suggests the same for medicine and architecture in that city.

d. Baltzell's study showed that one-fourth of the *Who's Who* listees from *Social Register* cities were in the *Social Register*.

e. Almost one third of the partners in the largest Wall Street law firms, a major source of American legal and political expertise, are listed in the *Social Register*. Baltzell's study of Philadelphia revealed several upper-class law firms in that city.

4. The major producers of expertise — *e.g.*, Harvard, Yale, Princeton, Columbia, Penn, and Stanford — are controlled by members of the American upper class. This implies at the very least the power to select and train those who will be experts.

5. Military experts are selected by the Department of Defense, which is dominated by members of the upper class and by high-level corporate executives.

6. Experts are advanced and acclaimed in accordance with their success in solving problems posed by a system which disproportionately benefits members of the upper class.

For all of these reasons, we do not believe that experts from the middle class have somehow displaced the American upper class as a governing class. They are well rewarded for their services to this group, however.

CONFLICT WITHIN THE UPPER CLASS

Do the disagreements within the upper class contradict the notion that it is a governing class? Is such disagreement evidence for a pluralistic model? The answer is that it is very possible for members of a governing class to disagree as to what long-range strategies should be, not to mention short-range tactics. Nor is the day-to-day reality of conflict, as depicted so beautifully in the case of the federal government by Cater in *Power in Washington*, necessarily in conflict with a governing-class theory. Sweezy believes that the pluralistic model integrates "a considerable body of observed fact" in a "tolerably satisfactory fashion." However, he also believes that "the state has a function in society which is prior to and more fundamental than any which present-day liberals attribute to it."[9] He is referring to the protection of private property as a system.

SO WHAT?

Another objection would run as follows. So what if the upper class controls a disproportionate amount of the wealth, and controls the corporations and the federal government? The important thing is whether or not their decisions are in the interest of the country as a whole. Would members of other classes make similar decisions on key issues? The answer to this question, above and beyond the special interests that are implied by disproportionate income and wealth, is that it is not really pertinent. This book has not tried to show that the rule of the American upper class has been a benevolent one or a malevolent one. Rather, it is concerned with the existence and the mechanics of the national upper class, not with an interpretation of the impact of its rule on American civilization for better or for worse. Whether decisions by members of the upper class are "good" for the whole country or only for themselves is difficult to answer in any case, but it is not relevant to the existence of a governing class by our definition. Such a criticism assumes that a study of social structure implies an attack on that social structure, but that is only the case, to quote Mills, under certain circumstances: "When little is known, or only trivial items publicized, or when myths prevail, then plain description becomes a radical fact — or at least is taken to be radically upsetting."[10]

RESTRAINTS

An objection closely related to the one immediately above could be formulated as follows. Even if it is true that one socioeconomic group owns a disproportionate share of the wealth and contributes a considerable percentage of national leaders, the fact remains that there are restraints on decision-makers. There are opposing interest groups and opposing socioeconomic classes, such as workers, farmers, small businessmen, and consumers, and there are restraining cultural values, as manifested in the Constitution, the Bill of Rights, civil rights laws, and the golden rule. Most of all, there is the right to vote, which means that the leaders are accountable to all the people. After showing that blue-collar

[9] Paul Sweezy, *The Theory of Capitalist Development* (New York: Monthly Review Press, 1942), pp. 240–241; see also Sweezy, "Has Capitalism Changed?" in *Has Capitalism Changed?* ed. Shigeto Tsuru (Tokyo: Twanami Shotin, 1962), pp. 87–90.

[10] C. Wright Mills, "Comments on Criticism," *Dissent*, V, I (1957), 33.

workers are almost totally excluded from decision-making roles in New Haven, Dahl points to their restraining powers:

> Nonetheless, it would be wrong to conclude that the activities and attitudes of people in these strata have no influence on the decisions of governmental officials. Though wage earners lack social standing, they are not without other resources, including the ballot, and what they lack as individuals they more than make up in collective resources. In short, although their direct influence is low, their indirect collective influence is high.[11]

We would agree, in Dahl's terms, that the underlying population's "potential for control" is infinitely greater than that of the upper class, but we would add that the "potential for unity" is much greater in the latter than it is in the former, which is hopelessly divided into income classes, religious groups, ethnic groups, and racial groups.[12] We also would agree that there are restraints on the power of the governing class, for the governing class is part of a system which includes other nation-states as well as other socioeconomic groups. We would even agree that members of the power elite often try to anticipate the reactions of other groups when they make their decisions. The potential power of angry, organized masses is well known in twentieth-century America thanks to foreign revolutions, the battle over women's suffrage, labor strikes, and the civil rights movement.

BUT BUSINESSMEN HATE GOVERNMENT

The final, and most important, objection that is usually raised against a governing-class model concerns the apparent autonomy of the federal government. Critics point to the New Deal, the Democratic Party, anti-business legislation, and the intense hostility of business to government in support of the idea that the federal government is a relatively autonomous institution that adjudicates disputes among various interest groups. Talcott Parsons finds business opposition to government "impossible to understand" unless we assume "genuine, and in some sense effective" governmental control of business.[13] Similarly, economist Edward S. Mason, an expert on corporations and a former president of the American Economic Association, was paraphrased as follows in *Business Week:* "Business' intense opposition to every proposed surrender of power to Washington is hardly consistent with the view that it itself dominates the U.S. government."[14]

In answer to these objections, this study has shown who controlled the New Deal — liberal elements of the American upper class, including many ex-Republicans. We have stressed that the New Deal created a split within the power

[11] Robert Dahl, *Who Governs?* (New Haven: Yale University Press, 1961), p. 233.

[12] Robert Dahl, "A Critique of the Ruling Elite Model," *American Political Science Review*, LII, 1958, p. 465.

[13] Talcott Parsons, *Structure and Process in Modern Societies* (New York: The Free Press, 1960), pp. 213–214.

[14] "Viewing U.S. Economy With a Marxist Glass," *Business Week*, April 13, 1963.

elite which has not yet healed. Many members of the upper class remain unreconciled to the New Deal, believing that aristocrat Franklin Roosevelt ("Rosenfelt") was a traitor to his class who was part of an international Communist-Jewish conspiracy. However, this does not mean that other members of the upper class did not control the New Deal. As Baltzell documents, the New Deal was actually the beginning of a more ethnically representative establishment within the governing class which pushed aside the Protestant Establishment made up of heavy industrialists, fiscal conservatives, and prejudiced personalities. On a larger time scale, 1932–1964, this study has answered the claim that the federal government is autonomous by showing that the now-dominant Executive branch is honeycombed to an overwhelming degree by members of the power elite. This same evidence, buttressed by studies of campaign financing, also disposes of the myth that the Democratic Party is not controlled by elements of the American upper class. As to the charge that the upper class is not omnipotent, and therefore not a governing class, the fact remains that a very wealthy upper class which makes concessions remains a wealthy upper class. It stoops to conquer, taking the advice of its English counterparts rather than the foolhardy path of the French landlords. Perhaps Joseph P. Kennedy put this point as well as anybody could in discussing his reaction to the Depression, a time of genuine panic and confusion for many members of the upper class:

> I am not ashamed to record that in those days I felt and said I would be willing to part with half of what I had if I could be sure of keeping, under law and order, the other half. Then it seemed that I should be able to hold nothing for the protection of my family.[15]

WHY BUSINESSMEN COMPLAIN

There are several very good reasons why businessmen complain about the government, the first of which requires a slight detour into history. The original American political and economic system battled for many years against a centralized government in England. As Baltzell puts it, American institutions were "born in a revolt from the tyranny of a centralized government symbolized in the British monarchy and mercantilism. . . ."[16] We would add that this long and bitter struggle created an anti-government ideology, especially against a strong central government, and that this hostility has remained one of the most prominent features of American thought, if not of American practice. In short, there are historical and ideological reasons why businessmen would verbalize hostility toward the federal government. This ideological hostility, we would argue, does not answer the question of whether or not members of the American upper class of rich businessmen control the government they criticize. A second "historical" reason for hostility to the federal government has been noted in the previous paragraph; that is, many businessmen do not accept the New Deal. They remember the good old days before the De-

[15] Richard Whalen, *The Founding Father* (New York: New American Library, 1964), p. 112. This is the difference between a New Dealer and a member of the old guard.
[16] E. Digby Baltzell, *Philadelphia Gentlemen* (New York: The Free Press, 1958), p. 429.

pression, and they deny the claim by some of their colleagues that changes were necessary in order to forestall more serious socioeconomic and political difficulties. However, on this point it is necessary to emphasize that not all businessmen are hostile to a strong central government and the innovations of the New Deal. Some even find labor unions a useful stabilizing influence.[17] We believe that these business liberals are coming to be the dominant influence within the upper class, as symbolized in the views of the CFR, FPA, CED, BAC, and NAC.

A third factor in understanding business hostility to the federal government is the fact that most businessmen are not part of the group that controls the government. The federal government is controlled by the corporate rich, and only a small percentage of American businesses are even incorporated, let alone large enough to sustain the owners as members of the national upper class. In short, it is necessary to specify *which* businessmen are complaining about the federal government. Small businessmen, for example, have good reason to complain. For them the government is largely an expensive nuisance which makes them keep annoying and costly records while doing very little for them. Needless to say, some of these small businessmen line up with the anti-New Deal members of the upper class to form the conservative wing of the Republican Party, which is very vocal in its hostility to a strong federal government. We suspect that this coalition would be the origin of most of the examples that Parsons and Mason could give in supporting their claim that businessmen are hostile to the federal government.

Other factors must be considered in explaining business hostility toward the federal government. First, much of this hostility is really hostility toward other businessmen, especially in the case of the regulatory agencies. For example, we have cited the case of the fight over an increase in natural gas prices, which was opposed by the other elements of the business community who would pay most of the increase in higher production costs. The FPC nonetheless took the brunt of the hostility. Along this same line, McConnell points out that "some industries, including the radio industry, the airlines, the railroad and trucking industries, and the oil companies, have actively sought regulation."[18] Then too, many businessmen are temperamentally unsuited for the give-and-take of the political world. Nor are they comfortable with the hoopla of electioneering. They see government as a bureaucratic tangle opposed to the orderly, efficient atmosphere of the corporate world. Osborne Elliott (SR, NY) goes so far as to call the corporate structure "authoritarian" in making this point.[19] This would suggest that members of the upper class with temperaments and interests different from those of most businessmen would be more successful as political leaders. Neither President Roosevelt nor President Kennedy, for example, could get very enthusiastic about business careers.

As still another factor in considering business hostility to the federal government, it must be realized that even a government controlled by the corporate rich

[17] Osborne Elliott, *Men at the Top* (New York: Harper & Bros., 1960).

[18] Grant McConnell, *Private Power and American Democracy* (New York: Alfred A. Knopf, 1966), p. 284. What the businessman objects to in regulation is that it clashes with his ideology (Dahl, 1959, p. 38, quoting R. E. Lane's *The Regulation of Businessmen*).

[19] Elliott, 1960.

will often take measures which are distasteful to many corporations and corporate executives. Good examples from the mid-1960's would be the need to curtail overseas spending to halt the outflow of gold to other countries, and the need to curtail investment spending to discourage the inflationary tendencies which developed in an economy that was spending increasing sums on national defense. While both of these measures were in the interests of the system as a whole, they were not in the interests of the individual corporations, and many seemed to ignore the pleas of Secretary of Commerce John T. Connor, the former president of Merck and Company, and Secretary of Defense Robert McNamara, the former president of the Ford Motor Company.

Finally, there are good reasons why businessmen well aware of their power would pretend that they did not control the government. This is such a charged point, impugning as it does the motives of our corporate leaders, that we would not make it ourselves. Instead, we will let a respectable political scientist, Grant McConnell, and a highly regarded reporter, Bernard Nossiter, speak for themselves. After pointing to business antagonisms as the first element in explaining hostility to government, McConnell goes on as follows:

> Second, whether the issue is understood explicitly, intuitively, or not at all, the denunciations serve to establish and maintain the subservience of governmental units to the business constituencies to which they are actually held responsible. Attacks upon government in general place continuing pressure on governmental officers to accommodate their activities to the groups from which support is most reliable. Third, and probably most important, is that business attacks upon government are directed at any tendency toward the development of larger constituencies for the government units.[20]

After noting that "some businessmen believe the myths cultivated by the imagemakers of both major parties," and that pressure on President Kennedy brought the best results for business interests, Nossiter makes this important point:

> A second and related reason has to do with business sensitivity about its own power. To proclaim the triumph of business doctrine on the New Frontier might invite retaliation and counterpressure by organized labor, farmers, and other interest groups. Overt display of power in the corporate world is not only vulgar, it is unprofitable.[21]

We believe the above arguments are an adequate explanation as to why many businessmen would express hostility toward the federal government. However, even if they were not, we would still argue that a decision about business domination of the government cannot be based upon the subjective feelings of the corporate executives, corporate lawyers, and aristocrats who provide the leadership of the State Department, Defense Department, and Treasury Department. We thus conclude from our empirical evidence that many social scientists are mistaken in their respective emphases on the New Deal, the Democratic Party,

[20] McConnell, 1966, p. 294.
[21] Bernard D. Nossiter, *The Mythmakers* (Boston: Houghton, Mifflin, 1964), pp. 40–41.

and business hostility as considerations which are contrary to the notion of a governing class.

CONCLUSION

Now the reader has been introduced to the main arguments raised in the past when the upper reaches of society have been studied with the sociology-of-leadership methodology. He must re-assess these arguments in the light of the empirical evidence presented in the previous chapters. For ourselves, we conclude that the income, wealth, and institutional leadership of what Baltzell calls the "American business aristocracy" are more than sufficient to earn it the designation "governing class." As Sweezy would say, this "ruling class" is based upon the national corporate economy and the institutions that economy nourishes. It manifests itself through what the late C. Wright Mills called the power elite.

The revisionist currents of recent years have not all run in the direction of class or elite analysis. In the following selection from his book, The Power Structure: Political Process in American Society, *the late Arnold Rose charts a course for those who remain unpersuaded by radical interpretations of power. His "multi-influence hypothesis" is a synthetic effort deriving largely from pluralism, although it also incorporates dichotomous perspectives of antipluralist lineage. Rose focuses on political power and, as a former state legislator, brings the bias of a sympathetic insider to his study of the political process. He begins with a profound distrust of scholars like Hunter and Mills who reject the democratic pretensions of American politics. Yet Rose has also been deeply influenced by the verisimilitude of elite theory, and the ghost of a power elite persistently haunts his analysis.*

These conflicting forces are apparent in Rose's conclusions, which frequently are marked by a peculiar ambivalence or duality. On one hand, each of his sixteen concluding assertions emphasizes the democratic or pluralistic elements in the political process. In particular, Rose finds that the political sector and political elites now dominate national life. The increased democratization of the political process, the decline of economic power blocs, and other changes have forged a new balance of forces congenial to the public interest. On the other hand, Rose often admits that the elitist critique of pluralism is partly valid. The economic elite has had some success in conditioning certain government decisions; a few small and exclusive groups have played a lamentably large role in formulating foreign policy; the proliferation of bureaucracies and of complex organizations does increase the general importance of elites; and campaign contributions do affect the decisions of legislators. In each case, however, Rose believes that countervailing forces restrain the growth of an undemocratic elitism. In his emphasis, then, Rose is basically a pluralist rather than an elitist.

In several respects this revision is quite plausible. Political power today may, in fact, be more significant than it was during the Eisenhower administration, although this does not necessarily mean that it now overshadows both economic and military power. Rose also implies, with some justification, that contemporary worries about power have intensified precisely because new and previously quiescent pressure groups now believe they have a reasonable chance of changing the distribution of power. In this sense, rising expectations regarding the accessibility and importance of political power are themselves perhaps partly responsible for renewed public concern about its misuse.

Rose's optimism, however, may be premature. The current wave of public dissent seems to denote a general disillusionment with the political process as well as a widespread conviction that established elites still monopolize the implements of political power. There is a look of desperation rather than confidence on the face of contemporary protest, and this hardly suggests a flowering of political democracy. Further, many of Rose's conclusions rely on four rather disconnected case studies — of political structure and influence in Texas, public perceptions of power in Minnesota, John F. Kennedy's quest for the 1960 Democratic presidential nomination, and the passage of medicare legislation — and this limited research may not sustain large generalizations about the prevalence of political pluralism. Were he to demonstrate his case conclusively, Rose would have to expand his narrow concern with the political process and political power.

Finally, the uneasy coexistence of elitism and pluralism throughout his analysis forces Rose to a curious justification of his pluralist sympathies. Scholars like Mills and Hunter, he seems to suggest, have measured American democracy against overly rigorous, utopian criteria of democracy. Rose, conversely, believes that our society is comparatively democratic and pluralistic when realistically judged by the standards of other nations. This difference in evaluative touchstones allows Rose to admit much of the elitist critique of pluralism and yet ultimately to deny its implications. The reader himself must decide whether Rose is justified in rejecting idealistic standards of evaluating and judging the distribution of power in American society. In a useful critique of The Power Structure, G. William Domhoff details a number of other objections to Rose's multi-influence hypothesis: "Where a Pluralist Goes Wrong," The Berkeley Journal of Sociology, XIV (1969), pp. 35–57, also in The Higher Circles, op. cit.

ARNOLD M. ROSE
The Multi-Influence Hypothesis

Political power in the United States, like any other social phenomenon, is changing its locus of concentration, its distribution, and its manifestations constantly.[1] Some of the observations and generalizations made in this book will be out of date by the time the reader is able to analyze and criticize them. Recent changes, for example, have occurred in the rural-urban distribution of power in state legislatures, in the strength of the Republican–Southern Democratic "coalition" in Congress, and in the extent to which businessmen are to be found in key positions in the national Administration. Nevertheless, most aspects of power have remained sufficiently stable for a student of the power structure to draw generalizations and to note slow-moving trends. In contrast to the major theses of C. Wright Mills and Floyd Hunter — that there is a secret, hierarchical, and unified power structure in the United States headed by an economic elite, that the political elite occupies only a secondary position in the power structure, and that the masses are apathetic and act in terms of false consciousness of their interests — we would assert the following propositions. Most of them are based on studies reported or summarized in this book; others are based merely on general or participant observation.

1. There is a power structure in every organized activity of American life and at every level — national, regional, state, and local. Power is the major means used by a large, heterogeneous society to effect or to resist change, and — except in simple face-to-face relations — power is structured, which is to say that there are different roles and role relationships, and a pattern into which these roles and relationships fit.

2. There are varying degrees of relationship and agreement among these varied power structures. They are certainly not unified into a simple power structure, even *within* the categories of the economic and the political, although occasionally semi-permanent liaisons develop among them. Nor are they usually countervailing, because each operates primarily within its own sphere of influence, although countervailing (or check-and-balance) relationships occasionally do occur. The political party power structures — there are at least four major ones on the

From Chapter XIV, "Conclusion," in *The Power Structure: Political Process in American Society*, by Arnold M. Rose. Copyright © 1967 by Oxford University Press, Inc. Reprinted and retitled by permission.

[1] Even from the time the present study was begun, in 1960, until it was sent to the publishers, in 1966, there were so many significant changes that additions, corrections, and qualifications had to be made regularly in the manuscript.

national level alone — probably have the largest number of relationships with other power structures, both because one of their specific roles is to mediate conflicts and because they have a large degree of control over the bureaucratic machinery of government, which — in turn — monopolizes most of the instruments of organized physical force.

3. Within each power structure, a small number of persons hold the largest amount of power. In community studies, this has been estimated to constitute less than 1 per cent of the population, but such estimates refer to those who lead in community-wide political decisions, and not to power *within* the spheres of business, unions, voluntary associations, schools, churches, etc. While in any sphere of activity there are "leaders," who constitute a tiny proportion of all those affected by the activity, this does not mean that the others have no power whatsover. Opposition groups occasionally form, and sometimes succeed in overturning the existing elite. In all cases where there are elections, the rank-and-file voters exercise some restraining and modifying power over the elite. Their power is a function of the extent to which they have interacted to create a public opinion, the extent to which the election machinery is honest, and the extent to which voters are equal. Under these criteria, most governmental elections accord a good deal of power to the electorate, most business corporation elections accord practically no power to the electorate, and labor union and voluntary association elections vary between these two poles. But even in government and in actively democratic trade unions, there is an ever-changing elite which exercises most of the power at any given moment.

4. Each elite manifests its power mainly within its own domain. That is, the strongest powers of businessmen are exercised within their own businesses, and the strongest powers of politicians and public administrators are exercised within government. But particularly the political and economic elites, among all the elites, influence each other's spheres. Especially since the 1930's the government has set various restrictions and controls on business, and has heavily taxed business and the public to carry out purposes deemed to be for the general good —welfare programs, education programs, highways, war and military defense activities, etc. Business leaders use lobbyists, "business representatives" in legislatures, contributions to campaign funds, publicity designed to influence public opinion, the "political strike," and other lesser techniques to influence government. Businessmen influence government more effectively than most non-businessmen — not only because they can afford lobbyists, advertisements and other costly techniques — but also because they are more educated, more knowledgeable, more articulate, and more activist than average citizens. The latter qualities give them an advantage quite compatible with a democratic society.

5. The economic elite has its greatest success in influencing government where there are no counter-pressures — from other sectors of the economic elite, from other non-economic elites, and from public opinion. The result has been that the economic elite has been relatively successful in influencing government purchasing agents and the independent regulatory commissions. This is not quite an accurate way of stating the facts, however, since individual businesses often compete strongly with each other in influencing these factors of government, and there is a considerable turnover in the individual businesses benefited by these

sectors of government. In pressuring or appealing to the top levels of the federal administration, to the Congress, or even to many state legislatures (especially outside the South), businessmen have been much less successful since the 1930's. In fact, as far as general legislation is concerned, they have had an almost unbroken series of defeats, although they have succeeded in *delaying* the passage of certain bills for years. Thus, while businessmen have gained certain economic benefits from government, their typical ideology — in favor of businessman leadership in the society and of a minimum of government activity for the benefit of other segments of the population — has made no progress.[2]

6. While the federal government has been gaining ascendancy over the state and local governments, and while the office of the President has been gaining power at the expense of Congress, it is far from true that the state governments and the Congress are powerless. Rather, it could be said that the "balance of power" doctrine envisaged in the Constitution has come into operation only since 1933, because the federal government (except for military activities) and the presidency (except in wartime) were relatively weak institutions before then. These two trends in political power have reduced the influence of the economic elite, for the federal government is less susceptible to influence from businessmen than are most of the state governments, and the presidency is less susceptible to such influence than are many of the congressmen.

7. In the early 1960's a coalition of several decades' duration between two major political power structures — the conservative leadership of the Republican party and the Democrats in power in most of the Southern states — largely broke down. The Southern Democrats, changing in membership and reduced in number by Republican inroads on their constituencies, drew closer to the Northern Democrats, except publicly over the issue of civil rights. The South was rapidly becoming like the North — in its industrialization, urbanization, patterns of race relations permitted by Negro voting, and development of a two-party system.[3] The Republican party was sharply divided between its conservatives and liberals, on the one hand, and a smaller group of right-wing extremists with a vigorous ideology who seized control of the party's grassroots structures in the majority of states. The extremists — while occasionally ideologically supportive of business — were not as willing to make political compromises in behalf of business or as willing to trust leading businessmen, as had been the previous conservative leaders of the Republican party. All these developments, coupled with the political skill of President Lyndon B. Johnson, permitted the passage of a great deal of "liberal" legislation in the 1964–65 sessions of Congress — including "Medi-

[2] It has been argued that this businessman's ideology represents a "false consciousness" — that is, it claims to represent an economic interest, but is in fact, contrary to the economic interest of businessmen. The factual argument is that businessmen gain most economic benefits when the government actively promotes the welfare and education of even its poorest citizens, when it maintains a regularly unbalanced budget, and when it reduces tariffs — all policies which most businessmen oppose.

[3] The decline in the number of "safe" Democratic House seats has been documented by Raymond E. Wolfinger and Joan Heifetz, "Safe Seats, Seniority, and Power in Congress," *American Political Science Review*, 59 (June 1965), 337–349.

care" for the elderly . . . federal aid to education, the anti-poverty program, tax reduction without a balanced budget, a comprehensive civil rights act, a voting rights act, elimination of national quotas for immigrants, creation of a new Department of Housing and Urban Development, aid to urban mass-transit programs and to highway and city beautification efforts, and a National Foundation on the Arts and Humanities. Further, the President had an unofficial price control policy which worked for a few years to keep major industries from raising prices.

8. In the passage of the above-mentioned legislation, interested economic elite pressure groups were mostly defeated. On the other hand, the major legislation sought by organized labor — repeal of Section 14(b) of the Taft-Hartley Act — was also defeated in the Senate. The one economic elite group that continued to reap major economic benefits from government activity was the armaments and space-exploration supply industries, although the Secretary of Defense made certain decisions on procurement — such as in favor of competitive bidding rather than cost-plus contracts — even in this area which were not favored by the leading manufacturers.

9. Through the Voting Rights Act of the Congress and the *Baker v. Carr* and *Reynolds v. Sims* decisions of the United States Supreme Court — including the giving of permission to the Attorney General to seek a Court review of the poll tax (which was consequently outlawed by the Supreme Court) — a major democratization of voting for state legislatures was occurring in many states. Both state and local government activities were increasingly influenced by standards set by federal aid programs that covered ever wider spheres.

10. The pattern of legislation at both federal and state levels revealed the emergence of new popular pressure groups with considerable power, partly because of demographic shifts and partly because of growing political consciousness among these groups. These groups are the elderly, a portion of whom are now organized into many associations, the most politically active of which is the National Association of Senior Citizens; the Negroes, possibly a majority of whom are organized into various civil rights associations and activist churches; and the "resentful disaffected," practically all organized into a variety of leftist and rightist extremist organizations, of which the John Birch Society is the largest and the wealthiest. The political organization of voluntary associations representing these three categories of the "masses" provides increasing evidence of a thesis expounded in an earlier section on "Reactions against the Mass Society" (pp. 196–212).

11. The major area of small-group control of national policy remaining in the country was that of foreign policy. The most powerful arm of this small group — namely the President and his official advisers — are quite exposed to the public. But there are secret decision-makers operating in this area also — secret in that their influence and processes of decision-making are not accessible to the public. These decision-makers are the CIA, the foreign policy "experts" in the universities and in such organizations as the Foreign Policy Association and the Council on Foreign Relations, and the military supplies industrialists who exert their influence mainly through the military leaders. The last-named

are the ones whom Mills placed at the pinnacle of the power elite in the United States; we identify them rather as one influence among several affecting the nation almost exclusively in the area of foreign policy. We are entirely skeptical about Mills's contention that the other "members" of the economic elite — say, for example, those organized in the Chamber of Commerce — have more influence on foreign policy than the workers organized into trade unions, especially when they engage in shipping boycotts.

12. Despite the fact that the Republican party's ideological move to the right after 1962 left the Democrats securely in command of the center, the program of the Democratic party remained as liberal as it had ever been. This can be seen not only by comparing national party platforms over the years, but by reviewing the legislation supported (and usually passed) by the majority of Democrats in Congress and by the Democratic Presidents Kennedy and Johnson. This can be explained either as a long-run trend — in terms of the increasing strength of voters who favor liberal measures and generally support the Democratic party as the instrument to achieve them — or as part of a structural cycle. Lipset specifies a version of the latter theory:[4] Republican Presidents seek center support and so force Republican congressmen from safe conservative seats to behave in a more liberal fashion. When a Republican holds the presidency, the Southern contingent of conservative Democrats have more power in their party. Thus, in a Republican presidency, the two congressional parties are not so far apart. But when a Democrat holds the presidency, he pulls his congressmen to the left, to respond to the needs of the greater number of voters there, while the Republican congressmen are free to follow their ideological inclination toward the right, and the two parties are quite far apart. It is difficult to judge from the facts which theory is correct, but this author tends to regard the former theory as more persuasive, especially in view of the decline of differences between South and North. In any case, there has been a significant difference between the platforms and policies of the two national parties at least since 1932,[5] and the difference in the mid-1960's was as great as could be found between democratic political parties anywhere in the Western world. The increasing number of differences between the two major political parties, and the growing ideological framework for those differences, will probably have profound implications for the political future of the United States — but it is still too early to foresee the future development. Nevertheless, from the standpoint of the thesis of this book, we can say that there is little evidence that business is playing any significant role in the development of these trends. Business is a declining influence on the political power structures, except in the narrow area of its relationship to govern-

[4] Seymour Martin Lipset, *Political Man* (New York: Doubleday, 1960), pp. 306–307.
[5] The basic ideological difference between the leadership of the two parties, on the average, has been demonstrated by Herbert McClosky, Paul J. Hoffman, and Rosemary O'Hara, "Issue Conflict and Consensus Among Party Leaders and Followers," *American Political Science Review*, 54 (June 1960), 406–427. The public, also, sees ideological differences between the two parties. See, for example, the report of the Minnesota Poll in the *Minneapolis Sunday Tribune*, November 3, 1963, p. UM2.

ment procurement officials and the independent regulatory commissions —
largely because business exerts its strongest efforts on these and because there
are few countervailing influences on them, as we pointed out in Chapter III.

13. The public's and the formal leadership's image of the power structure —
if we can generalize from a study of the one state of Minnesota — does not include many people as seeing the economic elite as all-powerful, although the
extent to which they do see business as influential may be somewhat exaggerated
in terms of the facts. Judging from their public pronouncements, it is the political extremist — of both the right and the left — whose image of the American
power structure includes a conspiratorial and all-powerful role for the economic
elite. The extremist groups have different names for this "all-powerful group"
but they refer to the same business elite: The "lunatic fringe" rightists call them
"the hidden group behind the communists," the more rational extreme rightists
call them "the Establishment"; the more rational extreme leftists also call them
"the Establishment" or "Wall Street," but are more likely to use the Mills-
Hunter terms "the power elite" or "the power structure," while the less rational
extreme leftists either use the same terms or refer bluntly to "the big business
conspiracy." While it is of considerable interest that the political extremists of
both right and left — apparently along with many non-extremist intellectuals
influenced by Mills and Hunter — have the same image of the top business elite
as being all-powerful, it is of greater importance to note that the majority of the
people and of the positional leaders of American organized society do not have
this image. We have adduced much evidence in this book that the top business
elite are far from having an all-powerful position; that power is so complicated
in the United States that the top businessmen scarcely understand it, much less
control it; and that since 1933 the power position of businessmen has been
declining rather than growing.

14. Because the spheres of their organizations have grown in recent decades,
the elites of the federal administration (including the military), of the federal
courts, of certain voluntary associations, and of certain educational and scientific
institutions, have grown more powerful. While on rare occasions they supersede
in power the top political elites — as when the United States Supreme Court
ordered the state governments to end racial segregation and to reapportion their
legislatures in accord with population, or when the same Court declares uncon-
stitutional a federal statute, or when the civil rights associations pressure Congress into voting for a statute as sweeping as the Civil Rights Act of 1964, or
when the labor and old-age groups pressure Congress into voting for a statute
as sweeping as the Medicare Act of 1965 (although both these statutes had the
full support of that significant political elite — the President) — the political
elites are usually ascendant over them. The political elites control the agencies
of force and the instruments of legislation, have considerable access to the mass
media, and have the support of public opinion. The political elites — the two
major parties, the President, the factions in the houses of Congress, the executives and legislatures of the states and large cities — are not unified of course,
and they check-and-balance each other to a considerable extent.

15. While the two major political parties are listed by us as among the most
powerful groups in the United States, their structures are quite generally mis-

understood by the public and by nonspecialized intellectuals and other leadership groups. They are structured mainly as voluntary associations, with grass-roots
elections that range from being wholly democratic to being "controlled" from
a self-perpetuating group at the top. In some states (e.g., Texas) they are highly
fractionated and schismatic. They are structured on the layer principle: ward or
county, municipality, district, and state. They scarcely exist as voluntary associations at the national level — except for the quadrennial national nominating
conventions — but they exist in the caucuses of Congress, where they are the
most important single influence on congressmen's voting behavior despite the
bifurcation within both political parties.

16. While money in the hands of rich people opens special opportunities to
democratic political processes — such as through the use of lobbyists, advertisements, and campaign contributions — these processes are by no means closed to
poor people. A volunteer campaign worker for a congressman will have more
influence on him than most lobbyists, and as much influence on him as a campaign contribution equivalent to the voluntary labor, roughly speaking. The fact
that the political party in most states is an open, if not entirely democratic,
voluntary association, and the fact that it is the single most important influence
on most elected officials, also gives the non-wealthy citizen access to political
power often greater than that of the wealthy, but not politically active, citizen.
In this context it should be understood that most elected officials, especially at
higher levels, are only partially open to pressures of any kind. Practically all congressmen, and probably most state legislators, vote for bills in accord with their
own personal convictions — when they have convictions with regard to specific
bills — most of the time. Where they do not have convictions regarding a specific
bill, the most important influence on them are the caucus leaders or committee
chairmen of their own political party who are representing the party leadership's
position. The "personal convictions" factor suggests that the *initial* selection of
candidates and the means which they use to get elected to Congress are the two
most important links in the chain leading to the passage of bills where influence
can be most effectively applied. It is for this reason that we say that voluntary
campaign labor, participation in the grass-roots party (as voluntary association),
and monetary campaign contributions are the most powerful instruments to
influence a legislator (or probably any other elected official).

In sharper summary, the conclusions of this book — in contrast with those
of Mills and Hunter — are that the power structure of the United States is
highly complex and diversified (rather than unitary and monolithic), that the
political system is more or less democratic (with the glaring exception of the
Negro's position until the 1960's), that in political processes the political elite
is ascendant over and not subordinate to the economic elite, and that the political elite influences or controls the economic elite at least as much as the economic elite controls the political elite. To arrive at such conclusions we must
in part have a contrast conception: What should the American political power
structure be compared to? We believe that Mills has implicitly compared the
existing American power structure to some populist or guild socialist ideal, which
has never existed and which we believe could never exist considering basic socio-

logical facts — such as the existence of culture, of the value of money to most people, etc. Our implicit comparison in this book has been to any known other society — past or present (with the possible exception of the contemporary Scandinavian countries). We do not say that the multi-influence hypothesis is entirely the fact, or that the United States is completely democratic; we simply say that such statements are more correct for the United States today than for any other society.

While the whole first chapter of this book might be repeated in the summary, we wish merely to repeat in conclusion the statement of the multi-influence hypothesis which has guided the studies reported in this book: Segments of the economic elite have violated democratic political and legal processes, with differing degrees of effort and success in the various periods of American history, but in no recent period could they correctly be said to have controlled the elected and appointed political authorities in large measure. The relationship between the economic elite and the political authorities has been a constantly varying one of strong influence, co-operation, division of labor, and conflict, with each group influencing the other in changing proportion to some extent, and each operating independently of the other to a large extent. Today there is significant political control and limitation of certain activities of the economic elite, and there are also some significant processes by which the economic elite use their wealth to help elect some political candidates and to influence other political authorities in ways which are not available to the average citizen. Further, neither the economic elite nor the political authorities are monolithic units which act with internal consensus and co-ordinated action with regard to each other (or probably in any other way): in fact, there are several economic elites, which only very rarely act as units within themselves and among themselves, and there are at least two (we prefer to think of them as four) political parties which have significantly differing programs with regard to their actions toward any economic elite and each of these parties has only a partial degree of internal cohesion.

The power structure of the United States is indeed so complex that this book only touches on certain aspects of it, rather than providing full empirical evidence for these aspects. We believe, however, that enough empirical documentation has been provided to give basic support to the multi-influence hypothesis as a general statement about what is true of the power structure of the United States.

WHAT IS THE EXTENT
OF CORPORATE POWER?

The degree of economic concentration in America is a central topic
in most discussions of the national power structure. Virtually all scholars
agree that major economic inequalities exist. Both elite and class analysts
tend to argue, however, that economic concentration and corporate power
have increased substantially since the end of World War II. Many, but certainly not all, pluralists conclude on the other hand that countervailing forces,
such as government antitrust policies, have brought economic concentration
to heel. Thus Talcott Parsons, in his critique of Mills, contends that "the
relative share of the largest firms in the production of the economy has
remained essentially stable for more than a generation." This, Parsons
believes, "points to some kind of equilibrium condition with respect to the
degree of concentration in the system as a whole."

This debate is complicated by subtle issues of statistical interpretation
and has by no means been resolved. Conclusions about the trend of economic concentration, for example, often depend on whether scholars
attempt to measure overall concentration (the share of the largest corporations, usually defined as the top 50, 100, 200, or 500), concentration within
individual industries, or the size inequality of firms. There is, moreover, no
consensus about the usefulness of absolute as opposed to relative measures
of economic concentration. These and other methodological problems are
discussed by G. Warren Nutter, "Industrial Concentration," in The International Encyclopedia of the Social Sciences (New York: Macmillan and
the Free Press, 1968), Vol. 7, pp. 218–222; Gideon Rosenbluth, "Measures
of Concentration," in the National Bureau of Economic Research, Business
Concentration and Price Policy (Princeton: Princeton University Press,
1955), pp. 57–95; and, briefly, by William G. Shepherd in his essay
"Trends of Concentration in American Manufacturing Industries, 1947–
1958," Review of Economics and Statistics, XLVI (May 1964), pp. 200–
212.

The dispute over economic concentration itself has not quieted since the early thirties, when Adolph Berle and Gardiner Means first suggested, in The Modern Corporation and Private Property, that America's largest 200 nonfinancial corporations would control a growing percentage of total corporate assets. After World War II John Blair concluded, in several reports written for the Federal Trade Commission, that concentration had greatly increased during the war and, if the trend continued, that "either the giant corporations will ultimately take over the country, or the government will be compelled to step in and impose some form of direct protection." (These reports included The Present Trend of Mergers and Acquisitions [Washington, 1947] and Report of the Federal Trade Commission on the Merger Movement, A Summary Report [Washington, 1948].) Blair's findings were soon challenged by John Lintner and J. Keith Butters, "Effect of Mergers on Industrial Concentration," Review of Economics and Statistics, XXXII (February 1950), pp. 30–48. The strongest rebuttal, however, was presented by M. A. Adelman in his essay, "The Measurement of Industrial Concentration," Review of Economics and Statistics, XXXIII (November 1951), pp. 269–296. Adelman found "a slight de-concentration during the wartime period," and denied, in addition, that there was any long-term trend toward greater concentration in the American economy. Some experts, like G. Warren Nutter and Henry Adler Einhorn (Enterprise Monopoly in the United States, 1899–1958 [New York: Columbia University Press, 1969]) have since agreed with Adelman that, in important sectors of the economy, concentration has either remained constant or decreased during most of the twentieth century.

Other economists, however, continue to challenge the idea of economic de-concentration or stability. Disagreeing with many of his fellow pluralists, A. A. Berle contends — in his essay Economic Power and the Free Society (New York: The Fund for the Republic, 1957) — that the dominance of a few hundred corporations controlled by a small group of men represents "the highest concentration of economic power in recorded history." Likewise, economist Gardiner Means, in testimony delivered before the Senate Judiciary Committee in 1964, argues more specifically that "manufacturing concentration, whether measured by total assets or by net capital assets, has increased greatly since 1929 and . . . without taking account of joint ventures or companies controlled through less than a majority ownership, somewhere in the close vicinity of 58 percent of the net capital assets of manufacturing are controlled by 100 companies," compared with perhaps 44 percent in 1929. A number of reports issued by the Federal Trade Commission suggest that the recent proliferation of "conglomerate" mergers has abetted the trend toward increasing economic concentration. See, for example, Concentration Trends and Merger Activity in U.S. Manufacturing Industry Since World War II (Washington, 1967), The Corporate Merger Movement, Its Dimensions and Impacts (Washington, 1969), and Corporate Mergers (Washington, D.C., 1969).

In the testimony reprinted here, Willard F. Mueller, director, Bureau of Economics, Federal Trade Commission (accompanied by Stanley E. Boyle, chief, Division of Economic Reports, Bureau of Economics) documents recent trends in the concentration of American manufacturing. Mueller finds that economic concentration has increased significantly during recent decades and that concentration today is alarmingly great. Yet, despite his convincing data, Mueller's conclusions should be embraced with due restraint. His thesis of increasing concentration is rejected, for example, by M. A. Adelman in later testimony before the Subcommittee on Antitrust and Monopoly, printed in Economic Concentration, Part I, Overall and Conglomerate Aspects, (Washington, 1964), pp. 223–248 (which includes a colloquy with John Blair), although Adelman's data are in turn criticized by the Federal Trade Commission, Corporate Mergers (Washington, D.C., 1969), pp. 730–736. Whatever the trend of concentration may be, however, Mueller does demonstrate the significant amount of inequality in the American economy, and this fact itself carries major significance for the student of national power.

WILLARD F. MUELLER

Concentration in American Manufacturing

INTRODUCTION

The data on manufacturing corporations for the fourth quarter of the year 1962 are based on information submitted to the Securities and Exchange Commission and the Federal Trade Commission and used in the preparation by these agencies of the *Quarterly Financial Report for Manufacturing Corporations.*

In a few instances, these special tabulations have been adjusted to include certain items which some companies omitted from their quarterly reports but which they included in their annual consolidated income and operating statements. No adjustments have been made in these preliminary figures which would consolidate companies under common ownership. . . .

From testimony of Willard F. Mueller (accompanied by Stanley E. Boyle), *Economic Concentration: Part I. Overall and Conglomerate Aspects.* Hearings before the Subcommittee on Antitrust and Monopoly of the Committee on the Judiciary, United States Senate, 88th Congress, 2nd Session (Washington, D.C.: Government Printing Office, 1964), pp. 113–129. Some footnotes have been omitted.

Also, the data which I shall summarize do not consolidate the assets of joint ventures. A brief examination of the largest manufacturing corporations indicates that, at a minimum, 15 joint ventures with combined assets of almost $900 million are included among the 1,000 largest U. S. manufacturing corporations. Thus, the following preliminary asset concentration figures underestimate the degree of concentration actually present in American manufacturing. Throughout this statement newspapers are not included among manufacturing companies.

Concentration of Assets in Total Manufacturing

In 1962, the population of American manufacturing enterprises consisted of about 180,000 corporations and 240,000 partnerships and proprietorships. These approximately 420,000 business units had combined assets of about $296 billion as of the fourth quarter of 1962. About 98.4 percent of these assets were held by corporations.

Table 1 and Figure 1 show the ownership distribution of manufacturing assets. The 20 largest manufacturing corporations (all of which had assets of more than $1.5 billion at year-end 1962) had $73.8 billion in assets, or an estimated 25 percent of the total assets of *all* U.S. manufacturing companies. The 50 largest corporations accounted for 35.7 percent, the 100 largest for 46.1 percent, the 200 largest for 55.9 percent, and the 1,000 largest for almost three-fourths (74.8 percent) of the total assets of all manufacturing companies. These data demonstrate quite clearly the high degree of concentration in American manufacturing. In fact, whereas the 20 largest companies held 25 percent and the 1,000 largest held 74.8 percent of all manufacturing assets, the 419,000 smallest companies accounted for only 25.2 percent of total manufacturing assets. Thus, the total assets of the 20 largest manufacturing corporations were approximately the same as those of the 419,000 smallest.

Asset and Profit Concentration among Manufacturing Corporations, 1962

Three financial items were used to measure concentration among manufacturing corporations: total assets, net capital assets, and net income. The results of these comparisons are shown in Table 2 and Figure 2.

When concentration is measured in terms of net capital assets, it is greater than when total assets are used. Concentration measured in terms of net profits is greater than when either asset measure is used. For example, the 20 largest manufacturing corporations, with 25.4 percent of total corporate assets, accounted for 31.3 percent of total net capital assets and 38 percent of profits after taxes. The 100 largest manufacturing corporations in 1962 accounted for 57.6 percent of net profits, compared with 55.1 percent of net capital assets and 46.8 percent of total assets. The 1,000 largest corporations accounted for 86.4 percent of profits after taxes, 82.2 percent of net capital assets and 76 percent of total assets.

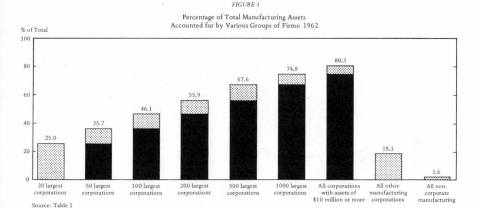

FIGURE 1

Percentage of Total Manufacturing Assets
Accounted for by Various Groups of Firms: 1962

Source: Table 1

The approximately 2,041 corporations with assets of $10 million or more earned 89.3 percent of all corporate profits whereas the about 178,000 remaining corporations earned 10.7 percent. Also of significance, the net profits of the 5 largest corporations were nearly twice as large as those of the about 178,000 smallest corporations.

These data indicate unmistakably that, regardless of the measure used, a relatively few immense corporations hold the great bulk of the financial resources of American manufacturing.

TABLE 1

Concentration of total manufacturing assets, fourth quarter, 1962

Corporate size group	Assets (millions)	All manufacturing (percentage)	Corporations only (percentage)
5 largest	$36,447	12.3	12.5
10 largest	54,353	18.4	18.7
20 largest	73,825	25.0	25.4
50 largest	105,421	35.7	36.2
100 largest	136,222	46.1	46.8
200 largest	165,328	55.9	56.8
500 largest	199,894	67.6	68.7
1,000 largest	221,279	74.8	76.0
Corporations with assets over $10,000,000[a]	237,410	80.3	81.6
All corporations[b]	291,022	98.4	100.0
Total manufacturing businesses[c]	295,690	100.0	—

[a] There were 2,041 manufacturing corporations in operation the first quarter of 1963.
[b] This group includes about 180,000 manufacturing corporations.
[c] Includes asset estimates for approximately 240,000 manufacturing proprietorships and partnerships.

Source: Bureau of Economics, Federal Trade Commission.

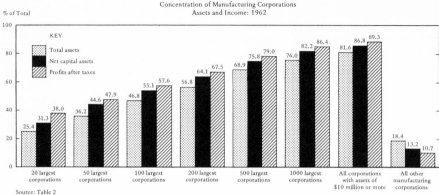

FIGURE 2

Concentration of Manufacturing Corporations
Assets and Income: 1962

Source: Table 2

TABLE 2

Concentration of assets and income, all manufacturing corporations,
fourth quarter, 1962

Corporate size group	Total assets		Net capital assets		Profit after taxes	
	Millions	%	Millions	%	Millions	%
5 largest	$36,447	12.5	$17,502	15.3	$957	19.8
10 largest	54,353	18.7	27,783	24.3	1,434	29.6
20 largest	73,825	25.4	35,840	31.3	1,839	38.0
50 largest	105,421	36.2	51,057	44.6	2,315	47.9
100 largest	136,222	46.8	63,128	55.1	2,788	57.6
200 largest	165,328	56.8	73,447	64.1	3,265	67.5
500 largest	199,894	68.9	86,818	75.8	3,821	79.0
1000 largest	221,279	76.0	94,178	82.2	4,178	86.4
All over $10,000,000[a]	237,409	81.6	99,443	86.8	4,321	89.3
All corporations[b]	291,022[c]	100.0	114,589	100.0	4,837	100.0

[a] *There were 2,041 corporations in this size class in the first quarter of 1963.* Quarterly Financial Report, *1963, p. 61.*
[b] *There were approximately 180,000 manufacturing corporations at the end of 1962.*
[c] *Adjusted. See text for explanation of adjustment.*

Source: *Bureau of Economics, Federal Trade Commission.*

Concentration in 28 Industry Groups, 1962

These are the 28 industries which appear in the Federal Trade Commission-Security and Exchange Commission's *Quarterly Financial Report on Manufacturing Corporations.*

The 20 largest manufacturing corporations, at year-end 1962, accounted for 25 percent of the total assets, 31 percent of the net capital assets and 38 percent of profits after taxes of all manufacturing businesses. While these data demonstrate that there is a high degree of concentration of economic resources, they tell us little of the degree of concentration in individual industries. To enlarge this area of the analysis, concentration measures have been computed for 28 individual industry groups. Tables 3 and 4 contain estimates of the share of each industry group's sales, total assets, net capital assets and income after taxes that are held by the 4 and 20 largest companies.

These data, while for broader industry groups than generally used to measure product concentration, do provide interesting insights into the relative strength of the major producers in each industry group. Most major producers confront their competitors in a number of different related industries and produce a large number of common products. Also, while almost all of the companies covered by this analysis are diversified to some extent, the bulk of the diversification of these companies has been into related product areas.

TABLE 3

Concentration of sales, total assets, net capital assets, and profits after taxes, for 27 selected industry groups, fourth quarter 1962[a]

NUMBER OF INDUSTRIES

Percentage of industry	Sales		Total assets		Net capital assets		Profits after taxes	
	4 largest	20^b largest	4 largest	20^b largest	4 largest	20^b largest	4 largest	20^b largest
90 to 100	—	4	—	4	—	4	—	5
80 to 89	1	1	—	3	1	5	1	6
70 to 79	1	2	2	4	—	3	2	2
60 to 69	—	4	—	4	1	4	1	7
50 to 59	1	5	2	2	3	5	6	—
40 to 49	6	2	8	6	7	3	4	5
30 to 39	5	5	5	2	9	1	5	—
20 to 29	6	2	4	1	1	2	4	2
10 to 19	5	2	4	1	4	—	2	—
Less than 10	2	—	2	—	1	—	2	—

[a] Based on the data appearing in Table 4 except that textile products are not included.
[b] Includes 2 industry groups with less than 20 companies.

Source: *Bureau of Economics, Federal Trade Commission.*

Table 3 provides a brief summary of the individual industry group data contained in Table 4. Again, as in Table 2, the degree of concentration in each industry group may vary depending upon the financial variable employed. These data, like those in Table 2, reveal that profits and net capital assets are more concentrated than total assets. In every industry group, sales are the least concentrated. Regardless of the variable selected, however, in more than half the industry groups the 20 largest companies account for 50 percent or more of total sales, total assets, net capital assets, or profits after taxes.

In 23 of the 28 industry groups (about 82 percent), profits after taxes show either the highest concentration or concentration within 1 percentage point of the highest figure. In 20 of the industry groups, the 20 top companies earned over 60 percent of industry profits.

TABLE 4

Concentration of sales total assets, net capital assets, and profits
after taxes for the 4 and 20 largest firms in 28 selected industry groups,
fourth quarter, 1962

INDUSTRY GROUP I

| | Percentage of total | |
	4 largest	*20 largest*
Motor vehicles and equipment:		
Sales	80.8	93.1
Total assets	79.7	93.9
Net capital assets	83.1	95.5
Profits after taxes	89.1	96.9
Aircraft and parts:		
Sales	47.3	92.4
Total assets	41.9	92.5
Net capital assets	32.6	90.5
Profits after taxes	46.6	92.9
Other transportation equipment:		
Sales	30.3	62.2
Total assets	44.2	76.2
Net capital assets	59.9	82.1
Profits after taxes	51.6	107.6

INDUSTRY GROUP II

Electrical machinery and equipment:		
Sales	34.4	57.5
Total assets	35.6	61.2
Net capital assets	41.5	63.0
Profits after taxes	44.4	64.8
Metalworking machinery and equipment:		
Sales	14.5	36.8
Total assets	16.3	42.8
Net capital assets	18.5	39.3
Profits after taxes	19.1	45.1
Other machinery except metal working and electrical:		
Sales	20.6	39.4
Total assets	24.3	46.0
Net capital assets	31.5	50.4
Profits after taxes	39.6	61.2

TABLE 4 — *cont.*

INDUSTRY GROUP III

	Percentage of total	
	4 largest	*20 largest*
Primary iron and steel:		
Sales	40.2	66.8
Total assets	48.0	77.7
Net capital assets	48.8	82.3
Profits after taxes	44.3	82.4
Primary nonferrous metals:		
Sales	27.3	65.0
Total assets	41.1	81.9
Net capital assets	47.7	87.0
Profits after taxes	37.1	88.9
Other fabricated metal products:		
Sales	14.7	26.5
Total assets	19.9	33.4
Net capital assets	30.3	42.4
Profit after taxes	17.7	41.4

INDUSTRY GROUP IV

Stone, clay, and glass products:		
Sales	18.1	40.2
Total assets	19.9	48.8
Net capital assets	19.8	52.3
Profits after taxes	23.4	63.7
Furniture and fixtures:		
Sales	5.2	14.4
Total assets	8.4	24.1
Net capital assets	9.6	27.8
Profits after taxes	5.3	23.7
Lumber and wood products except furniture:		
Sales	21.2	31.6
Total assets	31.0	45.7
Net capital assets	41.5	57.7
Profits after taxes	48.6	64.5

TABLE 4 — *cont.*

INDUSTRY GROUP V

	Percentage of total	
	4 largest	*20 largest*
Instruments and related products:		
Sales	37.9	56.9
Total assets	41.2	63.4
Net capital assets	50.2	72.5
Profits after taxes	56.6	74.0
Miscellaneous manufacturing and ordnance:		
Sales	16.3	29.1
Total assets	33.1	45.9
Net capital assets	34.3	48.2
Profits after taxes	25.2	43.5

INDUSTRY GROUP VI

	4 largest	*20 largest*
Dairy products:[a]		
Sales	42.9	59.1
Total assets	48.8	66.0
Net capital assets	47.4	64.4
Profits after taxes	73.9	87.8
Bakery products: [b]		
Sales	33.6	56.8
Total assets	39.6	64.3
Net capital assets	38.2	66.2
Profits after taxes	52.8	62.5
Food, excluding beverages, dairy, and bakery products:		
Sales	12.5	34.0
Total assets	13.2	38.8
Net capital assets	14.9	40.1
Profits after taxes	20.1	44.4

[a] *Data available for only largest 17 companies.*
[b] *Data vailable for only largest 18 companies.*

TABLE 4 — *cont.*

INDUSTRY GROUP VII

	Percentage of total	
	4 largest	*20 largest*
Textile mill products:[a]		
Sales	22.0	31.8
Total assets	26.1	38.4
Net capital assets	25.7	38.6
Profits after taxes	30.5	44.9
Apparel and other finished products:		
Sales	4.9	12.0
Total assets	7.7	18.0
Net capital assets	11.4	24.7
Profits after taxes	7.4	21.8
Paper and allied products:		
Sales	20.7	46.9
Total assets	23.2	53.5
Net capital assets	22.3	55.4
Profits after taxes	35.0	65.5

INDUSTRY GROUP VIII

Basic industrial chemicals:		
Sales	42.0	77.8
Total assets	45.5	82.4
Net capital assets	44.6	82.0
Profits after taxes	64.6	89.7
Drugs and medicines:		
Sales	31.0	81.5
Total assets	29.2	83.4
Net capital assets	33.3	88.6
Profits after taxes	32.6	86.8
Chemical except industrial chemical and drug and medicine:		
Sales	28.5	50.8
Total assets	30.0	54.8
Net capital assets	33.6	62.3
Profits after taxes	35.8	67.2

[a] *8 largest rather than 4 largest.*

TABLE 4 — *cont.*

INDUSTRY GROUP IX

	Percentage of total	
	4 largest	*20 largest*
Petroleum refining:		
Sales	50.3	90.7
Total assets	50.1	93.2
Net capital assets	47.7	93.6
Profits after taxes	54.3	94.9
Rubber and miscellaneous plastic products:		
Sales	48.1	69.0
Total assets	55.0	74.3
Net capital assets	56.4	74.5
Profits after taxes	51.6	74.3
Leather and leather products:		
Sales	26.7	37.9
Total assets	32.1	46.3
Net capital assets	35.4	52.2
Profits after taxes	28.8	49.9

INDUSTRY GROUP X

Alcoholic beverages:		
Sales	41.4	70.8
Total assets	47.2	75.8
Net capital assets	30.8	70.6
Profits after taxes	58.3	86.8
Tobacco:		
Sales	70.9	97.9
Total assets	72.7	98.5
Net capital assets	69.8	98.4
Profits after taxes	72.5	98.8

Source: *Bureau of Economics, Federal Trade Commission.*

Considerable variations in the degree of concentration exist among industry groups. For example, the four largest producers of motor vehicles and parts accounted for 79.7 percent of that industry's total assets and 89.1 percent of its net profits; the four largest producers of tobacco products accounted for 72.7 percent of total assets and 72.5 percent of total net profits of that industry group (Table 4). Both industries are highly concentrated and there is considerable disparity between the size of the four largest and all other producers of these products.

Rather high degrees of concentration also exist in rubber and miscellaneous plastic products, dairy products, primary iron and steel, alcoholic beverages, petroleum refining, industrial chemicals, other transportation equipment, and instruments and related products. In each one of these relatively broad industry groups, the four largest companies accounted for more than 40 percent of the total assets and more than 50 percent of the profits after taxes (Table 4).

On the other hand, there are seven industry groups in which the four largest companies accounted for less than 20 percent of total assets. These include stone, clay, and glass products, fabricated metal products, textile products, metalworking machinery, other food products (except alcoholic beverages, dairy and bakery products), furniture and fixtures, and apparel. However, in all but 2 of the above industry groups the 20 largest companies in each group accounted for 40 percent or more of the profits after taxes.[1]

Concentration in Manufacturing, 1950 and 1962

In addition to the above estimates of concentration in 1962, we have prepared estimates of the share of total manufacturing assets held by the 200 largest manufacturing corporations in 1950 (Table 5). These data show that between 1950 and 1962 a substantial increase in total manufacturing assets occurred in this country.[2] During the period, the total assets of all manufacturing businesses increased by 106 percent and the total assets of all manufacturing corporations grew by 111 percent. However, the assets of the 200 largest manufacturing corporations increased by 141.3 percent during the same period.

The data presented in Table 5 reflect the relatively more rapid growth of the 200 largest American manufacturing corporations (all with assets of $200 million or more in 1962). In 1950, for example, the 20 largest companies accounted for 21.5 percent of total *corporate* assets. By 1962, the 20 largest companies' share had grown to 24.8 percent — an increase of 3.3 percentage points. The share of the 100 largest companies increased from 40.2 percent in 1950 to 45.7 percent in 1962 — an increase of 5.5 percentage points, while that of the 200 largest companies increased from 48.9 percent in 1950 to 55 percent in 1962 — an in-

[1] Although we have presented sales concentration figures for each industry group, they were not included in the above comparisons because of the limited usefulness for the analysis of broad industry groups.

[2] The 1950 and 1962 data presented in this section were taken from corporation annual reports and *Moody's Industrial Manual*. Therefore, the 1962 figures contained in Table 5 are slightly lower than those contained in Tables 1 and 2.

TABLE 5

Concentration of total assets, 200 largest manufacturing corporations,
1950 and 1962 (in millions of dollars)

Corporate size group	1950, total assets [a]	Percentage of total		1962, total assets [a]	Percentage of total	
		All corporations	All manufacturing		All corporations	All manufacturing
5 largest	13,711	10.0	9.6	35,299	12.3	11.9
10 largest	20,759	15.7	14.5	52,924	18.9	17.9
20 largest	29,682	21.5	20.7	72,179	24.8	24.4
50 largest	43,353	31.8	30.2	103,560	35.8	35.0
100 largest	55,388	40.2	38.6	133,000	45.7	45.0
200 largest	66,931	48.9	46.7	161,531	55.0	54.6
All corporations	137,719 [b]	—	—	291,022 [b]	—	—
All manufacturing	143,396 [c]	—	—	295,690 [c]	—	—

[a] *These asset figures differ from those appearing in Tables 1 and 2 because the asset data used here are those reported in* Moody's Industrial Manual *rather than those reported in the* FTC-SEC Quarterly Financial Report.

[b] *Estimate. (See text for explanation for basis of estimates.)*

[c] *Estimate of the total assets of all incorporated and unincorporated manufacturing corporations. (See text for explanation of basis of estimates.)*

Source: *Bureau of Economics, Federal Trade Commission.*

crease of 6.1 percentage points. These data show that concentration in manufacturing has increased substantially since 1950.

When noncorporate manufacturing companies are included in the comparison, the increase in concentration is even more pronounced. Whereas in 1950 the 100 largest corporations held 38.6 percent of all manufacturing assets, by 1962 they held 45 percent of such assets — an increase of 6.4 percentage points. The share of the 200 largest companies increased from 46.7 to 54.6 percent, an increase of 7.9 percentage points. Hence, in just 12 years, their share of all manufacturing assets grew by about 17 percent.

Moreover, it must be recalled that this may well represent a minimum estimate of the actual increase in concentration of the period. As noted earlier, the assets of a number of joint ventures have not been credited to their parents.

Concentration in Manufacturing, 1947, 1950, and 1962

In 1950 the Federal Trade Commission published concentration estimates for the 113 largest manufacturing corporations of 1947 with assets of $100 million or more. That study showed that in 1947 the 113 largest manufacturing corporations controlled 40 percent of the total assets and 46.1 percent of the net capital assets of all U.S. manufacturing businesses.

Table 6 presents estimates of the share of all manufacturing assets held by the 113 largest manufacturing corporations in each of the years 1947, 1950, and 1962. Considerable care should be taken in drawing any precise comparisons between these estimates. In 1951 substantial changes were made in the sample design of the *Quarterly Financial Report* program; therefore, we have adjusted the 1950 asset data on the basis of the 1951 change. However, we have no logical basis on which to make a similar adjustment in the 1947 data.

TABLE 6

Concentration of total assets, 113 largest manufacturing corporations, 1947, 1950, and 1960 (in millions of dollars)

Year	Total manu-facturing assets [a]	113 largest corporations	
		Total assets	Percentage of total manufacturing
1947[b]	105,369	42,197	40.0
1950	132,032[c]	57,430[d]	43.5
1950	143,396[ef]	57,430[d]	40.0
1962	295,690	137,786[d]	46.6

[a] *Includes estimates of unincorporated manufacturing firms.*
[b] *Federal Trade Commission,* Report on the Concentration of Productive Facilities, 1947, *1949, p. 16.*
[c] *Unadjusted.*
[d] Moody's Industrial Manual.
[e] *Adjusted.*
[f] *1950 data adjusted to allow for 1951 change in sample design.*
Note. *The data for the 3 years may not be compared directly because of the noncomparability of the total asset figures due to differences in sampling procedures. However, substantial comparability exists between the 1947 and the 1950 (unadjusted) figures, and between the 1950 (adjusted) and the 1962 figures.*

Source: *Bureau of Economics, Federal Trade Commission.*

These data show that between 1947 and 1950 the share of all manufacturing assets held by the 113 largest companies increased from 40 to 43.5 percent (the 1950 unadjusted figure). It is further shown that between 1950 and 1962 the 113 largest increased their share from 40 (adjusted 1950 figure) to 46.6 percent. While the data for the 3 years are not directly comparable, they show quite clearly that between 1947 and 1962 the share of all manufacturing assets held by the 113 largest manufacturing corporations *probably* increased by about 10 percentage points, or by about 25 percent. . . .

The data contained in Tables 5 and 6 show that over the past 15 years the degree of concentration in the manufacturing segment of our economy increased at a rate comparable to increases in concentration which occurred in the 1920's. At this time we have no data which indicates that this growth is subsiding. In fact, according to the latest copy of *Fortune* magazine which came to my attention yesterday, between 1962 and 1963 the assets of the 500 largest industrial corporations as measured by *Fortune* grew more rapidly than did all manufacturing assets during that period, suggesting that an additional increase in concentration occurred between 1962 and 1963. . . .

I would like now to turn to some information which we developed on certain aspects of the current merger movement.

THE SCOPE OF THE CURRENT MERGER MOVEMENT

American industry is undergoing another important merger movement, and I am reasonably confident that this movement has played a major role in the post-World War II increases in overall concentration discussed earlier. I regret that we are unable, today, to provide you with very complete information of the scope and comparative significance of this movement. We are currently in the process of compiling and summarizing the merger information in our files. Although we have not completed this compilation, the information developed to date indicates some of the important dimensions of the current merger movement. We shall provide later this summer the remainder of the information you requested, consisting of a more detailed treatment of the structure of the current merger movement.

Acquisitions of Large Manufacturing and Mining Concerns

As we pointed out earlier (Table 2), in 1962 the approximately 2,000 manufacturing corporations with assets of $10 million or more held about 81.6 percent of the total assets and 89.3 percent of the total profits of all manufacturing corporations.

This, then, is really the heart of American manufacturing — about 2,000 companies with assets of over $10 million. Consequently, substantial merger activity among firms in this size class could have a significant impact upon the structure of the American economy.

Table 7 summarizes the total number and value of assets for manufacturing and mining acquisitions occurring since 1948 in which the acquired concern had assets of $10 million or more in the year prior to acquisition. Although these "large" acquisitions represented only about 6 percent of all acquisitions recorded by the Federal Trade Commission since 1948, they very likely accounted for well over half of the value of assets of all recorded acquisitions.[3]

The first point to be noted from these statistics is the rising tide of merger activity among large concerns following 1948–50. From a low of under 10 per year during 1948–50, mergers moved upward, reaching a postwar peak of 66 in 1955; they then declined to 33 in the recession year of 1958. Beginning with 1959, there were over 60 large mergers each year.

During the entire 1948–63 period at least 591 manufacturing and mining corporations with assets of $10 million or more merged or were acquired. These merged[4] corporations had total assets of $19.5 billion in the year prior to acquisition (Table 7).

---

[3] In 1963 the Federal Trade Commission recorded 1,018 manufacturing and mining acquisitions. The 62 of these with assets of $10 million or more had combined assets of $2.5 billion; 198 other acquisitions for which asset information could be obtained, or could be estimated, had combined assets of about $500 million.

[4] Throughout this discussion the terms "merger" and "acquisition" are used interchangeably to mean the disappearance of the whole or substantial part of a previously

One way to gauge the magnitude of these mergers is to compare them with the total number and assets of firms in this size class. Had these "large" firms not been acquired, and had they continued to operate in this size class in 1963, there would have been at least 26 percent more firms[5] in this size class in 1963 than there actually were (about 2,230).[6]

TABLE 7

Acquisitions of mining and manufacturing corporations with assets of $10,000,000 and over, 1948-63 (dollars in millions)

Year	Number of acquisitions[a]	Total assets of acquired corporations[b]	Year	Number of acquisitions[a]	Total assets of acquired corporations[b]
1948	2	$39.6	1957	44	$1,304.1
1949	1	21.5	1958	33	943.1
1950	3	135.7	1959	61	1,790.7
1951	12	257.3	1960	61	1,861.0
1952	12	313.8	1961	66	2,569.3
1953	24	713.6	1962	61	1,651.6
1954	30	1,165.4	1963	62	2,490.5
1955	66	2,202.1			
1956	53	2,052.9	Total[c]	591	19,512.2

[a] See App. A [in original publication] for sources of merger data.
[b] Includes consideration paid, when asset data not available.
[c] Total does not include 10 nonmining and nonmanufacturing acquisitions with total assets of $265,700,000.

Source: *Bureau of Economics, Federal Trade Commission.*

More significant, during each of the last 5 years, over 60 "large" firms were acquired each year. Whether or not this is a high merger rate is a question of judgment; but certainly, compared to the recorded wartime and immediate postwar merger rates, this is a high rate. During 1940–47, 81 concerns with assets of $10 million or more were acquired,[7] and during 1948–50 only 6 additional

---

independent business entity, or a stock acquisition involving purchase by one company of over 50 percent of the stock of another company.

[5] Of course, had they not been acquired, some of the firms may well have dropped from this size class because they failed or declined in size after 1948. On the other hand, an unknown — but perhaps larger — number of firms (not included in this count) with assets under $10 million when acquired, would have been in the $10 million class by 1963 had they not been acquired in the meantime.

[6] There were in this size class 2,041 manufacturing corporations in the first quarter of 1963 (FTC–SEC, *Quarterly Financial Report, op. cit.,* 61) and 189 mining corporations in fiscal 1961–62, the last year for which the Internal Revenue Service has such information.

[7] *Report of the Federal Trade Commission on the Merger Movement,* 1948, 27. Lintner and Butters place the number of such acquisitions at 58. Lintner and Butters, "Effect of Mergers on Industrial Concentrations, 1940–47." *Review of Economics and Statistics,* February 1950, 38.

firms of this size class were acquired (Table 7). Clearly, the annual rate of the 1940–50 period fell far short of current levels.[8]

The total value of assets acquired during 1948–63 was equal to about 22 percent of total manufacturing and mining assets in 1948 and 8 percent of such assets in 1963.

Perhaps the most meaningful measure of the relative magnitude of these mergers is to compare them with the assets of all firms in the size class of firms with assets of between $10 and $250 million, since all but three of the acquired concerns fell in this size class.[9] Such a comparison reveals that the assets of acquired concerns were 20 percent as great as the assets of all firms in the $10 to $250 million size class in 1963. And in recent years, the merger mortality rate (measured by assets) among firms in this size class exceeded 2 percent annually.

Acquisitions Involving the 1,000 Largest Manufacturing Corporations of 1950

Another indication of the relative volume of larger mergers is the number of the 1,000 largest manufacturing corporations of 1950 which have disappeared because of mergers. Since December 31, 1950, at least 216, or over 1 in 5, of the 1,000 largest manufacturing corporations of 1950 have merged or been acquired (Table 8). These merger-caused disappearances were especially heavy among the companies ranking in the 501 to 1,000 largest class. A total of 139 corporations, or 27.8 percent, of those in this class were acquired. The comparable percentages for the 201 to 500 class were 20.7 percent, and for the top 200 class, 7.5 percent. These tabulations further reveal that over one-third of the disappearing companies were acquired by companies which ranked among the 200 largest corporations in 1950. The assets of the firms acquired by these 200 corporations represented about 66 percent of the total assets of all acquisitions involving the 1,000 largest corporations of 1950.

Finally I would like to discuss the pattern of acquisitions made by the 200 largest manufacturing corporations of 1962.

Acquisitions of the 200 Largest Corporations

Between January 1, 1951, and the end of 1963, the 200 largest manufacturing corporations made at least 1,956 acquisitions (Table 9). Asset estimates could be made for 1,080 (55 percent) of these; we believe that most of the 876 for which no asset estimates have been made were very small.

Of those acquisitions for which we have asset estimates, 308 (28 percent)

---

[8] During 1940–47, 139 manufacturing and mining corporations with assets of $5 million or more were acquired. *Report of the Federal Trade Commission on the Merger Movement,* 1948, 27. Since there were in 1947 about the same number of corporations with assets of $5 million or more as there were corporations with $10 million or more in 1963, the current merger rate among "large" firms clearly is higher than during the wartime merger movement.

[9] Three acquired concerns had assets of over $250 million in the year prior to being acquired. The total assets of these three concerns were $839.5 million.

TABLE 8

Companies ranked among the 1,000 largest manufacturing companies in 1950 disappearing through mergers during 1951-63

Nature of acquiring company	Total	Rank of acquired company, 1950		
		1 to 200	201 to 500	501 to 1,000
Company rank in 1950:				
1 to 200	82	8	35	39
201 to 500	52	4	12	36
501 to 1,000	29	1	6	22
Total by 1,000 largest of 1950	163	13	53	97
Other manufacturing companies	37	2	6	29
Companies not principally engaged in manufacturing	16	—	3	13
Total number of disappearances	216	15	62	139

Source: *Bureau of Economics, Federal Trade Commission.*

had assets below $1 million and 611 (56 percent) had assets below $5 million; these 611 acquired units involved assets of about $875 million. On the other hand, the 339 acquired units with assets of $10 million or more involved total assets of over $13 billion, or about 88 percent of all assets acquired between 1951 and 1963 by the 200 largest manufacturing corporations.

Table 10 summarizes the asset values of acquisitions made by the 200 largest

TABLE 9

Size of acquisitions made between 1951 and 1963 by the 200 largest manufacturing corporations of 1962

Asset size of acquired units	Number of acquisitions	Total acquired assets[a]	Percentage of total
(Millions)		(Millions)	
Unknown	876	—	—
Under 1	308	$100.7	0.7
1 to 4.9	303	773.9	5.1
5 to 9.9	130	918.9	6.1
10 to 24.9	183	2,799.4	18.5
25 to 49.9	85	3,006.4	19.9
50 to 99.9	45	3,176.1	21.0
100 to 249.9	23	3,479.7	23.1
250 to 1,000	3	839.5	5.6
Total	1,956	15,094.6	100.0

[a] *These figures include all acquisitions (including partial acquisitions) made by the acquiring companies during the period 1951-63 and are not limited to acquisitions of mining and manufacturing companies. In instances where asset data were unavailable, consideration paid has been used.*

Source: *Bureau of Economics, Federal Trade Commission.*

TABLE 10
Acquisitions made between 1951 and 1962 by 200 largest manufacturing corporations of 1962

Size of acquiring corporation a	Assets of group		Asset growth, 1950-62	Number of acquisitions	Total assets acquired b	Acquired assets as percentage of total		
	1950	1962				1950	1962	Asset growth
	(Millions)	(Millions)	(Millions)		(Millions)			
Largest 4	13,274.9	36,447.3	23,172.4	30	651.1	4.9	1.8	2.8
5 to 10	7,403.3	17,905.8	10,502.5	35	782.5	10.6	4.4	7.5
11 to 20	8,237.0	19,471.6	11,234.1	47	278.3	3.4	1.4	2.5
21 to 50	12,389.0	31,597.0	19,208.0	232	2,905.8	23.5	9.2	15.1
51 to 100	11,910.7	30,625.9	18,715.0	709	4,888.9	41.0	16.0	26.1
101 to 150	6,833.3	17,654.8	10,821.4	434	2,223.0	32.5	12.6	20.5
151 to 200	4,305.4	11,625.1	7,319.6	382	2,052.8	47.7	17.7	28.0
Total 200	64,353.6	165,327.5	100,973.1	1,869	13,782.4	21.6	8.4	15.7

a Companies ranked by total assets in 1962.
b These figures include all acquisitions (including partial acquisitions) made by the acquiring company during the period 1951-63 and are not limited to acquisitions of mining and manufacturing companies. In instances where asset data were unavailable, consideration paid has been used. Asset information was available for 1,016 of these acquisitions.

Source: Bureau of Economics, Federal Trade Commission.

manufacturing corporations and compares the acquired assets with the 1950 and 1962 assets of the acquiring corporations, as well as with the growth in their assets between 1950 and 1962.

Firms in all size classes made a substantial volume of acquisitions (measured in assets) during the period (Table 10). The 10 largest corporations acquired the greatest volume of assets per firm, averaging about $143 million each; and as a group their acquired assets totaled $1,436 million.

The contribution of assets to the asset growth of the 200 largest firms varied, generally being relatively more important to firms in the smaller size classes. For example, acquired assets were equal to 2.8 percent of the asset growth of the 5 largest corporations and over 20 percent of the asset growth of the 51st to 200th largest corporation (last column, Table 10).

As shown earlier (Table 5), between 1950 and 1962 the 200 largest corporations' share of the total assets of manufacturing corporations increased by about 6.1 percentage points. Clearly, acquisitions played a central role in this increase in concentration. The $13,782,400,000 of assets acquired by these corporations were equal to 21.6 percent of their 1950 assets, 8.4 percent of their 1962 assets, and 15.7 percent of the growth in their assets between 1950 and 1962 (Table 10).

Only 16 of the 200 largest manufacturing corporations made no acquisitions during the period 1951–62 (Table 11); another 15 companies made acquisitions, but asset information was available for none of these (Table 11); and for 69 other companies the value of assets acquired was less than 10 percent of their total asset growth between 1950 and 1962. However, for 35 companies acquired assets exceeded 40 percent of the total growth in their assets between 1950 and 1962, and in the case of 23 companies acquired assets exceeded 50 percent of their asset growth during the period (Table 11).

TABLE 11

Acquired assets as percentage of asset growth from 1950 to 1962
of the 200 largest manufacturing corporations of 1962

Acquired assets as percentage of total assets growth[a] (percentage)	Number of acquiring corporations	Acquired assets as percentage of total assets growth[a] (percentage)	Number of acquiring corporations
0[b]	31	50 to 59.9	8
Less than 10	69	60 to 69.9	4
10 to 19.9	26	70 to 79.9	3
20 to 29.9	22	80 to 89.9	5
30 to 39.9	17	90 to 99.9	1
40 to 49.9	12	100 and over	2

[a] These figures include all acquisitions (including partial acquisitions) made by the acquiring companies during the period 1951-63 and are not limited to acquisitions of mining and manufacturing companies. In instances where asset data were unavailable, consideration paid has been used.

[b] Includes 15 companies which made acquisitions but for which asset data were not available and 16 companies which made no acquisitions.

Source: Bureau of Economics, Federal Trade Commission

These facts indicate that although mergers played a significant role in the growth of most large corporations, their relative importance varied substantially among corporations.

Although we have not completed our analysis of the impact of mergers on the changing mobility of firms, I think it will show that in a good many cases . . . the reason for mobility among the largest corporations is that some firms are making very extensive use of mergers.

Acquisitions by 25 Corporations

A relatively few corporations accounted for a large share of the assets acquired by the 200 largest corporations; 10 companies accounted for 25.5 percent and 25 companies acquired 47.8 percent of all the assets acquired by the 200 largest corporations (Table 12). These leading 25 acquirers made at least 477 acquisitions. The 159 of their acquisitions for which asset data are available, totaled $6,584 million. The 50 leading acquirers made 773 acquisitions; they acquired about 70 percent of the total assets of all companies acquired by the top 200 corporations.

TABLE 12
25 leading acquiring manufacturing corporations, 1951-62

Rank by volume of acquisitions[a]	Number of acquisitions	Number for which assets available	Total assets acquired[b] (millions)	Percentage of total assets acquired by 200 largest corporations
5 leaders	181	49	$2,216.4	16.1
6 to 10	103	33	1,293.9	9.4
11 to 15	84	37	1,215.0	8.8
16 to 20	48	15	994.5	7.2
21 to 25	61	25	864.3	6.3
Total 25 companies	477	159	6,584.1	47.8
Total 50 companies	773	289	9,621.6	69.8
Total 200 companies	1,869	1,016	13,782.4	100.0

[a] Acquiring corporations ranked by volume of assets acquired during 1951-62.
[b] These figures include all acquisitions (including partial acquisitions) made by the acquiring companies during the period 1951-62 and are not limited to acquisitions of mining and manufacturing companies. In instances where asset data were unavailable, consideration paid has been used.

Source: Bureau of Economics, Federal Trade Commission.

Financial Status of Large Acquired Concerns

One final aspect of recent mergers which may be of interest is the financial status of the large firms which were acquired.

We have found that very few large acquired corporations were failing concerns or even losing money in the year prior to being acquired. In fact, a substantial percentage were very profitable enterprises. As shown in Table 13, only 17 of the 165 acquired corporations for which we have financial information were losing money in the year prior to being acquired.[10] These concerns represented only 10.3 percent of all corporations for which we obtained such financial information.

On the other hand, 58 of the acquired corporations enjoyed earnings on net worth of over 10 percent and 90 of over 7.5 percent in the year preceding acquisition. This suggests that many of the acquired concerns were very profitable enterprises, and had they not been acquired they most likely would have continued as healthy economic enterprises capable of offering effective competition.

TABLE 13

Net income after taxes as percentage of net worth for 165 acquired corporations[a]

Rate of return[b] (percentage)	Number of companies		Number of companies
Negative	17	10.0 to 14.9	37
0.0 to 2.4	16	15.0 to 19.9	14
2.5 to 4.9	12	20.0 and over	7
5.0 to 7.4	30		
7.5 to 9.9	32	Total	165

a Shows rates of return for 165 of the 216 acquired corporations reported in table 8.
b Computed from data contained in Moody's Industrial Manual.

Source: Bureau of Economics, Federal Trade Commission.

Although there is clearly a great deal of economic concentration in America, which may or may not be increasing, this does not itself prove that economic power is necessarily vested in a privileged elite or class; nor does it mean that the collective power of American corporations is commonly used to violate the public interest. Indeed, pluralists frequently have tried to reconcile democracy and corporate power by arguing that safeguards prevent the misuse of concentrated economic resources.

A. A. Berle, for example, detects a major increase in economic concentration, yet he also believes there are effective restraints on the exercise of corporate power. (For a lucid summary, see his Power Without Property: A New Development in American Political Economy [New York: Harcourt, Brace, 1959], and The 20th Century Capitalist Revolution [New

10 The data in Table 13 are for the acquired corporations summarized in Table 8 for which we have developed financial information.

York: Harcourt, Brace, 1954].) He emphasizes that the managerial revolution has divorced property from power and helped to create a responsible
"people's capitalism." Berle finds, in addition, that economic power "is
actually controlled by the operation of the public consensus which can
engender public opinion leading to political intervention in any one of a
number of forms." There are also other limitations such as economic competition and economic pluralism. "No single organization," Berle writes,
"has been permitted to grasp more than a limited number of functions, or
even, as a rule, to achieve monopoly in any one function. In the main
(though not universally) the result at present is an equipoise of strong
organizations." A number of young scholars have sharply attacked this
somewhat sanguine interpretation. See, especially, Gabriel Kolko, Wealth
and Power in America: An Analysis of Social Class and Income Distribution (New York: Frederick A. Praeger, 1962), and Don Villarejo, "Stock
Ownership and Control of Corporations," New University Thought, II
(Autumn 1961), pp. 33–77, and II (Winter 1962), pp. 47–62.

John Kenneth Galbraith's concept of "countervailing power," developed
in his book American Capitalism (Boston: Houghton Mifflin, 1952), is
another significant liberal response to the reality of economic concentration.
"Countervailing power," Galbraith contends, is "a self-generating force. . . .
Power on one side of a market creates both the need for, and the prospect
of reward to, the exercise of countervailing power from the other side. This
means that, as a common rule, we can rely on countervailing power to
appear as a curb on economic power." In the selection reprinted here, economist Walter Adams convincingly disputes this theory, suggesting that automatic restraints on corporate power are far less effective than many pluralists
believe. Vertical integration, he observes, frequently can destroy the effectiveness of countervailing power. In addition, supposedly countervailing
sectors of the economy may actually unite and mutually exploit the consumer. Adams also questions Galbraith's assumption that intra-industry
competition is outmoded.

Further, Adams perceptively argues that the state is not always antago-
nistic to corporate interests, as pluralists frequently assume. Many corporations are political and can manipulate regulatory legislation to suit their
own ends. In essence, Adams concurs with those historians who believe
that many of the celebrated federal regulatory agencies actually advance
rather than restrain corporate interests. (Galbraith himself might now accept
the validity of such criticism. In his recent book, The New Industrial State
[Boston: Houghton Mifflin, 1967], he abandons pluralist faith in the "neutral" state, arguing, instead, that the state and the giant American corporations share personnel and common values. Galbraith's new idea that effective
power is possessed by the "technostructure," the "collective and imperfectly
defined entity" composed of "all who bring specialized knowledge, talent,
or experience to group decision-making," does, however, echo traditional
pluralist belief in the separation of ownership and control.)

Finally, Adams challenges the popular argument that increased corporate
size, and oligopoly or monopoly, are inevitable in any modern, industrial
society. Instead, Adams finds that monopoly has often resulted from coer-

cive business practices rather than from natural economic growth. His
example of defense contracts is especially apt, for such abuses still characterize the postwar American economy. Ironically, Adams, who is essentially
a laissez-faire liberal, is very close in this critique to members of the New
Left, although he differs from many leftists in advocating a return to a
free-and-open capitalist economy. The question that Adams does not directly
confront is whether such a return to open economic competition is any
longer possible without fundamentally restructuring the state and the
economy, as many radicals would contend. Adams, in sum, has presented
a telling critique of an important pluralist theory, but we may question
whether his idea of free competition between small economic units is any
less objectionable than that of countervailing power.

WALTER ADAMS
Competition, Monopoly and
Countervailing Power

INTRODUCTION

"Political liberty," a leading exponent of economic conservatism once remarked,
"can survive only within an effective competitive economic system. Thus, *the
enemy of democracy is monopoly in all its forms*: gigantic corporations, trade
associations and other agencies for price control, trade unions or in general, organization and concentration of power within functional classes."[1] Failure to check
the growth of concentrated economic power, he warned, would ultimately result
either in giant pressure groups controlling the government or in the direct regulation of pressure groups by the government. In either event, he concluded, the
result would be the triumph of collectivism over free enterprise and the destruction of a democratic society as we, in America, have known it.[2]

Reprinted by permission of the publishers from Walter Adams, *The Quarterly Journal of
Economics*, November, 1953. Cambridge, Mass.: Harvard University Press, Copyright, 1953,
by the President and Fellows of Harvard College.

[1] H. C. Simons, *Economic Policy for a Free Society* (Chicago: University of Chicago
Press, 1948), pp. 43–44. Italics in original.

[2] Mutual Security Administrator Harold Stassen supported this contention, when he
said: "World economic history has shown that nationalization and socialization have come
when there has been complete consolidation and combination of industry, not when enterprise is manifold and small in its units. . . . We must not permit major political power to
be added to the other great powers that are accumulated by big business units. Excessive
concentration of power is a threat to the individual freedoms and liberties of men, whether
that excessive power is in the hands of government or of capital or of labor." (Address
reprinted in *Congressional Record*, February 12, 1947, p. A545.)

The implications of this analysis for public policy were clear: economic power had to be dispersed among many buyers and sellers competing actively in open markets. While scrupulously avoiding any direct interference with private enterprise, the government had to provide and enforce certain basic rules of the game, so as to keep the channels of trade free; prevent monopolistic pre-emption of opportunity; preserve the incentives for efficiency and progress; and forestall the growth of both economic feudalism and political tyranny. This was the philosophy of America's antitrust laws — the core of our traditional belief in competition and hatred of monopoly.

Somehow, in spite of the efforts to translate this blueprint into reality, economic power became progressively more concentrated[3] and the decline of competition a common phenomenon in many industries. To the neoclassical economist, this fact was a cause for alarm and a source of despair. To the collectivist, it seemed but the manifestation of natural law — the operation of inexorable technological and economic forces which could not be reversed. To the defender of the status quo, however, it presented a unique challenge to explain the great transformation of the American economy — to demonstrate the compatibility of monopolistic and oligopolistic power aggregates with the stability and soundness of modern democratic capitalism.

In the advance guard of the "new enlightenment" was Professor J. M. Clark, who urged that the effectiveness of competition be judged in terms of its results, viz., the extent to which it promotes an efficient use of resources. It was Clark who suggested that the abstract theoretical model of "pure" competition be replaced by the more realistic concept of "workable" competition[4] as a gauge for judging the performance of specific industries in the public interest. Similarly, Professor E. S. Mason recommended that, in our public policy deliberations, we emphasize the constructive accomplishments and achievements of an industry rather than its market structure; that we accept an industry as workably competitive — regardless of its degree of concentration — if it evidenced, among other things, "a progressive technology, the passing on to consumers of the results of this progressiveness in the form of lower prices, larger output, improved

[3] For conflicting views on the extent of concentration in the American economy, see M. A. Adelman, "The Measurement of Industrial Concentration," *Review of Economics and Statistics*, XXXIII (Nov. 1951); and J. M. Blair, "The Measurement of Industrial Concentration: A Reply," *Review of Economics and Statistics*, XXXIV (Nov. 1952).

[4] J. M. Clark, "Toward a Concept of Workable Competition," *American Economic Review*, XXX (June 1940). It should be noted that the first significant and sophisticated departure from the use of pure competition as an "ideal" was made earlier than this. E. H. Chamberlin in his *Theory of Monopolistic Competition* (1933) had indicated (pp. 94 and 104) that the "ideal" was not to be identified with pure competition, and had developed the matter further in "Monopolistic or Imperfect Competition?", *Quarterly Journal of Economics*, LI (Aug. 1937), see esp. pp. 576 ff. (reproduced as chap. 9 of the 5th ed. of *Monopolistic Competition*, esp. pp. 213–15. See also his "Product Heterogeneity and Public Policy," *American Economic Review*, XL (May 1950), pp. 85–92.) Clark's references to Chamberlin would indicate an attempt to define *within* the area of monopolistic competition the conditions which would be "workably satisfactory" — to apply to this field the pragmatic criterion, a criterion, by the way, which leaves much to be desired.

products, etc."[5] And finally, Professor J. K. Galbraith — in an attempt to explain not just the workability of specific industries but of the whole economy — theorized that the American economy can perform quite brilliantly in spite of the widespread prevalence of industrial oligopoly. He tried to demonstrate that the American economy can provide better things for better living notwithstanding the fact that it operates in defiance of the rules laid down by "men of such Newtonian stature as Bentham, Ricardo and Adam Smith."[6]

In developing his theory, Galbraith credits Clark and Mason with a pragmatic concern for results — a recognition that "consequences, which in theory are deplorable, are often in real life quite agreeable." Yet Galbraith criticizes the exponents of workable competition for failing to make clear "why what is unworkable in principle becomes workable in practice," a failure which he attributes to their preoccupation with competition. He says:[7]

> In the competitive model the restraint on the power of any producer was provided by the competition of other producers — it came from the same side of the market. The tendency of any seller to exploit his customers was checked, not by the customers, but by another seller across the street and by many others in the same market. It was natural that in looking for restraints on the behavior of the large seller, who was one among few in the market, the search would be made in the same place. Competition, even though it might be different in kind from that of the competitive model, was still the object of the search. Indeed it was assumed that competition was the only possible restraint on private market power. This preoccupation with competition kept the investigators from seeing the actual restraints on market power — those that made not competition but the economy workable.

The *actual* or *real* restraints on a firm's market power are, according to Galbraith, vested not in its competitors but in its customers and suppliers; they are imposed not from the same side of the market, but from the opposite side. Thus "private economic power is held in check by the countervailing power of those who are subject to it. The first begets the second."[8] A monopoly on one side of the market offers an inducement to both suppliers and customers to develop the power with which they can defend themselves against exploitation. Thesis gives rise to antithesis, and there emerges a system of checks and balances which makes the economy as a whole workable, a *modus operandi* which lends stability to American capitalism. Most important of all, it relieves the government of its obligation — imposed by the now antiquated antitrust laws — to launch any frontal attack on concentrated economic power. No longer need there be con-

---

[5] E. S. Mason, "The Antitrust Laws: A Symposium," *American Economic Review*, XXXIX (June 1949), 713. See also C. E. Griffin, *An Economic Approach to Antitrust Problems* (New York: American Enterprise Association, 1951).

[6] J. K. Galbraith, *American Capitalism: The Concept of Countervailing Power* (Boston: Houghton Mifflin Company, 1952), p. 1. For a less sophisticated version of the Galbraith thesis, see D. E. Lilienthal, *Big Business: A New Era* (New York: Harper & Bros., 1953).

[7] Galbraith, *op. cit.*, pp. 61–62.

[8] *Ibid.*, p. 118.

cern about the decline of competition, the fewness of sellers in a particular market. Countervailing power (supported, where necessary, by government action) can be relied on to eliminate — through a process of creative destruction — the danger of any long-run exploitation by a private economic power bloc.

The following discussion will be concerned with an examination of the countervailing power thesis in terms of its practical as well as theoretical applicability.[9] Without attempting to discredit the fundamental plausibility and attractiveness of the thesis, we shall point to some of its limitations: (1) countervailing power is often undermined by vertical integration and top-level financial control; (2) bilateral monopolies created through the process of countervailance are not a happy solution of the economic power problem; (3) the countervailing influence of technological and inter-industry competition is not a meaningful substitute for competition in the neoclassical sense; (4) countervailance through government action is often subverted by unduly intimate affiliation between regulator and regulatee; and (5) the whole thesis rests on the dubious assumption that giant sized firms are the inevitable result of twentieth century technology and economics. These are the points which will now be discussed.

TOP-LEVEL FINANCIAL CONTROL AND VERTICAL INTEGRATION

According to Galbraith, the existence of concentrated power on one side of the market will eventually give rise to countervailing power on the other side of the market. Powerful sellers will cause the growth of powerful buyers and vice versa. As a result, the concentration of the steel barons will be offset by similar concentration among their automobile manufacturing customers, thus precluding, or at least reducing, the likelihood of monopolistic exploitation.

This argument leaves out of account the possibility of undermining and subverting the effectiveness of countervailing power as a regulatory mechanism. This objective can be accomplished by the co-ordination and centralization of both the buyer's and the seller's business policy within a single decision-making unit. It can be achieved through the common techniques of top-level financial control and vertical integration. Countervailing power can be exercised only so long as the forces on opposite sides of the market engage in arm's length bargaining, only so long as they are controlled by separate and financially independent decision-making units. Once we admit, however, the existence of economic interest groupings and giant vertical integrations, the opposing sides of the market are blended into one and any potential countervailance is automatically vitiated.

A fitting illustration of this process is Pullman Incorporated which, for many years, had a virtual monopoly over the manufacture and operation of sleeping car equipment.[10] Its customers were the nation's railroads, members of a highly concentrated industry. Here, then, was an almost perfect setting for the development of countervailing power — a monopolistic seller facing a number of

---

[9] It is of interest that the author served as economic counsel to the Senate Small Business Committee, 82d Congress. — Ed.

[10] U.S. v. The Pullman Company, 50 F. Supp. 123 (1943).

economically powerful buyers. The expected countervailance, however, never materialized. Its potential development was frustrated by the existence of an intricate maze of interlacing relations among several large investment banking concerns, insurance companies, the railroads, and Pullman Incorporated. The Morgan, Vanderbilt, and Mellon interests had a substantial representation on the boards of directors of Pullman, while simultaneously dominating a large number of major railroads — both through ownership and, more importantly, through the financial syndicates floating the securities of such railroads. Equally significant were the connections between Pullman Incorporated and several of the largest insurance companies holding considerable investments in railroad securities.[11]

It was through such banker and insurance nexus that the railroads were affiliated with Pullman Incorporated. It was through such relationships on the top level of big business finance, that the railroads — far from countervailing the power of the Pullman monopoly — were made an integral part of it. It is an ominous and perhaps ironic reflection on the inability of countervailing power to function in accordance with theoretical expectations[12] that, as a result of this interlocking control, the competition of progressive sleeping car manufacturers was stifled, and that the public, as well as the railroads, were detrimentally affected by the technological backwardness of sleeping car service.

Outright vertical integration between powerful suppliers and powerful customers is merely a variation on the above theme. It is but another technique for subverting the arm's-length-bargaining and countervailing power which may otherwise operate under conditions of bilateral monopoly and/or oligopoly. A case in point is the recent merger between Paramount Pictures Corporation and the Du Mont television network.[13] Here was a combination of the largest motion picture producer and the nation's fourth largest TV network; here was a union of a giant maker and a giant exhibitor of films — in short, the very kind of vertical arrangement which the Supreme Court had found prejudicial to the public interest in the motion picture industry.[14] Once the Federal Communica-

---

[11] As of 1945, fourteen major railroads had directors who also served on the directorate of one or more of seven investment banking houses; nine of the roads had directors who were also on the directorate of one or more of five big insurance companies; and four roads had directors who were also on the directorate of Pullman Incorporated. See Brief for the United States in Opposition to Offer of the Railroads to Purchase the Sleeping Car Business, U.S. v. The Pullman Company et. al., 1945, pp. 6–7.

[12] For other examples of how top-level financial control can actually or potentially subvert the operation of countervailing power, see L. D. Brandeis, Other People's Money and How the Investment Bankers Use It (New York: Frederick A. Stokes Company, 1932), pp. 52 ff.; Smaller War Plants Corporation, Economic Concentration and World War II, 79th Congress, 2d Session, Senate Document No. 206, 1946, pp. 354–56; Federal Trade Commission Report on Interlocking Directorates, 1951; Complaint in U.S. v. E. I. du Pont de Nemours et al., Civil Action No. 49C — 1071, filed June 30, 1949.

[13] See Federal Communications Commission, In the Matter of Allen B. Du Mont Laboratories, Inc., and Paramount Pictures, Inc., Docket No. 10032, 1953 (mimeographed edition).

[14] U.S. v. Paramount Pictures, Inc., 334 U.S. 131 (1948).

tions Commission approved this merger, any countervailance which Paramount might have exercised against Du Mont, and vice versa, was of course destroyed. Once the vertical control over motion picture *production* and *exhibition* was approved (by a government agency presumably intent on fostering countervailing power), the previous efforts of the Supreme Court to divorce these functions were effectively vitiated and boldly undermined.[15]

BILATERAL MONOPOLY AND COUNTERVAILING POWER

As pointed out above, countervailing power operates primarily through the creation of bilateral monopoly and/or oligopoly situations. A monopoly on one side of the market finds its power neutralized by the appearance of a monopoly on the other side of the market. There thus develops a system of checks and balances, built on the foundation of bilateral power concentrations.

The labor market is cited as an area where this process can be observed with the greatest clarity,[16] for it is in the labor market that giant unions bargain on a national, industry-wide scale against groups of employers acting jointly either through a trade association or an informal ad hoc bargaining committee. The countervailing power advocates defend this type of arrangement in highly concentrated industries like steel, rubber, automobiles, etc. They point out that "not only has the strength of the corporations in these industries made it necessary for workers to develop the protection of countervailing power; it has provided unions with the opportunity for getting something more as well. If suc-

---

[15] It is debatable whether from the consumer's point of view vertical integration is less desirable than bilateral monopoly (and the countervailing power situation inherent therein). In this connection, one careful student of the food industry has suggested that "(1) two successive monopolists, one above the other, would tend always to raise prices and limit supplies more than a single monopolist combining both their functions"; "(2) as the number of points of successive monopoly increases in the marketing system, the situation so far as the public is concerned becomes progressively worse"; and "(3) paradoxical as it seems at first thought, the public would probably be helped rather than injured by a conspiring between the successive monopolists to increase the amount of their combined profits." A. C. Hoffman, *Large-Scale Organization in the Food Industries*, T.N.E.C. Monograph No. 35, p. 85. In defending the integration activities of A & P, Adelman has argued along somewhat similar lines. See M. A. Adelman, "The A & P Case: A Study in Applied Economic Theory," [*Quarterly Journal of Economics*], LXIII (May 1949), 244-47.

[16] Oliver W. Holmes was perhaps the first judge to apply the theory of countervailing power to a case involving a labor dispute. Said Justice Holmes: "I have seen the suggestion made that the conflict between employers and employed is not competition. But I venture to assume that none of my brethren would rely on that suggestion. If the policy on which our law is founded is too narrowly expressed in the term free competition, we may substitute free struggle for life. Certainly the policy is not limited to struggles between persons of the same class competing for the same end. It applies to all conflicts of temporal interests. . . . One of the eternal conflicts out of which life is made up is that between the effort of every man to get the most he can for his services, and that of society, disguised under the name of capital, to get his services for the least possible return. Combination on the one side is patent and powerful. Combination on the other is the necessary and desirable counterpart, if the battle is to be carried on in a fair and equal way." 167 Mass. 92, 107-108 (1896).

cessful they could share in the fruits of the corporation's market power."[17] Bilateral monopoly in the labor market is thus justified on the grounds that it prevents unilateral exploitation, while simultaneously allowing one monopolist to share in whatever exorbitant gains may accrue to the other.

The fly in this ointment is self-evident, viz., that unions and management — without necessarily conspiring — can jointly exploit the consumer. This is true especially in times of inflation[18] when employers may grant wage increases with relative impunity, and then pass their higher costs on to the consumer in the form of higher prices. These higher prices thereupon become the basis for new wage demands, and the inflationary spiral is sent on another merry spin. The bilateral monopoly of union and management fuels the engine for accelerating and perpetuating inflation.[19]

The inadequacy of bilateral monopoly in the labor market is rather pointedly illustrated by the recent wage dispute in the stell industry. After collective bargaining procedures had broken down, the case was referred to the Wage Stabilization Board. The Board promptly recommended a wage increase which would have raised production costs by approximately $6 per ton. To offset these higher costs, industry representatives demanded a price increase of $12 per ton, a demand which the OPS was compelled to refuse. The agency did agree, however, to permit a $3 per ton price increase in line with the provisions of the Capehart amendment to the Defense Production Act. This increase would have yielded the industry a return of more than 28 per cent on stockholders' investment — a return which was far higher than the 1947–49 profit rate of 18½ per cent, which in turn was higher than any the industry had enjoyed since 1918.[20] In spite of its apparently generous terms, this OPS offer was rejected by the industry — thus precipitating a strike, the seizure of steel plants by the government, and the invalidation of this seizure by the Supreme Court. The result was that eventually the government was compelled — in the interests of uninterrupted production during the emergency period — to authorize both the requested wage increase and the $12 per ton price increase. The irresistible force had met the immovable object. Bilateral monopoly, instead of providing countervailing checks and balances, was instrumental in wrecking price controls and supporting the inflationary forces which drove the economy into dizzy spirals of ever higher prices, wages, costs and prices.

Given the existence of power concentrations on both sides of the market, this result was perhaps inevitable. Indeed it was predicted by Robert Liefmann, the great exponent of industrial cartels, as long ago as 1927. In justifying cartels

[17] Galbraith, op. cit., p. 122.

[18] In fairness to Galbraith, it must be pointed out that he recognizes inflationary periods as a special situation under which countervailing power tends to become inoperative. Galbraith, op. cit., pp. 195–208.

[19] For a further discussion of this problem, see W. Fellner, "Prices and Wages under Bilateral Monopoly," Quarterly Journal of Economics, LXI (Aug. 1947).

[20] For the economic facts of this dispute, see E. Arnall, Statement on Steel before the Senate Committee on Labor and Public Welfare, Senate Document No. 118, 82d Congress, 2d Session, April, 1952.

ex visu the workers, Liefmann pointed out that cartels were in a better position than competitive firms to grant wage increases, since they could more easily shift the resulting cost increases on to the consumer in the form of higher prices. Said Liefmann:[21]

> Where the firms are in a cartel, they are more inclined to concede the workers higher wages than in a state of free competition, because they find it easier to pass the increased costs on to their customers by charging higher prices. The workers will therefore, generally speaking, find it easier to impose higher wages upon organised firms, and it is in their power, at least if they can form strong trades unions, to demand wages increasing with the cartel's prices, i.e., a *"sliding wage-scale."*

Here indeed were prophetic words, foreshadowing the kind of escalator arrangements recently popularized by General Motors and the United Automobile Workers (CIO). Here were the naked implications of bilateral monopoly as a technique for wage determination — resulting not in the countervailance of power between union and management but rather in a *combination* of the two against the consumer. That such labor-management "co-operation" rather than widespread industrial strife is likely to become more common in the future, and that it might even be formalized by structural reorganization of the decision-making unit in the economy, is indicated by the spread of co-determination schemes in Germany and other countries where industrial monopoly is unchallenged by national economic policy.[22] Whether or not such arrangements will prove of long-run advantage to capital and labor is problematical; whether or not they will redound to the benefit of unorganized consumers, however, is a question which can — unfortunately — be answered with greater certainty.

TECHNOLOGICAL AND INTER-INDUSTRY COMPETITION

The advocates of the countervailing power thesis maintain that competition in the neoclassical sense, i.e., competition among sellers and among buyers within a particular industry, is outmoded. Their argument runs somewhat as follows. Old-fashioned intra-industry competition tends to promote maximum output, minimum prices, and optimum utilization of capacity; in short, it stimulates efficiency. But this efficiency is static and unprogressive in character. It makes no allowance for the research, development, and innovation required for economic growth. While it prevents concentration, it stifles progress. To have progress, we need more, not less concentration. Only bigness can provide the sizable funds necessary for technological experimentation and innovation in the industrial milieu of the twentieth century. Only monopoly earnings can provide the bait that lures capital on to untried trails. While progress may thus require high power concentration in many industries, this need not be a source of con-

---

[21] R. Liefmann, *Cartels, Concerns, and Trusts*, p. 80.

[22] For an incisive report on the implications of this new form of syndicalism see National Association of Manufacturers, *Co-Determination*, Economic Policy Division Series No. 42, 1951.

cern to society at large. Technological development will serve as an offset against any short-run position of entrenchment which may be established. The monopoly of glass bottles will be countervailed by the introduction of the tin can; and the dominance of the latter will in turn be undermined by the introduction of the paper container. The consumer need not rely, therefore, on the static competition between large numbers of small firms as protection against exploitation. In the long run, he can find far greater safety — and better things for better living, to boot — the technological competition of a small number of large firms, which through research and innovation eventually destroy any position of market control that may be established.[23]

There are two basic flaws in this argument. The first is that history seems to contradict it. "As a general rule monopolistic combinations and cartels have followed, not preceded, periods of extensive capital investment. For example, before the American trust movement from 1897 to 1903, the merger movement of the twenties, and the widespread resort to cartels during the thirties, industrial expansion was rapid and the volume of new capital commitments large. Moreover, the biggest single expansionary influence in twentieth century industrial development has been the automobile industry and in that field monopoly has been conspicuously absent."[24] It must always be remembered that neither Morgan's rationalization of the railroad industry in 1889, nor Morgan's organization of the U.S. Steel combine in 1901, nor Roosevelt's NRA in 1934 were conspicuous for stimulating technological innovation or increased capital investment. It must always be remembered that the phenomenal performance of American capitalism over the last hundred years may have been achieved not primarily because of the behavior of well entrenched large-scale firms, but "because there was still enough virility left in the competitive process to permit innovations and the breaking into established fields to go on."[25] Certainly we would be guilty of the *post hoc ergo propter hoc* fallacy were we to argue that since monopolization accompanied the long-run growth of output, it also was its cause. Certainly, the European experience with the restrictionism of monopoly capitalism should give us pause before society places exclusive reliance on the countervailing influence of technological competition as a protective device against exploitation, inefficiency, and monopolistic retrogression.

There is another flaw in the argument that inter-industry, product, or technological competition is an effective offset against entrenchment or market domination in any one industry. The facts are that when the paper container began to threaten the tin can duopoly, Continental Can entered the paper container industry; when magnesium threatened the aluminum monopoly, Alcoa started its participation in the magnesium cartel;[26] when aluminum began to

[23] Galbraith, *op. cit.*, pp. 91–99. This argument is based largely on Schumpeter, *Capitalism, Socialism and Democracy*, pp. 79 ff.

[24] G. W. Stocking and M. W. Watkins, *Cartels or Competition?* p. 236.

[25] G. H. Hildebrand, "Monopolization and the Decline of Investment Opportunity," *American Economic Review*, XXXIII (Sept. 1943), p. 595.

[26] See the indictment in U.S. v. Aluminum Company of America, Criminal 109–89. The defendants pleaded nolo contendere and were fined $104,993 (April 15, 1942).

be used as a substitute for copper, Anaconda embarked on its venture in the aluminum industry.[27] Today, newspapers control radio stations, and TV outlets are operated by the licensees of AM stations. But most significant of all, perhaps, is the recent merger between the United Paramount Theatres, the largest motion picture theatre chain, and the American Broadcasting Company, the third largest radio and television network.[28]

Here is a combination between giant firms in two separate industries which formerly competed with one another both with respect to audience (people's time and money) and with respect to product (films, talent, stories, etc.). It seems hardly in doubt that this merger tends toward the elimination of inter-industry competition between TV broadcasting, theatre TV, theatre exhibition of motion pictures, and subscription TV (when developed) — to the end of obtaining the largest possible monopolistic benefit for UPT-ABC's over-all operations, As FCC Commissioner Hennock pointed out:[29]

> In such a situation there is a substantial risk that the merged company, through the medium of . . . restrictive practices, may subordinate its television interests to its motion picture exhibition interests, particularly so when the company's greater investments in theatres may be in an especially vulnerable or precarious position. Given the opportunity for economic gain through such restrictive practices, and in the absence of adequate safeguards against them it cannot be assumed that the merged company will push its motion picture theatre and television interests fully and independently of each other, or to anywhere near the same extent that completely unfettered business competitors normally would. . . .

It would seem too much to expect full, vigorous and unrestricted competition between different parts of the same company when the obvious result of such activity would redound to the disadvantage and loss of the company's total operations.[30] Truly, the Brandeis maxim that "one cannot be expected to com-

[27] Joint Committee on Defense Production, *Aluminum Expansion Program and Competition*, House Report No. 1, 83d Congress, 1st Session, 1953, p. 12.

[28] In 1952, ABC operated 4½ AM, 5 FM and 5 TV outlets, all in key cities; in addition, ABC had 298 AM affiliates, 113 FM affiliates, and 64 TV affiliates, and achieved a total net sales of $53 million for the first eleven months of 1951.

[29] Federal Communications Commission, *In the Matter of American Broadcasting Company, Inc. and United Paramount Theatres, Inc.*, Docket No. 10046, 1953, Dissenting Opinion, p. 13 (mimeographed edition).

[30] "Thus it seems clear that the merged company would be less likely to push the fullest development of television service (by station construction or the finest programming) in a city in which its theatre investments were substantial and/or on a comparatively unsound financial basis than it would in a city in which its theatre interests were non-existent, small or had already repaid investments and yielded large returns. Similarly, its presentations of theatre TV programs and the extent to which it promotes them by advertising, etc., would also quite naturally be affected by the existence and precise nature of its television interests in a particular city. Even the merged company's promotion of television service might in this same manner be aimed at accomplishing only personal gain to the company at the expense of overall TV service in general. Thus, in a city where the merged company has both television affiliates and its own theatres, it is only to be expected that it will arrange its special

pete against one's self" is as applicable today as it was forty years ago. Inter-industry competition and technological innovation become a farce when public policy permits them to be subverted by merger and combination. Yet that is exactly what has been happening recently to an increasing extent. That is exactly why the argument of the countervailing power advocates is unconvincing if not outright erroneous.

THE ROLE OF GOVERNMENT

According to its exponents, countervailing power does not always arise autonomously. Indeed, in some cases, its development may require positive promotion by government action. Galbraith looks upon this promotive activity as the main peacetime function of the federal government and applauds, for example, the enactment of New Deal measures designed to give a group market power it did not previously possess. As a rule of thumb, Galbraith simply suggests that the government "attack positions of original market power in the economy if these are not effectively offset by countervailing power.[31] He regards such action as neither adventitious nor abnormal, since its purpose is merely to support a "natural" economic process. Given the existence of private market power, Galbraith considers governmental countervailance a desirable technique for strengthening the "capacity of the economy for autonomous self-regulation," and deems it an indirect method for lessening the "amount of over-all government control or planning that is (eventually) required or sought."[32] So, at least, the countervailing power doctrine would have us believe.

This thesis rests on the doubtful assumption that there is a sharp dichotomy between the economy, on the one hand, and government, on the other. It assumes that government is an autonomous, monolithic, and self-contained organism. This view is, unfortunately, an intellectual amusement of the past. It ignores the fact that economic interest groups are today largely politicized units, making their claims upon and through the institutions of the state. As V. O. Key observes:[33]

> The dilemma of the politics of economic control comes from the fact that governments must keep in check the pressures of particularism, yet at the same time governments derive their power in no small degree from the support of particularistic interests. Government — that is, political parties, public agencies, the bureaucracy — has a social strength within itself, but

---

theatre events (either of feature films or theatre TV) on those particular nights when least likely to interfere with its own television programs and more likely to interfere with those of its broadcasting competitors, and vice versa. Such restrictive practices *ad infinitum* could be pursued by the merged company on a local as well as a national level and no theatre or station manager could be expected to manage his own particular operation in any way but to cause as great benefit and as little possible harm to the company as a whole." Federal Communications Commission, *op. cit.*, p. 14.

[31] *Op. cit.*, p. 144.
[32] *Ibid.*, p. 155.
[33] *Politics, Parties and Pressure Groups*, p. 204.

fundamentally its power comes from the support won for its policies among the organized and unorganized private interests of society. These are the groups whose activities the government must control in the general interest.

These are the groups against whom countervailing power must, at times, be brought into play. That this is a task of formidable proportions is indicated by an examination of governmental operations on the legislative, administrative, and quasi-judicial levels.

Legislation

In the legislative consideration of many economic measures, the absence of countervailing power is painfully apparent. In the enactment of tariff laws, for example, equal stakes rarely elicit equal pressures. Tariff duties are determined by a process of log-rolling and pressure politics, so that a few "control the process at the expense of the many. The inertia of the masses is so great that not even the strongest incitements of economic interest arouse them."[34] Since the majority is affected only indirectly and obliquely, it seems to acquiesce in the compromises and adjustments made to appease special interests. The result may be legislation devoid of public interest considerations, but the very forces which make such legislation bad economics, assure its political invincibility.

There is little doubt that particularistic, politically vocal economic pressure groups can use the legislative process for their own advantage. They can demand, and often obtain, governmental aid in countervailing the power of entrenched interests. This does not mean, however, that the form of this countervailance will redound to the general welfare as it does to a narrowly-defined private welfare. Nor does it mean, that the basic problems underlying the demand for governmental countervailance will thereby be solved. The NRA may have given businessmen what they wanted at the time; it did not, however, attack the basic causes of depression; nor did it stimulate economic recovery; and it certainly failed to promote the general welfare. The price support program for agriculture may have raised farm incomes, but it has hardly disposed of the farm surpluses rotting away in government warehouses.[35] The fiscal policy of the 80th Congress may have given tax relief to a variety of politically influential groups, but it did not counteract the postwar inflationary spiral nor effectuate a reduction in the national debt. The Capehart, Talle, and Herlong amendments to the Defense Production Act may have pleased the groups benefiting from their enactment, but the resultant emasculation of price controls was not what the majority wanted in a period of defense and inflation. In short, the countervailing action expected of government tends more often than not merely to be an appeasement

[34] E. E. Schattschneider, *Politics, Pressures and the Tariff*, p. 287.

[35] The government now holds 342 million bushels of wheat, 100 million bushels of corn, 464 million pounds of tobacco, 1.4 million bales of cotton, 6.8 million dozens of eggs, 42.5 million pounds of butter, 48.4 million pounds of turkey, etc. — an investment valued at $1.25 billion. The prospects are that the size of these agricultural surpluses will increase, rather than diminish, in the foreseeable future. See *U.S. News & World Report*, February 6, 1953, p. 21.

of special interest pressures. Legislation designed to countervail the power of "economic royalists" is not the product of an independent governmental unit functioning in a vacuum, but the result of a log-rolling process involving compromise with, adjustment to, and appeasement of a variety of special interest claims. Everybody who is somebody seems to get what he wants; only the sum total of these wants is not always equivalent to the needs and desires of the community as a whole.

Administration

The administration of economic laws by various branches of the Executive Department reveals similar limitations on the effective exercise of governmental countervailance. One Congressional investigation, for example, indicated that early in 1941 the Arabian-American Oil Company (a joint subsidiary of Standard Oil of New Jersey, Standard Oil of California, Socony-Vacuum, and Texas Co.) induced our government to extend $99,000,000 in lend-lease aid to Saudi Arabia. In return, the company promised to supply oil to the U.S. Navy at $.40 a barrel. In spite of this commitment, however, Aramco later demanded a price of $1.05 per barrel on a take-it-or-leave-it basis — terms which, under wartime conditions, the Navy could hardly decline. As a result, the Government was overcharged between $30 million and $38 million on oil purchases from Aramco and its affiliates between January 1942 and June 1947. These overcharges — this failure of the most powerful purchaser in the world to exert countervailing power against a dominant supplier — were not unrelated to the fact that the Government was represented in this transaction by persons connected with Aramco, its affiliates, and its parent companies.[36] As the Senate Committee investigating this matter was prompted to remark: "At times such personnel by reason of past association, training, and habit are susceptible of allowing their past background or thoughts of future benefits to color their official actions. In rare cases there have been a few who designedly sought key positions in Government service so that they could control situations for selfish interests."[37] The Committee which offered these findings and observations was the Brewster Committee of the 80th Congress — hardly a group of wilful and habitual muckrakers.

The employment of industry men in government agencies — many on a dollar-a-year basis — seems to have become standard operating procedure in periods of war or defense emergency. As of September 1, 1951, for example, twelve defense agencies had on their rolls 876 WOC's (without compensation

[36] The Director of the Foreign Division of the Petroleum Administration for Defense was a former Vice President of Aramco; the naval officer who wrote the purchase justification for Aramco oil at $1.05 per barrel was a former official of a Socony-Vacuum subsidiary; the admiral serving as executive officer of the Army-Navy Petroleum Board was a former president of a Texas-Socal subsidiary; and the Deputy Petroleum Administrator for War was a former officer of Standard Oil of California. See Special Committee Investigating the National Defense Program, *Navy Purchases of Middle East Oil*, 80th Congress, 2d Session, Report No. 440, Part 5, 1948, p. 26.

[37] *Ibid.*, p. 26.

personnel), many of whom occupied vital policy-making positions.[38] In the Petroleum Administration for Defense WOC's were at the head of ten divisions having operations service responsibility while only two such divisions had paid government personnel as their directors. WOC's were in positions of comparable responsibility in the Defense Production Administration, the Defense Transport Administration, and the National Production Authority. Many of these WOC's came from the country's largest industrial corporations. Thus, "as of April 20, 1951, 30 of the WOC's working in the National Production Authority were privately employed by the 100 largest manufacturing companies in the United States. This number had increased to 47 by June 25, 1951, or more than one-fourth of all WOC's employed by the NPA."[39]

That the results of these arrangements were not always calculated to bring countervailing power into play is illustrated in the following not unrepresentative cases. In one instance a $68,000,000 contract on vertical turret lathes for the Air Force was awarded to a General Motors subsidiary at a price of $90,000 per lathe, although a smaller firm — the Bullard Company of Bridgeport, Conn. — had submitted a lower bid at $38,000 per lathe. The contract award went to General Motors, however, on the recommendation of H. R. Boyer, a GM official, who was then serving as chairman of the Government's Aircraft Production Board.[40] In another instance, it was found that the commandant of the Army Tank Arsenal in Detroit had permitted a manufacturer who sought contracts with the Arsenal to pay for his travel and hotel expenses, while his subordinates borrowed a total of $200,000 from a number of government contractors. That the Arsenal, during the same period was accumulating a 104 year supply of some jeep replacement parts; that "in many instances the Government was actually gouged in the price paid . . . in the form of what might be considered a disguised subsidy to certain segments of the automotive industry"[41] — these were perhaps mere coincidences in the demonstration of countervailing power in action.

Regulation

The independent regulatory commissions are a third example of how difficult it is to achieve countervailing power through governmental action. The Interstate Commerce Commission is a case in point. This Commission, created to protect the public from the abuses of a highly concentrated power group, today seems mainly to protect the railroads against effective regulation by the public.[42] While

[38] Subcommittee on the Study of Monopoly Power of the Committee on the Judiciary, *The Mobilization Program*, 82d Congress, 1st Session, House Report No. 1217, 1951, p. 79.

[39] *Ibid.*, p. 81.

[40] House Committee on Armed Services, *Hearings on Military Waste*, 82d Congress, 2d Session, 1952; quoted in the *Detroit Free Press*, January 21, 1953, p. 6.

[41] Committee on Expenditures in the Executive Departments, *Inquiry into the Procurement of Automotive Spare Parts by the United States Government*, 82d Congress, 2d Session, House Report, No. 1811, 1952, p. 7.

[42] This state of affairs was foreseen as long ago as 1892 by Richard Olney, the Attorney General during the Cleveland Administration. In reply to his friend Charles E. Perkins, President of the Burlington and Quincy Railroad, who had recommended that Olney press for the abolition of the Interstate Commerce Commission, Olney wrote as follows: "My

it defends the railroads from encroachment by rival means of transportation, the Commission also serves as an effective lobby on behalf of railroad interests. It is the main spokesman for the railroads in their recurrent demands for rate increases; it shields them against efforts by the Post Office Department (acting on behalf of the taxpayers) to induce a reduction in the charges for carrying the public's mail; etc. — phenomena which one careful student has explained as follows:[43]

> The railroads are alone among the interests surrounding the Commission in their constant and comprehensive support of that body. By their continuous praise of the Commission, by their defense of its independence and by their efforts to protect and extend its authority the railroads have made the Commission the beneficiary of what has been their not inconsiderable political power. But in the rough world of competitive politics nothing comes free. Political support must be purchased, and the price which the ICC has paid for its railroad support may be traced through almost all important phases of its policy and behavior.

The result is so close an affiliation between regulator and regulatee, that some observers have recommended the abolition of the ICC as an independent regulatory agency and its replacement by "other instrumentalities better able to act in the public interest."[44]

A similar pattern seems to apply to other independent regulatory bodies. In the case of the Civil Aeronautics Board, its chairman, James Landis, was denied reappointment for objecting to the merger of Pan American and American Overseas Airlines. When he was replaced by Delos W. Rentzel, a brilliant young man who had served the previous fifteen years with the country's largest airlines, doubts were raised concerning the CAB's future exercise of countervailing power in the public interest. Unfortunately, the Commission's recent actions — both with respect to the subsidy-mailpay controversy[45] and with respect to the nonscheduled airlines[46] — have done little to dispel those doubts.

---

impression would be that looking at the matter from a railroad point of view exclusively it would not be a wise thing to undertake. . . . The attempt would not be likely to succeed; if it did not succeed, and were made on the ground of inefficiency and uselessness of the Commission, the result would very probably be giving it the power it now lacks. The Commission, as its functions have now been limited by the courts, is, or can be made, of great use to the railroads, at the same time that that supervision is almost entirely nominal. Further, the older such a commission gets to be, the more inclined it will be found to take the business and railroad view of things. It thus becomes a sort of barrier between the railroad corporations and the people and a sort of protection against hasty and crude legislation hostile to railroad interests. . . . The part of wisdom is not to destroy the Commission, but to utilize it." Quoted in M. Josephson, *The Politicos* (New York: Harcourt, Brace & Co., 1938), p. 526.

[43] S. P. Huntington, "The Marasmus of the I.C.C." *Yale Law Journal*, LXI (April 1952), p. 481.

[44] *Ibid.*, p. 509.

[45] House Committee on Interstate and Foreign Commerce, *Hearings on Air Mail Subsidies*, 82d Congress, 2d Session, 1952; L. P. Marvin, Jr., "Air Mail Subsidy Separation," *Georgetown Law Journal*, Vol. XL, January 1952, pp. 161–240.

[46] Senate Small Business Committee, *Report on Role of Irregular Airlines in United States Air Transportation Industry*, 82d Congress, 1st Session, Report No. 540, 1951.

The Federal Power Commission affords another example of how established interests have strengthened their position in the national economy by preventing the appointment of men they considered hostile to their interests. In this case, the target was Leland Olds who had spent a lifetime promoting natural gas conservation and resisting rate increases which influential producer groups and utility companies considered vital to their interests. When Olds was denied confirmation by the Senate, the way was clear for a Commission ruling that the FPC had no jurisdiction over the rates of nonintegrated natural gas producers[47] — a ruling that enacted by administrative fiat what the pressure groups had failed to obtain by legislation. Senator Kerr's Natural Gas Bill,[48] which Mr. Truman had previously vetoed, thus became — for practical intents and purposes — the law of the land. Countervailing power in the public interest had once again been frustrated by the action of an "independent" regulatory agency of the government. Perhaps it was this kind of experience which once prompted Senator Wheeler to remark sadly: "It seems to invariably happen, that when Congress attempts to regulate some group, the intended regulatees wind up doing the regulating."[49]

Senator Wheeler's remark is, of course, only one reaction to the ancient and universal problem: *quis custodiet ipsos custodies?* Painful experience would seem to indicate that governmental creation of countervailing power to curb the market entrenchment of "economic royalists" is more readily accomplished in theory than in practice. As Key points out:[50]

> The solution of the dilemma of controlling the controllers is not easy. Government can play one group against another. . . . Such deftness of political leadership, however, is not a dependable quality of government. The problem of organizing public power, adequate in strength yet responsibly exercised under public control, for the reconciliation of group conflict and the imposition of programs promotive of the general welfare will doubtless remain for some time without a completely satisfactory solution.

SIZE, TECHNOLOGY AND EFFICIENCY

The final limitation of the countervailing power thesis is inherent in its basic assumption, viz., that the giant size of America's dominant enterprises is the inevitable result of twentieth century technology and economics. The theory assumes that "the process by which the typical industry passes from the hands of the many to the few has not been well understood";[51] that the causes for

[47] Federal Power Commission, *In the Matter of the Phillips Petroleum Company,* Opinion No. 217, Docket No. G-1148, August 16, 1951.
[48] S. 1498, 81st Congress, 1st Session, introduced April 4, 1949.
[49] Quoted in B. Bolles, *How to Get Rich in Washington* (New York: W. W. Norton & Company, 1952), p. 23.
[50] *Op. cit.,* p. 204.
[51] Galbraith, *op. cit.,* p. 36.

this concentration are not to be found in the designs of individual empire builders; that, instead, these causes are deeply organic in the fabric of American industry. It contends that firms grow because they realize the technical economies of large-scale organization; the successful ones acquire the earnings, the reputation and the experience which permit them to expand further; and eventually, as a result of this process, there is no longer freedom of entry into industries where the scale of production is considerable. "At the same time that entry becomes difficult or impossible, the forces which tend to reduce the number already in the industry continue. Weaklings may still fail, and disappear, especially in bad times. Good times make it easy to finance consolidations and tempting for the strong company to expand and the weak to sell out. Thus . . . the combination of a low or zero birthrate and a continuing death rate must always be a declining population."[52] To the extent that this phenomenon is widespread in the American economy, it seems futile to counteract it by antitrust prosecution. "It is possible to prosecute a few evil-doers; it is evidently not so practical to indict a whole economy."[53]

This explanation of the concentration process is the cornerstone of the whole countervailing power theory. If it is valid, then antitrust litigation is obviously outmoded, and countervailing power becomes *one* — if not *the* — method of dealing with huge economic power aggregates. If the explanation is inadequate, however, other public policy alternatives may become more desirable. In any event, it is important to subject this basic assumption to empirical tests, for as Keynes once remarked, conclusions may be arrived at by clearness and consistency and by easy logic but be based on assumptions inappropriate to the facts.[54] We must examine, therefore, the crucial assumption of the Galbraith thesis, viz., that firms are big because they are efficient; that firms are big because consumers want them to be big; that bigness is little more than the natural result of modern technological and economic forces.

Elsewhere I have argued[55] that the data on the relation between size and efficiency are by no means conclusive; efficiency is not always the concomitant of giant size; in aluminum and steel, for example, the largest firms are neither great technical innovators nor the paragons of efficient operation; modern technology, far from giving industrial giantism its undivided blessings, may actually militate in favor of industrial deconcentration; and finally, in the one industry where the large-scale dissolution of giant enterprises has been attempted (under the Public Utility Holding Company Act), the result has been an increase rather than a decrease in the efficiency of the successor companies. There is additional evidence. Part of this evidence is submitted here merely to caution against accepting public policy changes on the basis of plausible, yet unsubstantiated, theories of industrial growth.

The record of antitrust prosecutions is replete with cases which demonstrate

[52] *Ibid.*, p. 38.
[53] *Ibid.*, p. 55.
[54] Keynes, *General Theory*, p. 371.
[55] See W. Adams, "The Dilemma of Antitrust Aims: A Reply," *American Economic Review*, XLII (Dec. 1952), 895–900.

that industrial pre-eminence is often achieved as much by resort to coercive practices as by "natural" growth processes. In the Tobacco case,[56] for example, a unanimous Supreme Court found that the exorbitant profits of the Big Three in the early thirties attracted the entry of the "10¢ brands"; the appearance of these venturesome newcomers precipitated a devastating price cutting campaign by the majors (which went so far that Camels and Luckies were being sold at a loss, while Liggett curtailed its normal business activities and cut its advertising to the bone); upon elimination of the new competitors, the old price and profit equilibrium of the cigarette oligopoly was successfully restored. Here certainly was one instance where the Big Three held their position, not through a decisive victory in the arena of free consumer choice, but through an aggressive campaign of restricting the range from which the consumer could select a genuine favorite. The victors in this popularity contest were chosen by a process not unlike the "free elections" held in the "people's democracies" of Soviet satellite states.

The more recent case against the United Shoe Machinery Corporation is another illustration of how a firm can enjoy a virtual monopoly, not only on the basis of efficiency but also because of a systematic resort to coercive practices. United used the kind of leasing system, for example, which effectively deterred and prevented their customers from replacing any United machine with that of a competitor. In addition, United apparently engaged in the systematic infringement of patents held by small undiversified competitors, and then cut the bottom out of the specialized market for the machines covered by these patents. So brazen and contemptuous was this practice that, in one of the resulting infringement suits (by N. W. Mathey against United), "the United States District Court for the District of Massachusetts found that United had *intentionally* infringed Mathey's patent, and that United 'knew or must have known' that the effects of the terms established by it on its heel flap trimming machine 'would ruin the plaintiff as its only competitor in a distinctive field.' "[57] This patent infringement, far from being an isolated occurrence, seemed to be just part of a comprehensive program to eliminate competition. It was the kind of competitive tactic which should have proved unnecessary for a company whose pre-eminence rested on technological superiority and/or consumer popularity.

Many cases could be cited to show that competition often dies from other than natural causes, while those responsible for its euthanasia advertise themselves as victors in an unfettered Darwainian struggle. There is evidence that at times the survival of the fittest is promoted, not alone through a process of natural selection, but with the helping hand of a benevolent authority. Government supported research activity is a case in point. Of the nearly 2,000 industrial organizations receiving government research contracts for the fiscal years 1940–44, the 10 largest corporations received 37 per cent of the funds; the 20 largest, 50 per cent; the 40 largest, 60 per cent; and the 60 largest, 65 per cent.[58]

[56] U.S. v. American Tobacco Company et. al., 328 U.S. 781 (1946).

[57] Complaint in U.S. v. United Shoe Machinery Corporation, Civil Action No. 7198, filed December 15, 1947, p. 27.

[58] See Smaller War Plants Corporation, *Economic Concentration and World War II*, 79th Congress, 2d Session, Senate Document No. 206, 1946, p. 52.

Yet in spite of the fact that government funds were expended, the patent rights and know-how on the commercial application of this research were not made freely available to industry in general but became the exclusive property of a handful of large corporations working under contract with the government.[59]

Similarly, during the period 1940–44, the 100 largest corporations received two-thirds of the prime contracts awarded, with more than 51 per cent of such contracts accruing to the top 33 corporations, and a major portion of the subcontracts also going to larger companies. The government permitted this concentration of war contracts despite the fact that smaller plants had a considerable amount of idle, but usable, capacity — despite the fact that "nearly one-third of these plants reported that they could increase their production by 50 per cent or more over January 1943 levels without adding new machinery or construction."[60] According to a report by the Senate Small Business Committee, the concentration of defense contracts as of July 19, 1951 was even greater than during World War II: "10 large manufacturing companies have been handed 40 per cent of the total dollar volume of defense contracts since Korea; 50 companies command almost two-thirds of the dollar volume of defense contracts."[61] Again, existing facilities of smaller manufacturers seem to be ignored, both in the award of prime and subcontracts. As a matter of fact, there are many instances where giant companies are subsidized in their expansion of plant facilities, while the plants of their smaller brethren languish in idleness.

An examination of the allocations and priority system,[62] the accelerated amortization program,[63] the disposal of war surplus establishments,[64] the structure of business taxes[65] reveals the same pattern of promoting concentration — at times through unconscious, at times through deliberate action by the most

[59] To correct this situation, the Attorney General has recommended that "Where patentable inventions are made in the course of performing a Government-financed contract for research and development, the public interest requires that all rights to such inventions be assigned to the Government and not left to the private ownership of the contractor. Public control will assure free and equal availability of the inventions to American industry and science; will eliminate any competitive advantage to the contractor chosen to perform the research work; will avoid undue concentration of economic power in the hands of a few large corporations; will tend to increase and diversify available research facilities within the United States to the advantage of the Government and of the national economy; and will thus strengthen our American system of free, competitive enterprise." U.S. Department of Justice, *Investigation of Government Patent Practices and Policies*, 1947, I, 4.

[60] Attorney General, *Report Prepared Pursuant to Section 708 (e) of the Defense Production Act of 1950*, December 1950, p. 14. See also H. R. Bowen, "Impact of the War upon Smaller Manufacturing Plants," *Survey of Current Business*, July 1943.

[61] Senate Small Business Committee, *Concentration of Defense Contracts*, 82d Congress, 1st Session, Report No. 551, 1951, p. 1.

[62] House Small Business Committee, *Hearings on the Problems of Small Business under the Controlled Materials Plan*, 82d Congress, 2d Session, 1952, Parts 1–4.

[63] Joint Committee on Defense Production, *Hearings on Tax Amortization*, 82d Congress, 1st Session, 1951.

[64] *Report of the Attorney General under Section 205 of the War Mobilization and Reconversion Act of 1944*, Reports 1–5, 1945.

[65] Senate Small Business Committee, *Hearings on the Tax Problems of Small Business*, 82d Congress, 2d Session, 1952.

powerful economic unit in the world. The net effect is that established giants remain dominant while the competition of newcomers is effectively handicapped. As Galbraith rightly points out, "in this race the horse with the poorest record, or no record, must carry the greatest weight."[66] In the present institutional framework this is practically inevitable, but — as Galbraith fails to point out — there is nothing inevitable about the framework itself. It might be well to remember that, given the status quo, horses are assigned their jockeys not by a system of natural law, but by the rules of men. A different weight distribution may result in different racing returns. A racing commission which is not loaded against the long-shot; a punctilious supervision of the track while the race is in progress — these changes may not alter the composition of the winner's circle; they will, however, shorten the odds. My point is simply this: the nature of the man-made handicaps has a more decisive influence than we are willing to concede. Until we know more about the correlation between handicaps and derby winners, it ill behooves us to consider racing results under current rules as inexorable, inevitable and unavoidable.

CONCLUSION

In conclusion, we can say that the countervailing power thesis is not without merit; that it rightly calls attention to the existence of potential checks and balances which, in our economy, supplement competition as a device for counteracting concentrated economic power. This does not mean, however, that countervailing power is a suitable substitute for competition; or that it can long survive in the absence of competition; or that it affords any clear and administratively feasible guidelines for public policy.

Some measure of countervailing power is obviously ubiquitous. It exists in a socialist state where the steel monopoly countervails the aluminum monopoly and where the trades union congress offsets the power of the central industry planning board. It is present, to some degree, in a fascist corporate state as well as in a sovietized society. This hardly affords any assurance, however, that the people will be protected against actual or potential abuse of concentrated economic power.

Before we discard competition as the cornerstone of national economic policy, we might well recall that even our socialist critics regard competition as the oldest and strongest defense of private capitalism and enterprise. As Herbert Morrison once observed:[67]

> Free competition, the intelligent anti-socialist used to argue, is the only way of bringing prices down to the level of costs and seeing that production is not unnecessarily restricted and the public overcharged. There was great force in this argument — but it is now dead, killed by events. When Lord McGowen defends the cartel, with often cogent arguments drawn

[66] Op. cit., p. 37.

[67] H. Morrison, Government and Industry (London: Fabian Research Group, 1944), p. 11.

from the benefits of large scale organization, research, etc., he is publicly consigning to the scrap heap the one powerful argument against socialism that ever existed.

It is to be hoped that we will not consign the most powerful defense of our economic system to what may prove to be a totalitarian scrap heap before a careful examination of all existing alternatives.

The interpenetration of economic and political power has been explored by many critics of the national power structure. Generally, these analysts have studied the similar social backgrounds of economic and political decision makers, or the more explicit coordination mentioned by Mills in The Power Elite. By contrast, economist Morton Baratz here examines the subtler coincidence of political and economic interests deriving from the rise of a new corporate economy.

The increase in conglomerate mergers and the attendant rise of super-oligopoly, Baratz contends, has strengthened centers of economic power. Pluralist regulatory mechanisms, he finds, are relatively ineffective. Increasingly, giant corporations are able to manipulate the rate of technological change, to control prices, and otherwise to affect the lives of countless citizens. In Baratz's view, the very existence of a few corporations with such extensive influence helps to translate economic power into political power. It is unlikely that political decision-makers will take steps that might significantly damage the interests of corporate giants. In many cases, solicitous politicians will, overtly or covertly, structure national priorities to meet the demands of the corporate economy. As a result, public policy seldom clashes with the vital needs of America's largest corporations.

Baratz's suggestive analysis does illustrate that the structure of an economy carries with it certain ideological implications. Still, if this tells us that government will not destroy, or intentionally weaken, corporate capitalism, it does not fully explain the development of specific policies. Neither, some critics would argue, does this analysis adequately explain certain government actions detrimental to business interests, such as the Kennedy administration's attack in 1962 on the price policies of U.S. Steel, or the apparent vigor of some antitrust prosecutions. In fact, only a more thorough examination of particular decisions can clarify the dynamic relation between economic and political power. One recent step in this direction is Jim F. Heath's study of John F. Kennedy and the Business Community (Chicago: University of Chicago Press, 1969).

146

MORTON S. BARATZ
Corporate Giants
and the Power Structure

Ideally, if not in reality, ours is a pluralistic society. Our concept of freedom is that power be decentralized, that influence over the process of decision-making be diffused.[1] It is this, of course, which explains our devotion to a political and economic system characterized by small units of control, functioning in fragmented structures. As norms for public policy, perfect competition and pure democracy have survived largely because they are models in which the discretionary authority of individuals and groups is sharply delimited.

Now it is eminently clear that atomized political and economic structures are incompatible with a modern industrial society. Does this mean that bigness and a pluralistic distribution of power are mutually exclusive? Are giant business enterprises which are pursuing their private interests steadily gaining a greater proportion of power both in the private and public sectors of the economy? Is the American economy truly pluralist or is it more nearly a "pluralism of elites," of which the corporate giants are one?

These questions have been examined by a large and growing number of analysts. In popular and academic publications there has been comment on the political, social, legal, and economic aspects of the problem of corporate giantism and its place in a free society. By and large, however, economists have dominated the discussion and set the boundaries within which it has been conducted. The emphasis, as a result, has been put upon the impact of the large-scale business unit on the allocation of resources, the level and distribution of income, and the rate of economic development.

While these are rather well-defined areas for analysis, they may be handled with different theoretical models. If, on the one hand, the theorist reasons from static assumptions — constant consumer preferences, resources, and technology — he is most likely to conclude that the behavior of large-sized enterprises, particularly where they have significant market power, will cause a less-than-

From *The Western Political Quarterly*, Vol. IX, No. 2, June 1956, pp. 406–415. Reprinted by permission of the University of Utah, copyright owners.

[1] "Power is participation in the making of decisions: G has power over H with respect to the values K if G participates in the making of decisions affecting the K-policies of H." H. D. Lasswell and A. Kaplan, *Power and Society* (New Haven: Yale University Press, 1950), p. 75.

optimum allocation of resources, a lower level and greater inequality in the distribution of income, and a slower rate of economic progress. This reasoning, firmly grounded on the classical theory of markets, is embedded in the voluminous monographs of the President's Temporary National Economic Committee of 1939–40.

If, on the other hand, the theorist assumes changing wants, resources, and technology, he will arrive at quite different conclusions. In the context of the long run the activities of the giant business firm tend to bring about a more nearly optimum allocation of resources, raise the level and reduce inequality in the distribution of income, and promote the secular rise in total output. This analysis, most clearly expounded by J. A. Schumpeter, has been embraced more or less by J. K. Galbraith, D. E. Lilienthal, and A. D. H. Kaplan, among others.[2]

Not all economists concerned with business power fit neatly into either of these two schools; some, like C. D. Edwards,[3] take a position somewhere between them. More importantly, however, there has been growing recognition that the fundamental issues are political rather than economic. Increasing attention has been paid to the tendency to resolve in the political arena problems which are primarily economic. This approach invokes questions concerning the impact of giant firms on legislators and legislation. It raises the specter of political competition as the principal means of settling economic conflicts and implies there is a developing movement in the United States toward syndicalism of one form or another.[4]

While power, economic and political, has been considered in greater or less degree by all the writers, none has explored fully the implications for the distribution of power within the business community of the multi-plant, multi-product ("conglomerate") firm. Nor has anyone examined the possibility that the very existence of giant business firms compels public officials more and more to adopt a view roughly approximate to "what is good for General Motors [or the equivalent] is good for the country." That is, I hope, the contribution of this paper.

One of the central themes of much recent literature is that interproduct com-

[2] J. A. Schumpeter, *Capitalism, Socialism and Democracy* (3rd ed., New York: Harper & Bros., 1950), chaps. vi–viii; J. K. Galbraith, *American Capitalism: The Concept of Countervailing Power* (Boston: Houghton Mifflin Co., 1952); D. E. Lilienthal, *Big Business: A New Era* (New York: Harper & Bros., 1953); and A. D. H. Kaplan, *Big Enterprise in a Competitive System* (Washington: Brookings Institution, 1954). Compare, also, C. Wilcox, "Concentration of Power in the American Economy," *Harvard Business Review*, XXVIII (November, 1950), pp. 54–60.

[3] C. D. Edwards, *Maintaining Competition* (New York: McGraw-Hill Book Co., 1949), especially pp. 100–108.

[4] See, for example, F. Machlup, *The Political Economy of Monopoly* (Baltimore: Johns Hopkins University Press, 1952), pp. 76–77; J. M. Clark, *Alternative to Serfdom* (New York: Alfred A. Knopf, 1948), chap. v; and H. C. Simons, *Economic Policy for a Free Society* (Chicago: University of Chicago Press, 1948), chap. vi.

petition affords restraints against concentrations of economic power similar to those provided in classical theory by intraindustry rivalry. No matter what its size, the argument runs, no firm can enjoy more than a temporary advantage so long as there is a continuing flow of innovation, particularly new products. To put it another way, the effect of innovation is to erode positions of market dominance, assuring that over the long run economic power will remain dispersed.

This reasoning depends in considerable measure on the presumption that innovation will spring from "new" firms, that is, business concerns other than the ones currently dominant. As the leading exponent of the thesis put it: "in capitalist reality . . . [the] kind of competition which counts [is] the competition from the new commodity, the new technology, the new type of organization (the largest-scale unit of control, for instance) — competition . . . which strikes not at the margins of the profits and the outputs of the *existing firms* but at their very lives."[5]

What is the unique role of the giant enterprise in the "New Competition"? Because of its immense technical and financial resources, it is said to be the veritable fount of innovation.

> The firm of the type that is compatible with perfect competition is in many cases inferior in internal, especially technological efficiency. If it is, then it wastes opportunities. It may also in its endeavors to improve its methods of production waste capital because it is in a less favorable position to evolve and to judge new possibilities. And . . . a perfectly competitive industry is much more apt to be routed . . . under the impact of progress than is big business. . . . What we have got to accept is that [the large-scale establishment] has come to be the most powerful engine of [economic] progress. . . .[6]

While product competition and innovation are constituent parts of classical theory, neither received there the stress currently accorded them. And from a dynamic orientation there is no denying that the thesis built around them is highly persuasive. Especially in recent years there have been numerous product innovations which have at once expanded the alternatives available to consumers and dissipated prior positions of market dominance. To cite a few representative examples: steel must now compete in many uses with copper, aluminum, and magnesium, among other metals; cotton and wool must contend with such synthetics as rayon, nylon, orlon, and dacron; plastics and paper are competitors with glass and "tin" in the container industry; bituminous coal's markets have been reduced sharply by competition from petroleum and natural gas; railroads, buses, and airplanes compete among themselves for passenger traffic and all three compete with private automobiles.

[5] Schumpeter, *op. cit.*, p. 84. Italics added.

[6] *Ibid.*, p. 106. It is worth noting that Schumpeter's language is somewhat more guarded than that of his disciples. Compare, for instance, the comments in Lilienthal, *op. cit.*, chap. vi and *passim*.

These illustrations seem to provide a basis for believing that, except in rare instances, bigness and competition are compatible. If this is so, does it portend that innovation will come to be concentrated in the hands of but a few giants? And beyond that, what situation will obtain if interproduct competition comes to be waged by a small number of diversified giant corporations? In other words, may not "all-pervading cartel systems"[7] be virtually unavoidable concomitants of developing giantism?

"Because development is costly," it has been said, "it follows that it can be carried on only by a firm that has the resources associated with considerable size."[8] This is undoubtedly too extreme a statement.[9] The impressive achievements of Du Pont, General Motors, Radio Corporation of America, and others suggest, nonetheless, some direct correlation between corporate size and the control of innovation. This implies, in turn, that truly effective challenges to the established market positions of the giants must come to a considerable extent from other giants. What assurances have we that such challenges will be forthcoming? Is there not a possibility that the major large-sized firms will come to recognize that it may be to their mutual advantage to retard the rate of technological change and to conserve their common vested interests?[10]

These questions would not arise were the principal large-sized firms producers of single products sold under oligopolistic conditions. In such a situation, as Schumpeter and others have argued, innovation originating elsewhere would limit if not destroy the market power of the oligopolists. The fact is, however, that the typical giant corporation produces a variety of products, many of them competitive with one another. Orlon, nylon, and dacron are substitutive in many uses and all are produced by or under license of Du Pont. General Electric, RCA, and Philco, among others, produce both radio and television sets. Anaconda is now a producer of both copper and aluminum. Alcoa is of major importance in both the aluminum and magnesium industries. The Container Corporation of America produces boxes, fiber cans, and paper containers. The Koppers Company is engaged in the sale of three competing fuels: coke, natural

[7] It was Schumpeter's contention that the problem for policy was simply to guard against the creation and perseverance of "an all-pervading cartel system [which] might sabotage progress." *Ibid.*, p. 91.

[8] Galbraith, *op. cit.*, p. 92.

[9] All large-sized firms do not innovate. Nor do all innovations originate with such enterprises. See, for example, G. W. Nutter, "Monopoly, Bigness and Progress," paper read at a joint meeting of the American Statistical Association and the American Economic Association, December 29, 1953.

[10] "The certainty of relative loss and the possibility of absolute reduction of earnings provide an inducement for extending quasi-agreements to cost-saving innovations, product variation and advertising." If the oligopolistic group "is not quite small," it is more realistic to assume that the quasi-agreements are "characterized by the placing of limitations on all varieties of competition rather than by the complete elimination of competition with respect to cost-saving innovation, product variation and advertising. In the passage of time all factors bearing on relative strength tend to change." W. J. Fellner, *Competition Among the Few* (New York: Alfred A. Knopf, 1949), pp. 188–89.

gas, and bituminous coal. The New England Transportation Company, an important operator of passenger buses and trucks, is a subsidiary of the New Haven railroad.

Though only a few of many possible, these illustrations indicate a tendency toward what may be called "super-oligopoly." There is a movement, that is, toward the domination of clusters of industries by the same giant corporations. In part, this is being brought about by merger activity,[11] in part by innovation or imitation. In all events, the indications are that a few conglomerate mammoths are emerging as virtual holding companies[12] of American business. Whether they use this power malevolently or benevolently is irrelevant. That they are in the process of gaining it is the matter of importance to a society which would remain free.

Most economists who acknowledge the political implications of big business enterprises concern themselves with the impact of the giant firms on legislative activity. These remarks are typical:

> Certainly, the argument that bigness threatens our political liberties is without foundation. If there is one handicap that bigness possesses, it is lack of political influence. Let any group or organization become large and economically powerful, and its political influence drops. That is true of both labor and business. The most powerful lobbies in Washington are those that represent the farmers and small business.[13]

There are no objective standards with which to evaluate these assertions. How does one measure the degree of legislative influence of one interest group relative to another? Are statutes comparable either in their number or importance of their provisions? May not the failure to legislate in certain circumstances be more significant in terms of power than the actual passage of a group of laws? These are questions which afford room for much interesting debate and analysis. But they are of secondary importance. The ability or inability of corporate giants profoundly to affect legislative proceedings is only a small part of a much broader issue. That is whether the rise of giantism in business has had an effect on the formulation and implementation of public policy in general.

It is indisputable that a comparatively small number of business concerns control a disproportionate share of the nation's real and money resources. It has been estimated, for example, that the largest two hundred employers accounted in 1948 for about 20 per cent of all employees in private nonagricultural establishments; the largest two hundred corporations (the "top two hundred" are not the same in each case) held about 40 per cent of total corporate assets and

[11] See especially W. Adams, "Competition, Monopoly and Countervailing Power," *Quarterly Journal of Economics*, LXVII (1953), 472–74.
[12] As here used, the term includes management as well as financial control.
[13] S. H. Slichter, "Is Bigness in Business a Problem?" Summary of an address before the Fourteenth Stanford Business Conference, Stanford University, California, July 26, 1955. Professor Slichter kindly sent me a copy of this summary. See also *The New York Times*, July 27, 1955.

between a fifth and a fourth of income-producing national wealth.[14] What these data clearly suggest is that the private decisions of a small number of business executives can alter the pattern of community or regional development, raise or lower the level of national income and employment, affect the level and structure of wage rates. In short, so strategic is their economic position and so dependent upon them are thousands of persons that what happens to any one of the giant firms is of the greatest moment to the entire population and, perforce, to the makers of public policy.

The extent to which large-sized firms condition the processes of governmental decision-making can be indicated by taking first an extreme illustration. Except in unusual circumstances, the financial collapse or disappearance of a small- or medium-sized business concern is of little importance to public policy-makers. The nature of the economic system is such as to require that some enterprises succeed and some fail. So long as the social impact of a given business failure is confined to local parts of the system, public policy need not be unduly tender toward the departed.

Suppose, on the other hand, that financial crisis grips a concern such as General Motors, Du Pont, United States Steel or the Metropolitan Life Insurance Company. Here the impact would be felt economy-wide. The effects on workers, shareholders, creditors, suppliers, and distributors of and tangent to the stricken organization would be intolerable. No government could stand idly by. What is more important, no government can ignore the possibility, no matter how remote, that such an incident can occur. Consciously or insensibly, its monetary and fiscal policies must increasingly be arranged with sufficient flexibility that at any time the federal government is in a position promptly to bail out the private managers of large enterprises situated in key positions in the economy.[15]

Moreover, the dominant position of the giant firms demands that public policy-makers avoid at all costs decisions which could conceivably jeopardize the financial integrity of the mammoths. As a practical matter this means that most doubts in divestment proceedings in antitrust prosecutions,[16] on levies on

[14] M. A. Adelman, "The Measurement of Industrial Concentration," *Review of Economics and Statistics*, XXXIII (1951), 276–77.

[15] The Reconstruction Finance Corporation in its early years, circa 1932–39, illustrates the principle. About 70 per cent of its industrial loans were extended, it is true, to small-sized firms, chiefly because most of the giants had the resources to weather the storm. Nevertheless, exactly 100 firms, or 1.2 per cent of all borrowers, received loans in excess of $500,000; they received 39.4 per cent of total sums authorized. *Quarterly Report of Reconstruction Finance Corporation*, quarter ending June 30, 1939 (Washington, D.C.: Government Printing Office, 1939), Table 9, p. 50. The modern bankruptcy system which permits reorganization of existing firms in financial straits is equally relevant.

[16] "In antitrust, however, what man hath joined together the courts still hesitate to put asunder. In the absence of flagrant abuse they are loath to modify established rights of property. Unable to foresee the consequences of disintegration, they are reluctant to risk impairment of efficiency." C. Wilcox, *Public Policies toward Business* (Homewood, Ill.: Richard D. Irwin, 1955), p. 249. Also W. Adams, "The Aluminum Case: Legal Victory — Economic Defeat," *American Economic Review*, XLI (1951), 915–23.

unreasonable accumulations of surplus,[17] on the vigor with which certain regulatory statutes will be applied[18] — most doubts will be resolved in favor of the corporation in question. In a real sense the giant enterprises have achieved many of the privileges accorded the publicly regulated utilities without at the same time being burdened even by the formal restraints imposed on the latter.

The impact of giant firms on the economy is best illustrated by the magnitude of their spending relative to the total for all firms. In 1953, for instance, net private domestic investment amounted to about $24 billions.[19] Of this the three largest firms in the steel, automobile, chemical, and oil industries together accounted for more than $2.7 billions, or approximately 12 per cent.[20] To public officials responsible for the making of fiscal and monetary policy, it is evident that the private decisions to spend or not to spend of but twelve huge enterprises have a profound effect on output and income in a wide segment of the economy.[21] To put it technically but more generally, the spending decisions of those concerns will be transmitted throughout the economy through the invest-

[17] Between July, 1939, and July, 1949, approximately 1500 cases were brought by the Bureau of Internal Revenue under section 102 of the Internal Revenue Code. In about 900 cases the tax was collected, though there are no figures to show in how many of these instances suit was brought to obtain a refund. The total amount collected from the 900-plus cases was $18,738,400. Tax Institute, *Economic Effects of Section 102* (Princeton: *Tax Institute*, 1951), p. 93. These figures add some weight to the assertion that "the history of the administration of section 102 and official policy statements seem to give the vast majority of executives little cause for concern. . . ." R. Goode, *The Corporation Income Tax* (New York: John Wiley & Sons, 1951), p. 199.

[18] An outstanding instance is the refusal of the Federal Power Commission to fix the producer's price of natural gas. See, for example, Wilcox, *op. cit.*, pp. 583–84. Less to the point but of some relevance, "disclosure of corporate structure is required under the Securities Act of 1933 and the Securities Exchange Act of 1934 . . . the enforcement of this requirement has not been systematic, and many of the more important facts about the structure of great corporations which have floated securities have remained secret." Corwin D. Edwards, *Maintaining Competition* (New York: McGraw-Hill Book Co., 1949), p. 138.

[19] U.S. Department of Commerce, "National Income," 1954 edition, Supplement to the *Survey of Current Business* (Washington, D.C.: Government Printing Office, 1954), p. 160.

[20] The figure was computed from data on additions to property at cost in *Moody's Industrial Manual* (New York: Moody's Investors Service, 1954). For at least two reasons it is only a crude approximation to net private domestic investment as calculated by the Department of Commerce: (1) it does not include a sum for the Ford Motor Company, which in 1954 was not required by law to submit financial statements to the Securities and Exchange Commission; and (2) the additions to property include in some cases purchases by or for foreign subsidiaries. Unhappily, individual company data reported in the capital expenditures survey of the Department of Commerce and the Securities and Exchange Commission are collected on a confidential basis and cannot be released.

[21] Direct purchases of the motor vehicle industry in 1947 constituted the following percentages of total output of these selected industries: metal stampings, 32.4 per cent; tires and inner tubes, 22.4; storage batteries, 80.4; synthetic rubber and miscellaneous rubber products, 11.7; machine shops, 29.4; lighting fixtures, 23.8; glass, 9.2; asbestos products, 26.7; ball and roller bearings, 27.1; nonferrous foundries, 14.5; steel springs, 7.0; and cutting tools, jigs, and fixtures, 34.4. Data from U.S. Bureau of Labor Statistics in Federal Reserve Bank of Cleveland, *Monthly Business Review*, XXXV (1953), 7.

ment multiplier and, to a lesser extent, the accelerator. They will, therefore, have a major impact on the present and prospective levels of national income and employment. While this situation makes economic forecasting easier, it remains true that the activities of the twelve giants will have a material influence on governmental policy with respect to the level and kind of public expenditures, the level and structure of tax rates, the quantity of money and credit, and the level and structure of interest rates. To put it less cautiously, public policy necessarily tends to be oriented, especially over the long run, in a direction which is fundamentally in line with the interests of the great corporate enterprises. And this will be true even if the interests of the giants are in conflict with other social goals.

This point is illustrated by recent changes in the tax laws. Except under conditions of national emergency, it was public policy until 1954 to require firms to depreciate their tangible assets over the expected life of the property. In the belief that there is a pronounced direct correlation between tax rates and the rate of business spending and between investment and the national income, the Congress provided in the Internal Revenue Code of 1954 that on new properties acquired business firms may take depreciation reductions at a rate considerably faster than previously.[22] Enacted with votes of Congressmen avowedly intent on eliminating the persisting federal deficit, this provision was expected even by its sponsors to reduce tax receipts in fiscal 1955 by $375 millions.[23] Of greater significance, the firms most likely to benefit from accelerated depreciation are the largest rather than the newest and smallest ones.

> It should be pointed out that the choice of accelerated amortization as the particular form of incentive [to encourage private investment] favors expansion of capacity by existing firms, rather than new firms. New firms

[22] Sec. 167 of the Internal Revenue Code of 1954, Public Law 591, 83rd Congress, 2d Session, provides for the use of any of the following methods for computing depreciation allowances: straight line, declining balance, sum of the years-digits, or "any other consistent method productive of an annual allowance which does not, during the first two-thirds of the useful life of the property, exceed the total of such allowances which would have been used had such allowances been computed under the [declining balance] method."

Chairman Reed (R., N.Y.) of the House Ways and Means Committee explained the purposes of the revision in these terms: "This provision of the bill [H.R. 8300] is anticipated to have far-reaching economic effects. Incentives resulting from the changes are vital in order to help create thousands of jobs each year and to maintain the present high level of investment in plant and equipment. The bill will make it possible for management to assume risks which they would otherwise not take. By allowing businesses to recover a large part of their costs more quickly, it will be of particular assistance to growing businesses in financing their expansion. Farmers and other small businessmen also have a particularly vital stake in this provision of the bill because the faster recovery of capital which it permits will enable them to secure short term loans which would otherwise not be available." 83 *Cong. Rec.* (March 17, 1954), 3424.

[23] The estimated loss for corporations was $300 millions; for individuals, $75 millions — though "according to the experts who prepared them, these estimates are dangerously misleading, because they do not take into account the increased activity which will result from the provision." *Ibid.*, p. 3421.

will generally find the tax concession of little value since the first few years of a new firm are likely to be years of losses or at least low profits. But an established and profitable firm can charge off accelerated amortization against its profits on other facilities even if its new facilities are not profitable. It is apparent, therefore, that the particular device chosen for providing incentives for expansion of industrial capacity is one which works contrary to a national policy of encouraging the birth and growth of new firms.[24]

There is another manifestation of the power of large-sized corporations. This is the tendency for the largest private corporations to serve as prime contractors for government procurement. In that role the giant firms are in fact serving as arms of government, empowered to distribute largess almost as they see fit. Subcontracts may or may not be granted to the lowest responsible bidder; they may be awarded with the view of building a ring of satellites, smaller firms which are to be made wholly dependent for their future survival on the giant company. Or, alternatively, the general contractor may use the lucrative subcontract as a means of promoting other aspects of its operations, e.g., tying a contract award to a promise to buy certain products. Once again, it is not particularly relevant whether the giant company abuses its powers as a general contractor. It is relevant to a free society, however, that private organizations have such power, no matter how it is used.

It has been said:

> There is an elusiveness about power that endows it with an almost ghostly quality. It seems to be all around us, yet this is "sensed" with some sixth means of perception rather than with the five ordinary senses. We "know" what it is, yet we encounter endless difficulties in trying to define it. We can "tell" whether one person or group is more powerful than another, yet we cannot measure power. It is as abstract as time, yet as real as a firing squad.[25]

Undeniably, power relationships are highly complex, the more so because individual or group behavior through time is a composite of intention and reaction. Thus, for example, business firm A may attempt to influence the behavior of firm B, but the activities of A itself will be conditioned by the actual and expected reactions of B.[26] If for only this reason, attempts to trace shifts in the power structure must yield results which are very imprecise.

Cautiously as the case must be presented, however, the indications are unmistakable that giant business concerns have unusual influence over the processes of decision-making in both the private and the public sectors of the economy. To the extent that this power is exercised, the giant corporations can alter the

[24] J. P. Miller, "The Pricing Effects of Accelerated Amortization," *Review of Economics and Statistics*, XXXIV (1952), 16.
[25] H. Kaufman and V. Jones, "The Mystery of Power," *Public Administration Review*, XIV (1954), 205.
[26] *Ibid.*, pp. 207–208.

allocation of resources, the level and distribution of income and the rate of economic development. Under certain circumstances, the interests of the corporate giants may well coincide with those of other groups in the society ("the public interest"). And the giants may utilize their power moderately or not at all. But this is hardly a satisfactory arrangement for a society which places a high value on a decentralized power structure. It has wisely been said that "the important fact about 'enlightened despotism' — also the one fact 'enlightened despots' always forget — is that, while it appears as enlightenment to those in power, it is despotism pure and simple to those under it."[27]

To summarize, the contention here is decidedly not that "Big Business" is a rampant ogre, coldly bidding for greater and greater power. In largest part, the enhanced influence of the giant enterprises over the decision-making processes has come without their intention. Nor can it accurately be said that the largest corporations do now or will ever have absolute dominion over the society. Even the pure monopolist of classical price theory cannot charge *any* price he wishes; the range of his discretion, while broader than that of the firm in a purely competitive market, is not unlimited. In brief, the argument here is that bigness in business, together with parallel developments in other sectors of society, has moved us away from a pluralist toward a structure of power best described as a pluralism of elites.[28] This is an alternative foregone, i.e., a cost, of giantism which the members of society may or may not be willing to bear. Policy decisions must, in any event, be made in the light of *all* the implications, political as well as economic.

[27] P. F. Drucker, *Concept of the Corporation* (New York: John Day Co., 1946), p. 72.

[28] Some contend that big corporations themselves are pluralist, decentralized structures and so offset the tendency toward élitism. See, for instance, Kaplan, *op. cit.*, pp. 175–78. "But though [intracorporate] rivalry may be effective as a means of inducing hard work and identifying ability, it serves merely to intensify the performance of the participants along lines prescribed by the corporation. In a concern that has chosen to raise prices, restrict output, avoid improvements in the product, or limit new investment, internal competition does nothing to overthrow these decision." Edwards, *op. cit.*, p. 117.

IS THERE A
MILITARY-INDUSTRIAL COMPLEX?

Following World War II, military influence on national affairs seemed to increase with startling rapidity. Americans for the first time accepted the burden of a large standing army, a massive, permanent military establishment, and peacetime military conscription. After 1947, the military budget increased several times over, causing many to fear that the United States had generated a war economy. Further, military officers participated more frequently in important sectors of government and business, thereby playing a more visible role in the exercise of power. In response to such developments, some concerned intellectuals have suggested that America is becoming a "garrison state" (an idea originally developed by Harold Lasswell, "The Garrison State and Specialists on Violence," American Journal of Sociology, XLVI [January 1941], pp 455–468) or, with Mills, that a "military ascendancy" has made military leaders part of the power elite.

A singular statement by a public figure, rather than a sustained intellectual analysis, however, first truly captured the popular imagination and unleased latent fears about the growth of military power. President Dwight D. Eisenhower's timely warning about the "military-industrial complex," excerpted below, is one of those curious political orations which gain significance more from a memorable turn of phrase than from striking intellectual content. In assessing Eisenhower's address, moreover, students should realize that it generally lacks those radical overtones often attributed to it.

Unlike radical critics such as Mills, Eisenhower projects the danger from a military-industrial complex into the future. In addition, the pluralist theme of balance echoes through his speech, and it is clear that Eisenhower believes in the descriptive accuracy of pluralist rather than radical theory. Next, Eisenhower's rhetoric is far more conservative and belligerent than has generally been realized. Thus, he speaks of a "hostile ideology —

global in scope, atheistic in character, ruthless in purpose and insidious in method." Such bellicosity, with its attendant call for continual sacrifice, may not be altogether consistent with reprobation of the military-industrial complex. Many revisionist scholars would argue, in fact, that precisely this sort of condemnatory Cold War ideology has driven a fearful American nation to establish and to maintain dangerous liaisons between the military and industry. Eisenhower's apt phrase, then, may actually have entered the lexicon of American reform more by inadvertence than design. Nevertheless, the president clearly merits praise for bringing a neglected issue to public attention.

DWIGHT D. EISENHOWER
The Military-Industrial Complex

. . . We now stand ten years past the midpoint of a century that has witnessed four major wars among great nations — three of these involved our own country.

Despite these holocausts America is today the strongest, the most influential and most productive nation in the world. Understandably proud of this preeminence, we yet realize that America's leadership and prestige depend, not merely upon our unmatched material progress, riches and military strength, but on how we use our power in the interests of world peace and human betterment.

Throughout America's adventure in free government, our basic purposes have been to keep the peace; to foster progress in human achievement, and to enhance liberty, dignity and integrity among peoples and among nations.

To strive for less would be unworthy of a free and religious people.

Any failure traceable to arrogance or our lack of comprehension or readiness to sacrifice would inflict upon us grievous hurt, both at home and abroad.

Progress toward these noble goals is persistently threatened by the conflict now engulfing the world. It commands our whole attention, absorbs our very beings.

We face a hostile ideology — global in scope, atheistic in character, ruthless in purpose and insidious in method. Unhappily the danger it poses promises to be of indefinite duration. To meet it successfully there is called for, not so much the emotional and transitory sacrifices of crisis, but rather those which enable us to carry forward steadily, surely and without complaint the burdens of a prolonged and complex struggle — with liberty the stake.

Only thus shall we remain, despite every provocation, on our charted course toward permanent peace and human betterment.

From Dwight D. Eisenhower, "Farewell Address," delivered to the nation, Washington, D.C., January 17, 1961.

Crises there will continue to be. In meeting them, whether foreign or domestic, great or small, there is a recurring temptation to feel that some spectacular and costly action could become the miraculous solution to all current difficulties. A huge increase in newer elements of our defenses; development of unrealistic programs to cure every ill in agriculture; a dramatic expansion in basic and applied research — these and many other possibilities, each possibly promising in itself, may be suggested as the only way to the road we wish to travel.

But each proposal must be weighed in the light of a broader consideration; the need to maintain balance in and among national programs — balance between the private and the public economy, balance between the cost and hoped for advantages — balance between the clearly necessary and the comfortably desirable; balance between our essential requirements as a nation and the duties imposed by the nation upon the individual; balance between actions of the moment and the national welfare of the future. Good judgment seeks balance and progress; lack of it eventually finds imbalance and frustration.

The record of many decades stands as proof that our people and their Government have, in the main, understood these truths and have responded to them well in the face of threat and stress.

But threats, new in kind or degree, constantly arise. . . .

A vital element in keeping the peace is our military establishment. Our arms must be mighty, ready for instant action, so that no potential aggressor may be tempted to risk his own destruction.

Our military organization today bears little relation to that known of any of my predecessors in peacetime — or, indeed, by the fighting men of World War II or Korea.

Until the latest of our world conflicts, the United States had no armaments industry. American makers of plowshares could, with time and as required, make swords as well.

But we can no longer risk emergency improvisation of national defense. We have been compelled to create a permanent armaments industry of vast proportions. Added to this, three and a half million men and women are directly engaged in the defense establishment. We annually spend on military security alone more than the net income of all United States corporations.

Now this conjunction of an immense military establishment and a large arms industry is new in the American experience. The total influence — economic, political, even spiritual — is felt in every city, every state house, every office of the Federal Government. We recognize the imperative need for this development. Yet we must not fail to comprehend its grave implications. Our toil, resources and livelihood are all involved; so is the very structure of our society.

In the councils of Government, we must guard against the acquisition of unwarranted influence, whether sought or unsought, by the military-industrial complex. The potential for the disastrous rise of misplaced power exists and will persist.

We must never let the weight of this combination endanger our liberties or democratic processes. We should take nothing for granted. Only an alert and knowledgeable citizenry can compel the proper meshing of the huge industrial

and military machinery of defense with our peaceful methods and goals, so that
security and liberty may prosper together. . . .

In the selection reprinted below, Senator William Proxmire of Wisconsin
presents data that lend substance to Dwight Eisenhower's vague anticipa-
tion, almost a decade before, of the military-industrial complex. This new
evidence indicates that the number of retired officers above the rank of
colonel or navy captain employed by major defense contractors approximately tripled during the 1960's. This fact may be interpreted in different
ways, of course, but it indicates to some observers, including Proxmire,
that a malignant community of interest between the military and the
defense industry not only exists but is growing stronger.

In 1959, the House Armed Services Committee stated, with due caution,
that the " 'coincidence' of contracts and personal contacts with firms represented by retired officers and retired civilian officials sometimes raise serious
doubts as to the complete objectivity of some of these decisions." By 1969,
the coincidence of economic and military interests seemed more explicit.
Not only, suggests Proxmire, do defense contractors and their military
employees "hold a narrow view of public priorities based on self interest"
and "a largely uncritical view of military spending," but they too often
"may see only military answers to exceedingly complex diplomatic and
political problems." Moreover, in a chart not reprinted here, the senator
shows that a disproportionate amount of defense contract spending goes to a
relatively few firms and their subsidiaries: in fiscal year 1968, over 67 per
cent of prime contract spending was paid to one hundred contractors and
their subsidiaries, 50 per cent to thirty-three, and almost 30 per cent to the
top ten alone. Unlike Eisenhower, then, Proxmire indicates that the
military-industrial complex is a matter of immediate rather than future
concern. The Senator from Wisconsin further elaborates these views in
Report From Wasteland: America's Military-Industrial Complex (New
York: Praeger, 1970). Students may also profit from the House Committee
on Armed Services, Report No. 1408, Employment of Retired Commissioned Officers by Contractors of the Department of Defense and the
Armed Forces, 86th Congress, 2nd Session (Washington, D.C., 1960).
Although the evidence of increasing military-industrial collusion is powerful,
not every scholar would uncritically agree with these alarming analyses; for
different interpretations, see Emile Benoit and K. E. Boulding, eds., Disarmament and the American Economy (New York: Harper & Row, 1963);
M. J. Peck and F. M. Scherer, The Weapons Acquisition Process (Cambridge: Harvard University Press, 1962), and Murray L. Weidenbaum,
"Concentration and Competition in the Military Market," Quarterly Review
of Economics and Business, 8 (Spring 1968), pp. 7–17.

WILLIAM PROXMIRE

The Community of Interests

in Our Defense Contract Spending

. . . Recently I asked the Department of Defense for a list of certain high ranking retired military officers employed by the 100 companies who had the largest volume of military prime contracts. I did this in connection with the hearings of the Subcommittee on Economy in Government of the Joint Economic Committee.

In fiscal year 1968 these 100 companies held 67.4 percent of the $38.8 billion of prime military contracts, or $26.2 billion.

The Defense Department has now supplied to me the list of high ranking military officers who work for these 100 companies. They include the subsidiaries. In one case, that of the 35th ranking contractor, four firms were involved in a joint venture.

I asked only for the names of those retired military officers of the rank of Army, Air Force, Marine Corps colonel or Navy captain and above. Excluded are all officers below those ranks. I asked for only retired regular officers and not reserve officers, although in a very few cases the reserve officers may be included.

TOP 100 COMPANIES EMPLOY OVER 2,000 RETIRED OFFICERS

The facts are that as of February, 1969, some 2,072 retired military officers of the rank of colonel or Navy captain and above were employed by the 100 contractors who reported. This is an average of almost 22 per firm. I shall ask to have printed in the *Record* as exhibit A of my statement a list of the 100 companies, ranked according to the dollar volume of their prime military contracts, and the number of high ranking retired officers they employ.

TEN COMPANIES EMPLOY OVER 1,000

The 10 companies with the largest number on their payrolls employed 1,065 retired officers. This is an average of 106 per firm. These 10 companies employed over half the total number of high ranking former officers employed by

From *The Congressional Record*, March 24, 1969, pp. S 3072–S 3078.

all the top 100 defense contractors. These companies, listed according to the number of retired officers employed by them, are given in Table 1, as follows:

TABLE 1

Ten military prime contractors employing largest number of high ranking retired military officers, and value of their fiscal year 1968 contracts

Company and rank by number of high-ranking retired officers employed	Number employed, Feb. 1, 1969	Net dollar value of defense contracts, fiscal year 1968
1. Lockheed Aircraft Corp.	210	$1,870,000,000
2. Boeing Co.	169	762,000,000
3. McDonnell Douglas Corp.	141	1,101,000,000
4. General Dynamics	113	2,239,000,000
5. North American Rockwell Corp.	104	669,000,000
6. General Electric Co.	89	1,489,000,000
7. Ling-Temco-Vought, Inc.	69	758,000,000
8. Westinghouse Electric Corp.	59	251,000,000
9. TRW, Inc.	56	127,000,000
10. Hughes Aircraft Co.	55	286,000,000
	1,065	9,552,000,000

KEY ABM CONTRACTORS EMPLOY 22 PERCENT OF TOTAL

Among the major defense contractors involved in producing the key components of the anti-ballistic-missile system — ABM — nine of them employ 465 retired officers. This is an average of 51 each.

In 1968 they held contracts valued at $5.78 billion and, of course, will receive many billions more if the ABM system is deployed. These companies and the number of retired officers they employ are given in Table 2, as follows:

TABLE 2

Major prime contractors involved in ABM system and number of high ranking retired military officers employed by them

1. McConnell Douglas	141
2. General Electric	89
3. Hughes Aircraft	55
4. Martin Marietta	40
5. Raytheon	37
6. Sperry Rand	36
7. RCA	35
8. AVCO	23
9. A. T. & T.	9
Total	465

COMPARISON OF 1969 WITH 1959

Almost 10 years ago in connection with hearings before the Senate Finance Committee on the extension of the Renegotiation Act, former Senator Paul H. Douglas asked for and received a similar list from the Pentagon. We can, therefore, make comparisons over a decade as to what has happened with respect to the employment of high ranking retired military officers by the top 100 defense contractors.

In 1959, the total number employed was only 721 — 88 of 100 companies reporting — or an average of slightly more than eight per company.

In 1969 the 100 largest defense contractors — 95 of the 100 companies reporting — employed 2,072 former high military officers, or an average of almost 22 per company.

In 1959 the 10 companies with the highest number of former officers employed 372 of them.

In 1969 the top 10 had 1,065, or about three times as many.

Some 43 companies which reported were on both the 1959 and 1969 list of the top 100 largest contractors. There were several more who were on the list in both years but failed to report in one or the other year. But we can compare the 43 companies. These 43 companies employed 588 high ranking former officers in 1959. In 1969 these same companies employed 1,642 retired high ranking retired officers.

In each case where a comparison can be made, namely, in the total number of former high ranking officers employed by the top 100 contractors, the top 10 contractors employing the largest number, and the number employed by firms reporting in both 1959 and 1969, the number employed has tripled. It has increased threefold.

Roughly three times the number of retired high ranking military officers are employed by the top 100 companies in 1969 as compared with 1959.

SIGNIFICANCE

What is the significance of this situation? What does it mean and what are some of its implications?

First of all, it bears out the statement I made on March 10 when I spoke on the "blank check" for the military, that the warning by former President Eisenhower against the danger of "unwarranted influence, whether sought or unsought, by the military-industrial complex," is not just some future danger.

That danger is here. Whether sought or unsought there is today unwarranted influence by the military-industrial complex which results in excessive costs, burgeoning military budgets, and scandalous performances. The danger has long since materialized. The 2,072 retired high-ranking officers employed by the top 100 military contractors is one major facet of this influence.

NO CONSPIRACY OR WRONGDOING

Second, I do not claim nor even suggest that any conspiracy exists between the military and the 100 largest defense contractors. I do not believe in the conspiracy theory of history. I charge no general wrongdoing on the part of either group.

In the past many of the officers have performed valiant and even heroic service on behalf of the United States. The country is indeed grateful to them for their past service and for their patriotic endeavors.

We should eschew even the slightest suggestion of any conspiracy between the Pentagon, on the one hand, and the companies who hire former employees, on the other. There is not a scintilla of evidence that it exists.

COMMUNITY OF INTEREST

But what can be said, and should properly be said, is that there is a continuing community of interest between the military, on the one hand, and these industries on the other.

What we have here is almost a classic example of how the military-industrial complex works.

It is not a question of wrongdoing. It is a question of what can be called the "old boy network" or the "old school tie."

This is a most dangerous and shocking situation. It indicates the increasing influence of the big contractors with the military and the military with the big contractors. It shows an intensification of the problem and the growing community of interest which exists between the two. It makes it imperative that new weapon systems receive the most critical review and that defense contracts be examined in microscopic detail.

I am alarmed about this trend not because I question the integrity or the good will of the retired officers who have found employment with military contractors but because I believe that the trend itself represents a distinct threat to the public interest.

DANGERS WHEN COUPLED WITH
NEGOTIATED CONTRACTS

Third, this matter is particularly dangerous in a situation where only 11.5 percent of military contracts are awarded on a formally advertised competitive bid basis. It lends itself to major abuse when almost 90 percent of all military contracts are negotiated, and where a very high proportion of them are negotiated with only one, or one or two, contractors.

Former high-ranking military officers have an entree to the Pentagon that others do not have. I am not charging that is necessarily wrong. I am saying that it is true.

Former high-ranking officers have personal friendships with those still at the

Pentagon which most people do not have. Again, I charge no specific wrong-doing. But it is a fact.

In some cases former officers may even negotiate contracts with their former fellow officers. Or they may be involved in developing plans and specifications, making proposals, drawing up blueprints, or taking part in the planning process or proposing prospective weapon systems. And they may be doing this in co-operation with their former fellow officers with whom they served with and by whom, in some cases, even promoted.

With such a high proportion of negotiated contracts there is a great danger of abuse.

In addition, there is the subtle or unconscious temptation to the officer still on active duty. After all, he can see that over 2,000 of his fellow officers work for the big companies. How hard a bargain does he drive with them when he is 1 or 2 years away from retirement?

This danger does not come from corruption. Except in rare circumstances this is no more prevalent among military officers than among those with comparable civilian responsibilities.

MUTUAL INTERESTS — UNCRITICAL VIEWS

The danger to the public interest is that these firms and the former officers they employ have a community of interest with the military itself. They hold a narrow view of public priorities based on self-interest. They have a largely uncritical view of military spending.

As a group they have what has been termed "tunnelvision." But in this case their narrow training can be fortified by self-interest. In too many cases they may see only military answers to exceedingly complex diplomatic and political problems. A military response, or the ability to make one, may seem to them to be the most appropriate answer to every international threat.

SUMMARY

When the bulk of the budget goes for military purposes; when 100 companies get 67 percent of the defense contract dollars; when cost overruns are routine and prime military weapon system contracts normally exceed their estimates by 100 to 200 percent; when these contracts are let by negotiation and not by competitive bidding; and when the top contractors have over 2,000 retired high-ranking military officers on their payrolls; there are very real questions as to how critically these matters are reviewed and how well the public interest is served.

That . . . is the point. That is why I think it important that there be public disclosure of these facts so that the American public can know more about the community of interests involved in our huge defense contract spending. . . .

EXHIBIT A

A list of the 100 largest companies ranked by 1968 value of prime military contracts and number of retired colonels or Navy captains and above employed by them, February 1969

1	General Dynamics Corp.	113	51	Mobil Oil Corp.	(a)
2	Lockheed Aircraft Corp.	210	52	TRW, Inc.	56
3	General Electric Co.	89	53	Mason & Hanger Silas Mason	5
4	United Aircraft Corp.	48	54	Massachusetts Institute of	
5	McDonnell Douglas Corp.	141		Technology	5
6	American Telephone & Telegraph	9	55	Magnavox Co.	3
7	Boeing Corp.	169	56	Fairchild Hiller Corp.	7
8	Ling-Temco-Vought, Inc.	69	57	Pacific Architects & Engineering	16
9	North American Rockwell Corp.	104	58	Thiokol Chemical Corp.	3
10	General Motors Corp.	17	59	Eastman Kodak Co.	15
11	Grumman Aircraft Engineering		60	United States Steel Corp.	(a)
	Corp.	31	61	American Machine & Foundry	7
12	AVCO Corp.	23	62	Chamberlain Corp.	3
13	Textron, Inc.	28	63	General Precision Equipment	23
14	Litton Industries, Inc.	49	64	Lear Siegler Inc.	4
15	Raytheon Co.	37	65	Harvey Aluminum, Inc.	4
16	Sperry Rand Corp.	36	66	National Presto Industrial Inc.	0
17	Martin Marietta Corp.	40	67	Teledyne, Inc.	8
18	Kaiser Industries Corp.	11	68	City Investing Co.	4
19	Ford Motor Co.	43	69	Colt Industries, Inc.	4
20	Honeywell, Inc.	26	70	Western Union Telegraph Co.	5
21	Olin Mathieson Chemical Corp.	3	71	American Manufacturing Co. of	
22	Northrop Corp.	48		Texas	0
23	Ryan Aeronautical Co.	25	72	Curtiss Wright Corp.	1
24	Hughes Aircraft Co.	55	73	White Motor Co.	(a)
25	Standard Oil of New Jersey	2	74	Aerospace Corp.	6
26	Radio Corp. of America	35	75	Cessna Aircraft Co.	0
27	Westinghouse Electric Corp.	59	76	Emerson Electric Co.	3
28	General Tire & Rubber Co.	32	77	Seatrain Lines, Inc.	4
29	Int'l. Telephone & Telegraph Corp.	(a)	78	Gulf Oil Corp.	1
30	IBM	35	79	Condee Corp.	1
31	Bendix Corp.	25	80	Motorola, Inc.	3
32	Pan American World Airways	24	81	Continental Air Lines, Inc.	4
33	FMC Corp.	6	82	Federal Cartridge Corp.	1
34	Newport News Shipbuilding	6	83	Hughes Tool Co.	13
35	Raymond/Morrison, etc.[b]	6	84	Vitro Corp. of America	25
36	Signal Companies, Inc. (The)	9	85	Johns Hopkins Univ.	(a)
37	Hercules, Inc.	13	86	Control Data Corp.	14
38	Du Pont, E. I. de Nemours & Co.	3	87	Lykes Corp.	0
39	Texas Instruments, Inc.	7	88	McLean Industries, Inc.	2
40	Day & Zimmerman, Inc.	1	89	Aerodex, Inc.	5
41	General Telephone & Electronics		90	Susquehanna Corp.	7
	Corp.	35	91	Sverdrup & Parcel Assoc., Inc.	9
42	Uniroyal, Inc.	6	92	States Marine Lines Inc.	0
43	Chrysler Corp.	11	93	Hazeltine Corp.	7
44	Standard Oil of California	6	94	Atlas Chemical Indus., Inc.	0
45	Norris Industries	2	95	Vinnell Corp.	0
46	Texaco, Inc.	4	96	Harris-Intertype Corp.	4
47	Collins Radio Co.	3	97	World Airways, Inc.	4
48	Goodyear Tire & Rubber Co.	6	98	International Harvester Co.	6
49	Asiatic Petroleum Corp.	0	99	Automatic Sprinkler Corp.	3
50	Sanders Associates, Inc.	17	100	Smith Investment Co.	0
				Total	2,072

[a] *Not yet reported.*
[b] *Raymond Int'l, Inc.; Morrison-Knudsen Co., Inc.; Brown & Root, Inc.; and J. A. Jones Construction Co.*

EXHIBIT B

The 100 largest companies ranked by 1958 value of prime military contracts and number of retired colonels or Navy captains and above employed by them, June 1959

1	American Bosch Arma Corp.	0	51 Lear, Inc.	2
2	American Telephone & Telegraph		52 Lockheed Aircraft Corp.	60
	Co.	1	53 Marine Transport Lines, Inc.	1
3	Asiatic Petroleum Corp.	0	54 Marquardt Aircraft Co.	2
4	Avco Corp.	4	55 The Martin Co.	15
5	Bath Iron Works Corp.	2	56 Massachusetts Institute of	
6	Beech Aircraft	(a)	Technology	(a)
7	Bell Aircraft Corp.	3	57 Mathiasen's Tanker Industries, Inc.	1
8	Bendix Aviation Corp.	14	58 McDonnell Aircraft Corp.	4
9	Bethlehem Steel Co.	8	59 Minneapolis Honeywell Regulator	
10	Blue Cross Association	0	Co.	0
11	Boeing Airplane Co.	30	60 Motorola, Inc.	(a)
12	Brown-Raymond-Walsh	0	61 Newport News Shipbuilding and	
13	California Institute of Technology	0	Dry Dock Co.	6
14	Cessna Aircraft Co.	1	62 North American Aviation, Inc.	27
15	Chance Vought Aircraft Inc.	6	63 Northrop Aircraft Inc.	16
16	Chrysler Corp.	11	64 Olin Mathieson Chemical Corp.	6
17	Cities Service Co.	4	65 Oman-Farnsworth-Wright	0
18	Collins Radio Co.	5	66 Morrison-Knudsen Co., Inc.	1
19	Continental Motors Corp.	2	67 Pan American World Airways, Inc.	(a)
20	Continental Oil Co.	2	68 Philco Corp.	17
21	Curtiss-Wright Corp.	4	69 Radio Corp. of America	39
22	Defoe Shipbuilding Co.	0	70 The Rand Corp.	14
23	Douglas Aircraft Co. Inc.	15	71 Raytheon Mfg. Co.	17
24	E. I. du Pont de Nemours & Co.	1	72 Republic Aviation Corp.	9
25	Eastman Kodak Co.	12	73 Richfield Oil Corp.	4
26	Fairchild Engine & Airplane Corp.	7	74 Ryan Aeronautics Co.	9
27	Fairbanks Whitney Corp.	4	75 Shell Oil Corp.	0
28	Firestone Tire & Rubber Corp.	3	76 Sinclair Oil Corp.	1
29	Food Machinery & Chemical Corp.	6	77 Socony Mobile Oil Co.	1
30	Ford Motor Co.	5	78 Sperry Rand Corp.	12[b]
31	The Garrett Corp.	2	79 Standard Oil Company of	
32	General Dynamics Corp.	54	California	(a)
33	General Electric Co.	35	80 Standard Oil Company of Indiana	(a)
34	General Motors	(a)	81 Standard Oil of New Jersey	1
35	General Precision Equipment Corp.	(a)	82 States Marine Corp.	0
36	General Tire & Rubber Co.	28	83 Sundstrand Machine Tool Co.	(a)
37	Gilfillian Brothers Inc.	0	84 Sunray Mid-Continent Oil Co.	0
38	B. F. Goodrich Co.	1	85 Sylvania Electric Products, Inc.	6
39	Goodyear Tire & Rubber Co.	2	86 Temco Aircraft Corp.	6
40	Greenland Contractors	(a)	87 Texaco, Inc.	0
41	Grumman Aircraft Engineering		88 Thikol Chemical Corp.	8
	Corp.	1	89 Thompson Ramo Wooldridge, Inc.	6
42	Hayes Aircraft Corp.	3	90 Tidewater Oil Co.	3
43	Joshua Hendy Corp.	0	91 Tishman (Paul) Company, Inc.	0
44	Hercules Powder Co. Inc.	1	92 Todd Shipyards Co.	2
45	Hughes Aircraft Co.	7	93 Union Carbide Corp.	4
46	International Business Machine		94 Union Oil Company of California	0
	Corp.	3	95 United States Lines Co.	0
47	International Telephone & Telegraph		96 United Aircraft Corp.	15
	Corp.	24	97 Westinghouse Air Brake Co.	42
48	The Johns Hopkins University	16	98 Westinghouse Electric Corp.	33
49	The Kaman Aircraft Corp.	1	99 The White Motor Co.	0
50	Peter Kiewit Sons Co.	1	100 System Development Corp.	2
			Total	721

[a] Not available.

[b] Gen. Douglas MacArthur not included.

Source: Congressional Record, *June 17, 1959, pp. 11044-45. Statement by former Senator Paul H. Douglas.*

Harold D. Lasswell's garrison state, C. Wright Mills' military ascendancy, and Dwight D. Eisenhower's military-industrial complex have all, to a greater or lesser extent, struck responsive chords in the public mind and helped to make predatory military power part of the popular demonology. Yet the military has also had persuasive defenders. In his important study, The Professional Soldier (New York: The Free Press, 1960), sociologist Morris Janowitz disputes those who believe that military power is now covetous and unrestrained. The military profession, he argues, is not a monolithic power group, but rather "an administrative pressure group . . . with a strong internal conflict of interest." In addition, the military exercises influence over political matters "with considerable restraint and unease," while civilians retain ultimate control over military affairs. Until recently, this debate was monopolized largely by those, like Mills, who perceived a dramatic increase in the power of military elites and those, like Janowitz, who stressed the limits of military influence and the effectiveness of democratic controls.

In this selection, historian Gabriel Kolko presents quite a different analysis. His interpretation builds upon a large body of revisionist scholarship, which emphasizes the central place of corporate enterprise in recent American history. In The Triumph of Conservatism (New York: The Free Press, 1963) and other works, Kolko himself has described the growth of "political capitalism," or the systematic use of the state for the benefit of business. The policies of the liberal state, Kolko contends, are shaped by those with dominant economic power. In addition, Kolko accepts many conclusions of revisionist diplomatic historians like William Appleman Williams who believe that American foreign policy has been greatly influenced by the need for economic expansion into new foreign markets. (See Kolko's own revisionist study, The Politics of War [New York: Random House, 1968].)

Kolko rejects both the idea of a military ascendancy and the optimistic pluralist alternative. Power is not dispersed and balanced but instead resides in a ruling class concerned primarily with the interests of American business. At the same time, interservice rivalry, the lack of an articulate military ethic, and the military's dependence upon industrial technology and civilian skills, has prevented a military ascendancy and made the armed services mere instruments of those civilian groups actually holding the reins of power. Business and not the military, therefore, is primarily responsible for the military-industrial complex, the war economy, and America's interventionist foreign policy. In addition to stressing the economic roots of military power, Kolko emphasizes the significance of economic imperialism and the importance of business values in American liberal ideology.

Kolko at times moves rather abruptly from limited empirical evidence to sweeping generalization. He also rests much of his case upon an analysis of career lines and the social backgrounds of certain decision-makers, although this can only suggest rather than prove the existence of common interests. Nevertheless, Kolko uncovers vital weaknesses in traditional interpretations of military power. He intelligently assails several cherished radical assumptions about the pervasiveness of military influence in American society. Yet he is equally critical of those pluralists who prescribe increased civilian control over foreign and military affairs as a sure protection against the military-industrial complex and the spread of military power. In short, Kolko's challenging interpretation raises important and difficult questions often overlooked by those of more conventional views. Students may also wish to consult the important radical critique by Marc Pilisuk and Thomas Hayden, "Is There a Military-Industrial Complex Which Prevents Peace?" Journal of Social Issues, 21 (July 1965), pp. 67–117, William Phelan, Jr.'s, essay, "The 'Complex' Society Marches On," Ripon Forum, V (January 1969), pp. 9–20, and Irving Louis Horowitz's analysis, The War Game: Studies of the New Civilian Militarists (New York: Ballantine, 1963).

GABRIEL KOLKO
The American Military
and Civil Authority

In the United States the civilians, the self-styled "liberals" and "democrats," finally direct the application of American power in all its forms throughout the world. Despite the dramatic and sinister overtones in the phrase "military-industrial complex," or C. Wright Mills' vision of the "military ascendancy," the fact is that the nature of global conflict and the means of violence are so thoroughly political and economic in their essential character, so completely intricate technologically, that it is probably more correct to argue the case for the declining importance of the military in the decision-making structure. For military power is the instrument American political leaders utilize to advance their enormous and ever-growing objectives, and that they require a vast Military Establishment is the logical, necessary effect rather than the cause of the basic objectives and momentum of American foreign policy since 1943. Civilians formulated that policy, in the context of the critical postwar period, when the

From *The Roots of American Foreign Policy* by Gabriel Kolko. Reprinted by permission of the Beacon Press, copyright © 1969 by Gabriel Kolko.

Military Establishment was docile and relatively starved. Belligerence requires generals and arms as tools for the advancement of permanent objectives.

The critics of America's policies in the world have focused their attacks on the visibility of the military, as if its "liberalization" would transform the reality of America's global role. The notion of an independent military dynamic and ethic occludes the real interests and purposes of American foreign policy, which is not to fight wars but to gain vital strategic and economic objectives that materially enlarge American power everywhere. That the military is a neutral instrumentality of civilian policy is inherent in the fact that increasingly the major object of strategic military policy is how to avoid using suicidal nuclear armaments while successfully advancing American economic and political goals. These ends are active, the struggle for them the potential cause of nuclear conflict that could destroy the world; only the most extreme imperatives ever led the civilians to consider this risk and option. If a distinctive military ethic, a regenerative theory of bloodletting and heroism, has ever existed, it has not caused a war in which civilian men of power did not first conceive of some more rational, material goals. This is no less true of the Cold War than of the Spanish-American War, when Washington used an essentially civilian-inspired theoretical school of heroism, which Theodore Roosevelt, Henry and Brooks Adams, and their friends led, as an ideological frosting for advancing American colonialism and global economic power.

Modern warfare is utilitarian to the furtherance of present American objectives, but only so long as it is combat between unequals and excludes great nuclear powers. This means, in brief, that in a world of revolutionary nationalist movements there are many small wars that the United States may choose to fight without confronting the U.S.S.R. or China, and that the strategic and most expensive section of the American Military Establishment will remain restrained and passive, as it has in a disciplined fashion in the past. What is left, from the numerous alternatives to anti-peasant, anti-revolutionary warfare with tiny powers, is a choice of political options for relating to the Third World, policies that civilian political leaders and their experts always determine and often call upon the military to implement. In some instances, such as Iran, Indonesia, Greece, and Cuba, the half-political, quasi-military C.I.A. has offered policy-makers more graceful-appearing means for attaining goals while skirting the more cumbersome and overt regular military. Indeed, the very existence of the C.I.A., completely removed from the military services, has increasingly strengthened the total control of the civilians over physical power and military intelligence. If the constantly changing technological escalation of the arms race has given the Military Establishment a dynamic and ever-growing appearance, we must never forget the fact that this is an effect rather than a cause of political policy, an appearance and instrumentality rather than the full nature of reality. If this were not the case, and the American military were all that the naïve element of the Left has blandly claimed, it would have destroyed the world some years ago.

So long as specialists in violence apply it only where and when higher authorities tell them to, a "garrison state" involving the disciplining of society and the politically-based unification of major economic and social institutions will be a rather different type of system than Harold D. Lasswell outlined nearly three decades ago.[1] Indeed, a coercive elite quite willing to undermine democracy at home as well as abroad will rule the society, even in the name of "liberalism," and it will permit global necessities to define its priorities internally, but contrary to Lasswell and Mills, the elite will not base its supremacy only on skill and efficiency — the qualifications of able bureaucrats — but also on the control or servicing of the economic, business sector of power. This dual relationship — one which uses the political structure to advance the domestic and global economic interests of American capitalists — has characterized Washington leaders for the better part of this century.

The fascination with the alleged expertise of the military, as if control of technique is equivalent to real power and implies a political conflict with existing authority, was the major defect in Mills' work no less than Lasswell's. Quite apart from the fact that the labyrinthine technological and political nature of modern warfare makes the professional soldier increasingly dependent on scientists and diplomats, Mills assumed that since the military sector generated vast economic demand, it somehow gave generals and admirals equal power, or near parity, with big business in the permanent war economy, merging their identities and interests in a distinctive, new fashion.[2] Yet how and what the government orders to attain its military goals is a much more complex process than he acknowledged, and that this created a war economy or sector should not obscure the fact that how and where — and how much — money was spent is always a decision of civilian political men as well as interested economic groups. My aim in this essay is to show that the military has always been the instrument, the effect rather than the cause of this policy. That the military intermingled with business and political leaders, and indeed shared a common social origin and outlook, is less consequential than the actual power of the various designers of American policy in the world. Quite apart from the alleged existence of what Mills called "military capitalism," the major issue is: Does this relationship serve the real interests of the military, the capitalists, or both?

BUSINESS DEFINITION OF THE MILITARY STRUCTURE

Business is both a fount and magnet for the Military Establishment. The "military-industrial complex" that exists in the United States is a lopsided phenomenon in which only businessmen maintain their full identity, interests, and commitments to their institution, while the military conforms to the needs of economic interests. Business careers are now part of the aspirations of thousands of military officers, while key businessmen and their lawyers continuously pass in and out of major bureaucratic posts in the Defense Department and national security agencies, usually remaining long enough to determine key policies and then return to business. The arms race, based on continuous technological innovations, originates as often with greedy arms firms as with generals — officers

---

[1] Harold D. Lasswell, *National Security and Individual Freedom* (New York, 1950), chap. II. See also Harold D. Lasswell, "The Garrison-State Hypothesis Today," in *Changing Patterns of Military Politics*, Samuel P. Huntington, ed. (New York, 1962), 51–70.

[2] C. Wright Mills, *The Power Elite* (New York, 1956), 28, 198–201, 214–15, 274–78, 292–96.

who are the instruments of the arms producers insofar as the military's strategic doctrines give the Services need for appropriate hardware. Perhaps most important, at no time has the military fully controlled or defined the budget and the vital strategic assumptions that have guided its size and allocation, for in this regard their internal bickering over limited resources has greatly diminished their ability to dictate to the civilians.

Historically, the military has always depended on business to a great extent. The Government left the mobilization of industry for military purposes during the First World War primarily in the hands of businessmen, and the interwar mobilization plans followed the wartime precedents. Corporate executives and business school social scientists dominated and lectured to the Army Industrial College for the decade and one-half after its founding in 1924. When the Roosevelt Administration finally drew up and implemented mobilization plans for the Second World War, businessmen played the vital role in its critical economic aspects, and at no time during the war did any military leader attempt to utilize the vast procurement power to foster a distinctive ideology or collective policy in the postwar period.[3]

One can hardly exaggerate the importance of the specific arms producers and industries in guiding the action of their respective, allied Services, both from the viewpoint of their making available new technical means for advancing Service strategies and eventually incorporating key military men into the military-based economy. Until about 1960, when missiles became the overlapping jurisdiction of all three major Services and traditional lines broke down somewhat, the industries supplying various modes of warfare — on the land, strategic airpower, and naval — all vied with each other for the largest possible slice of the limited military budgets. "The aircraft industry," Senator Barry Goldwater once remarked, "has probably done more to promote the Air Force than the Air Force has done itself." ". . . What appears to be intense interservice rivalry," General James M. Gavin has observed, ". . . in most cases . . . is fundamentally industrial rivalry."[4] In its ultimate and always prevalent form, such business competition determines precisely which weapons systems — which often perform essentially identical functions — the government will purchase. Indeed, in the case of the B-36 bomber and TFX plane, the existence of a firm with problems and traditional Service connections may be the primary reason for the procurement of a weapons system in the first place, even at a greater cost than is necessary. In this process of competition, the officers of various Services may line up with different companies, often merely as fronts.

To survive, weapons producers, and particularly aerospace firms, must constantly devise new weapons and systems to supersede those they have already

[3] Paul A. C. Koistinen, "The 'Industrial-Military' Complex in Historical Perspective: World War I," *Business History Review*, XLI (Winter 1967), 378–403; Albert A. Blum, "Birth and Death of the M-Day Plan," in *American Civil-Military Decisions*, Harold Stein, ed. (Montgomery, Ala., 1963), 63 ff.; Samuel P. Huntington, *The Soldier and the State: The Theory and Politics of Civil-Military Relations* (Cambridge, 1957), 315–16; Eliot Janeway, *The Struggle for Survival: A Chronicle of Economic Mobilization in World War II* (New Haven, 1951), 59–70.

[4] Quoted in Samuel P. Huntington, "Interservice Competition and the Political Roles of the Armed Services," *American Political Science Review*, LV (March 1961), 47.

built. In 1958–59, for example, the Navy received 486 unsolicited antisubmarine-warfare proposals from the industry, and agreed to fund 155 of them. Private risk capital first developed many of the major military aircraft, even though the Services did not see their immediate relevance, only because the corporations needed the final production contracts to operate their plants and make money. In the case of the semi-official Service associations that campaign for greater expenditures for their respective branches — the Navy League, Air Force Association, and Association of the United States Army — the financing of these lobbying activities comes from corporate dues and advertising in their journals.[5]

The ultimate discipline in making key officers subservient to the major arms firms is the hiring of retired officers, about two-thirds of whom left the military voluntarily to take up their new posts. Their ability to make favorable contacts for new careers while in the Services depends, in the last analysis, on avoiding conflicts with arms firms that can close off these lucrative posts. In 1959, the 72 largest arms suppliers alone employed 1,426 retired officers, 251 of them being of flag or general rank. Many of these former officers have special skills and background in procurement, modern weaponry, or the more technologically exotic aspects of warfare, and often meet their future employers in tax-deductible luxury. In effect, corporations are asking them to sell arms to their former military associates. "Every time I go to the Pentagon to obtain a contract for one of my constituents," one congressman complained in 1960, "I run into hundreds of retired officers."[6] Today congressmen and military officers both work for various, if competing, corporations.

THE MILITARY ETHIC

Radical social scientists such as Mills, and conservatives such as Samuel P. Huntington, nurtured the myth that a distinctive military ethic exists, common only to men in uniform. But the concept of aristocracy and discipline allegedly defining the military system hardly appreciates the decisive value of the military's inefficiency and incompetence in creating vast markets for civilian interests. In fact, the notion of an independent military sector, with its own codes and objectives, saves critical observers the trouble of viewing the nature of American power as a much larger integrated phenomenon. The military is a most conformist and pliable aspect of the power system, quite drably bureaucratic, and it serves the purposes of capitalists and politicians without much reticence.

[5] Merton J. Peck and Frederic M. Scherer, *The Weapons Acquisition Process: An Economic Analysis* (Boston, 1962), 237 n, 342, 366, 535–36; Charles N. Bernstein, "How to Propose a Research Program," *Missiles and Rockets*, VI (April 18, 1960), 32; Samuel P. Huntington, *The Common Defense: Strategic Programs in National Politics* (New York, 1961), 397–402; U.S. House, Committee on Armed Services, *Report . . . on Employment of Retired Commissioned Officers by Defense Department Contractors*. 86:1 (Washington, 1960), 16.

[6] *Army-Navy-Air Force Journal*, April 16, 1960, 921. See also U.S. House, *Report . . . on Employment of Retired Commissioned Officers*, 9–13; U.S. House, Committee on Armed Services, *Supplemental Hearings Released from Executive Session Relating to Entertainment Furnished by the Martin Company of Baltimore, Md., of U.S. Government Officers*. 86:1. September 10, 1959 (Washington, 1959), 29, 42 ff.

While it is true the technicians of violence are an intrinsic part of American leadership, these men begin with and often play many other roles as well, and as I have already argued, these roles are primary and a greater revelation of their true function. The ideologists of expansion and militarism in the United States have, with rare exceptions, been civilians in the tradition of what Huntington calls neo-Hamiltonianism, and not since Alfred T. Mahan has a professional officer penned a respectable rationale for the enlargement of American might that reflected distinctive ideological assumptions. Indeed, what is most significant about neo-Hamiltonianism is its role as a justification for the political capitalism that was the most critical outcome of American liberal reform, and its affinity for classic international expansion and adventure abroad. The failure of any significant sector of the military openly to rally to such theories of the positive and predatory state at any time reveals mainly that the American military is nonideological, even when civilians formulate a seemingly appropriate frame of reference for it.

There have been no coups, no hints of physical insubordination, no serious general political-military alliances. The one possible exception, the MacArthur controversy of 1951, was essentially a case of heading off the obvious political aims of a man whose overweening personal ambition and conceit was a quality of personality rather than a spearhead for a military alliance or a distinctive policy orientation. And it was a general, who, as President in 1961, warned of the dangers of the "military-industrial complex" *and* the "scientific-technological elite," and reaffirmed the virtue of civilian supremacy. Even MacArthur ended his days as an articulate opponent of total war, calling for nuclear disarmament.

No later than November 1947 the Army quietly informed its leading generals that they could neither write nor speak in a manner that contradicted the existing government policy toward Russia or the United Nations, an admonition that it often repeated. Publicly, in subsequent years such figures as General Omar N. Bradley, then head of the Joint Chiefs of Staff, stated that the function of the military was to assume responsibility for a military policy adequate for the implementation of the national political criteria and goals which the President and his chosen advisers defined. It was in this context during the Truman Administration that the State Department became the leading single exponent of expanded military power and the construction of an H-bomb, with the responsible military men operating within given and more stringent budgetary assumptions. "The Army respects its civilian leadership and abstains from any involvement in politics," General Maxwell D. Taylor, Army Chief of Staff, wrote to his major officers in September 1955.[7] When General Matthew B. Ridgway published his iconoclastic memoir the following year, he only revealed an intense

[7] *Army-Navy-Air Force Journal*, September 24, 1955, 91. See also Mills, *The Power Elite*, 174, 196, 222; Huntington, *Soldier and the State, passim*; Morris Janowitz, *Sociology and the Military Establishment* (New York, 1959), *passim*; *New York Times*, January 18, 1961, 22; Gen. Omar N. Bradley to Gen. Douglas MacArthur, May 20, 1948, and Memo on "Army Policy on Discussion of Russia," November 19, 1947, in Douglas MacArthur Papers, MacArthur Memorial Library, Norfolk, Va., Record Group 5; Gen. Omar N. Bradley, in *Department of State Bulletin*, XXVIII (March 16, 1953), 414–15; Huntington, *The Common Defense*, 47–53.

desire to permit his Service freedom to war with the Air Force and Navy for a larger portion of the military budget, and not ot be subjected to some "politico-military" party line before the civilians made their final decisions, at which point ". . . they could expect completely loyal and diligent execution of those decisions."[8]

There are, of course, the much publicized but ultimately unrepresentative extremes in the military viewpoint. At the one pole is the view of the professional nonideological technician of death, which the then head of the Marine Corps, General David M. Shoup, expressed in a statement in 1961: "We're professional soldiers. We fight any enemy the President designates. We don't have to develop hate. We don't just keep talking communism. . . . You might build up a hate against one enemy and find yourself fighting another."[9] The other position, even less consequential, is the jingoist reaction which so alarmed liberals in 1961 when the press revealed that John Birch and similar reactionary notions were a part of a military education program on about a score of bases, or a small minority of the total. What was truly significant about the phenomenon was that it was not more widespread, perhaps much less than in high schools and newspapers, and that it revealed how far the military had gone to censor the eccentric, idiosyncratic, and reactionary speeches of some of its generals. Such revelations were useful, for the fierce statements of a few impotent professorial geopoliticians, and the minor officers who used them, made the Kennedy Administration look relatively moderate at a time when it was advocating a vast civil defense program and a conventional military build-up, and attempting to create a first-strike nuclear strategy that, combined or individually, constituted a truly irrational new course in the arms race.

The moral of the few incidents of which we know is that the Birchite General Walker and those like him are summarily forced from the military and government service if their superiors cannot bring them into line. During the barely undercover "preventive war" discussions of August 1950, when Secretary of the Navy Francis Mathews publicly called for ". . . instituting a war to compel cooperation for peace," only the fact that he was "very contrite" when the President called him in saved Mathews his post.[10] While Hanson Baldwin claimed Mathews really reflected the views of Secretary of Defense Louis Johnson, thus posing a military challenge to civilian authority, what was most consequential was that all the personalities involved until that time were civilians. When shortly thereafter the head of the Air War College publicly urged preventive war against Russia, the Pentagon suspended him from his command.[11]

[8] Gen. Matthew B. Ridgway, *Soldier: Memoirs of Matthew B. Ridgway* (New York, 1956), 270.

[9] *New York Times*, October 29, 1961.

[10] *Time*, September 4, 1950, 12; Harry S Truman, *Memoirs* (Garden City, N.Y., 1956), II, 383. See also U.S. Senate, Committee on Government Operations, *Hearings, Organizing for National Security*. 87:1. January 1960 (Washington, 1961), 1206–09; U.S. Senate, Committee on Armed Services, *Hearings, Military Cold War Education and Speech Review Policies*. 87:2. January 1962 (Washington, 1962), *passim*; *New York Times*, January 28, June 18, November 1, 1961; U.S. Senate, *Congressional Record*, August 2, 1961, 13436–42.

[11] *New York Times*, September 1, 1950, 3; *Time*, September 11, 1950, 22.

The military, in brief, has been docile, its alleged "ethic" nebulous and meaningless. It has dissented no more than any other group of bureaucrats serving the state, and unquestionably it has been among the most restrained of those in power. A closer look at the manner in which the Military Establishment has operated only confirms this point.

THE MILITARY AFTER THE SECOND WORLD WAR

The central fact of the immediate postwar experience is that although the American Military Establishment was more than sufficient in regard to what Washington considered to be the major military problem — the Soviet Union — it was relatively starved not merely in contrast to the potential of the American economy, but also when measured against the actual as opposed to the perceived global challenges to American power abroad. Nearly everyone in Washington saw the question of communism and the Left as essentially a matter of the Soviet Union and Europe, and not until 1949 and thereafter did the question of Asia assume sufficiently high priority to warrant a shift toward a slightly more balanced military capacity. In reality, the American political definition of the world's main "problems" served as a usefully reinforcing underpinning to an almost universal desire to limit the military budget, for if Russia was the primary opponent, the relatively low cost of the strategic atomic theory of the Air Force made sense. The significant point is that the Air Force atomic strategy, which Congress endorsed, made it possible to place a ceiling on arms expenditures, and only the rude events of Korea, Indo-China, and the gradual shift of American priorities from Europe to Asia and Latin America inevitably forced arms expenditures ever upward.

In this process of changing concerns, lasting from 1946 to the beginning of the "New Look" under Eisenhower, Service divisions over fundamental strategic assumptions left the civilians quite free to continue to make the critical decisions regarding the extent and use of military power. It is this profound disunity that is the central fact of the potential political role of the military in the United States, and it was especially sharp during the lean years of 1946–50, when the military budget ranged from a low of $11.8 billion in 1948, or 4.5 percent of the gross national product, to a high of $14.4 billion in 1947, 6.2 percent of the GNP. In the context of opposition to Truman's two-year efforts to unify the military services into a single Department of Defense, eventually embodied in the National Security Act of July 1947, the Navy had overtly opposed any move toward reducing the future role of sea power. Less openly, the Army hoped to save its weakened position against the Air Force, which claimed total capacity to deter or win a war with Russia cheaply, by advancing a Universal Military Training bill in Congress, a politically unpopular proposal that Truman also mildly endorsed. And to relate itself to military probabilities, the Navy advanced plans for supercarriers capable of delivering bombs against the Soviet heartland.

Since all these conflicting strategic and organizational claims carried substantial price tags, and Congress was unwilling to pay for them all, the more attractive doctrine and political connections of the Air Force prevailed. Congress, with the Air Force's assistance, killed U.M.T., and the Army passively watched while the advocates of air power in Congress undercut the Navy supercarrier program. By the spring of 1949, when the Secretary of the Navy resigned in protest over the course of events, both the Air Force and Navy were engaged in a propaganda war against each other, unquestionably the most interesting and artful in the history of American strategic doctrine.[12]

A number of officers of the tactical fighter section of the Air Force, who resented the emphasis on big bombers, aided the Navy, but the furor over the B-36 bomber — on which the Air Force pinned its hopes for lack of a better plane — was the chief factor in strengthening the Navy's position. The Air Force's own experts privately had shown little enthusiasm for the B-36, which, with the aid of memos that Navy officers and competitive air frame producers distributed, correctly looked too much like an effort to bail out the sinking fortunes of the politically well-connected Consolidated Vultee Aircraft Company, whose links reached as high as Secretary of Defense Louis Johnson.[13] In the course of House hearings during October 1949 the Navy tendentiously advocated the value of carrier-based mobile air power and limited warfare, arguing the immorality of a city-busting atomic blitz as "morally reprehensible" and the illegal "mass killing of noncombatants." Such pleading was hollow, since the supercarrier was also useful mainly as a "city buster" against civilian populations. And as the Secretary of the Air Force, W. Stuart Symington maintained with greater consistency, the destruction of civilians is ". . . an unavoidable result of modern total warfare," and ". . . this opinion that war is immoral is a fairly recent one for anybody in the Military Establishment, and I wondered how and why it came up."[14]

No one in the Navy truly believed their moralistic contentions, and when eventually the Polaris submarine missile was invented, they too developed a strategic doctrine appropriate to that "city-busting" weapon. Truman was to fire at least one key Navy officer for his resistance to the official line, the Chief of Naval Operations, Admiral Louis E. Denfeld, and he disciplined others. What was at stake was not merely the independence of the various Services, but the belief, as General Bradley phrased it, that ". . . a nation's economy is its ultimate strength," and how they might obtain maximum security for the least expense remained the crucial issue.[15] Most of the Army generals who rose to prominence in the Joint Chiefs of Staff, as well as Herbert Hoover, Eisenhower, and the main

[12] Peck and Scherer, *Weapons Acquisition Process*, 100; Paul Y. Hammond, "Supercarriers and B-36 Bombers: Appropriations Strategy and Politics," in *American Civil-Military Decisions*, 481–91; Huntington, "Interservice Competition and the Political Roles of the Armed Services," 41; Truman, *Memoirs*, 53.

[13] U.S. House, Committee on Armed Services, *Hearings, Investigation of the B-36 Bomber Program.* 81:1. August–October 1949 (Washington, 1949), 13–20, 51–84, 477–92, 626–33.

[14] U.S. House, Committee on Armed Services, *Hearings, The National Defense Program—Unification and Strategy.* 81:1. October 1949 (Washington, 1949), 51, 56, 403, 436. See also *ibid.*, 45, 104, 185–89, 207–12, 238–41.

[15] *Ibid.*, 518. See also Truman, *Memoirs*, 53; Hammond, "Supercarriers and B-36 Bombers," 547.

forces of the budget-minded Republican Party, reinforced this assumption at the time. Congress itself has exerted control over the military not by aligning with it but rather by working within the President's broad guidelines and budgetary allocations to make certain that the Administration cut their constituents into as large a slice of the pie as possible. Other than this pork barrel impulse, which occasionally Congress translates into specific weapons systems that hardly alter the larger contours of the Executive branch's strategy, the role of Congress has merely been passively self-interested.[16]

If later the Army was to produce its own dissidents, the nature of the competitive struggle for limited budgetary resources in the 1950's meant that the profound divisions within the Military Establishment would always permit the civilians to play one Service bloc, consisting of the generals and their contractors, against the other. It is less significant to speculate what might have happened had the military assumed a common front, which is nearly impossible, than to realize that at no time did the political decision-makers lose control of the policy process.

America's civilian leaders applied the nation's policies within the informal and shifting committee-like structure that they organized into the National Security Council after mid-1947. United States leadership first defined those goals during the period 1896–1920, when McKinley, Roosevelt, and Wilson first scaled the objectives of American foreign policy to the capacity of American power to extend into the world. No later than the end of the Second World War those aims included a full-blown ideology of United States hegemony in the Western Hemisphere and Pacific, and primary leadership in the greater part of the areas that remained. Those goals reflected the American peace aims hammered out during the war, a process that excluded the Military Establishment on most of the key questions.

The very disunity within the military Services filled various key leaders in Washington with suspicion toward the consistency and reliability of the new Department of Defense, and they learned to depend on their own resources within the National Security Council and other committees. Although the original Council included the three Service secretaries, these men were all civilians; and while the Joint Chiefs attended meetings during the first years of the Council's existence, not until after the Korean War did they participate in the Council's vital staff functions. During 1949 Truman dropped the Service secretaries, and after the Korean War sharply cut back on the size of Council meetings, and the Defense Department has largely restricted itself to technical advice and analysis of the military implications of foreign policy decisions of the President, Secretary of State, or the advisers that the President uses informally. If Cabinet agencies set up independent planning committees from time to time, meshing foreign and military policy, the Executive ultimately considered

---

[16] U.S. House, *The National Defense Program*, 516–21, 545, 565, 638; Werner R. Schilling, Paul Y. Hammond, and Glenn H. Snyder, *Strategy, Politics, and Defense Budgets* (New York, 1962), 7–263; Elias Huzar, *The Purse and the Sword: Control of the Army by Congress Through Military Appropriations, 1933–1950* (Ithaca, 1950), *passim*; Huntington, *Soldier and the State*, 420–21; Huntington, *The Common Defense*, 387–91.

their recommendations in a manner that lowers the relative weight of Defense and military opinion. The Government, for the most part, has not determined basic foreign policy otherwise.[17]

Significantly, the civilians rather than the military attempted to break out of the traditional straitjacket of budgetary limitations to attain a force level equal to American political goals and ideological conceptions. During 1949 George Kennan argued for greater emphasis on mobile conventional armies. And it was with the budgetary restriction in mind that Dean Acheson, David Lilienthal, and Louis Johnson urged the President in January 1950 to authorize preliminary studies on the H-bomb, a weapon most of Washington then considered necessary in light of the Soviet discovery of the secret of making an A-bomb, to retain military superiority within a limited budget. The State Department, developing Kennan's original impulse and making it more grandiose, at the same time took the lead in a joint Defense-State committee to urge a vast increase in the military budget, which the State Department proposed to make between $35-50 billion, tying it to general ideological descriptions of the communist menace. The Joint Chiefs and Defense leaders, more modest and less ideological, and split within their own ranks due to Secretary Johnson's desire to cut the Defense budget, could propose only $17-18 billion, a modest increase over existing levels. At this juncture the Korean War began, with the conflicting positions in the policy paper now known as JCS 68 still unresolved.

By 1953 the military budget had grown to 13.8 percent of the gross national product, but in the White House a former general undertook to reduce the percentage with his "New Look" military policy of greater reliance on nuclear power. Eisenhower was concerned with the problem of how to maintain vast military power over a long period of time without overheating the nonmilitary economic sector and without assuming, as had the Democrats, that the danger of war with Russia increased with growing Soviet military and economic power. Above all, he wished to confront the extraordinarily difficult and ultimately unresolvable dilemma of how to combat or neutralize the diverse social revolutionary threats to the permanent strategic, political, and economic goals of the United States — a dilemma which has characterized American foreign policy since the fall of China. America's capacity to confront successfully the Soviet Union required a budgetary expenditure and strategic posture that was predictable. However, such a policy was inadequate to meet the challenge of the many, often yet unborn local revolutionary situations, where crude weapons made strategic nuclear weaponry inappropriate and potentially suicidal. America's economic and political limitations could not halt a world drifting beyond its control.

Ultimately, the Eisenhower Administration chose to confront Russia and to risk its ability effectively to respond militarily to the rest of the world. The General and his government rejected a full mobilization of American manpower and economic resources into a total warfare state capable of seriously retarding revolutionary movements everywhere. The result was a doctrine of massive re-

---

[17] David E. Lilienthal, *The Journals of David E. Lilienthal: The Atomic Energy Years, 1945-1950* (New York, 1964), 351; Truman, *Memoirs*, 59; U.S. Senate, *Organizing for National Security*, I, 154, 161-62, 563, 573, 673-74, 685, II, 431-33.

taliation appropriate for warfare against highly industrialized powers, which the
Government now frankly acknowledges as unlikely, and a beginning in the long-
term decline in the coveted American hegemony in the world. The upshot, too,
has been that in the rare instances which tempted factions of the military to
use nuclear weapons, such as in Indo-China during the spring of 1954, the
Army's fundamental skepticism toward this strategy made employment of it
impossible. Under the New Look policy, the absolute and percentage decline in
military expenditures and Army-Navy manpower continued, much to the disgust
of Army generals, until Kennedy came to office. In effect, military policy and
outlays were sufficient only to maintain a high level of economic activity at
home, but insufficient to cope with social revolution and guerrilla warfare, against
which missiles and atomic weapons were largely useless.[18]

THE "CIVILIZED" MILITARY

Within the context of these internal military divisions, the Services' lack of a
unified strategic doctrine, and the overriding limits of the budgetary process in
defining options, it would be difficult to prove C. Wright Mills' contention that
". . . as a coherent group of men the military is probably the most competent
now concerned with national policy; no other group has had the training in
co-ordinated economic, political, and military affairs. . . ."[19] On the contrary,
nothing in the operational structure of the Defense Establishment nor in the
changing character of military technology alters the fact that civilian, even
"liberal," leadership and civilian ideology have led the United States and the
world into its present morass of global crises and interventionism.

Each successive reorganization of the Defense Establishment since 1947 has
further consolidated the decisive role of civilians in military policy. In 1949
Congress deprived the Services of independent executive status and placed over
it a Defense Department structure with superior powers. In one of his first and
most critical acts, the stronger civilian Secretary created an independent, superior
office to control all missile developments within the three Services, thereby
dominating the most essential sector of future military technology. The Defense
Reorganization Act of 1953 further accelerated the civilian domination of the
Defense Department by increasing the number of civilian assistant secretaries
from three to nine and assigning them many responsibilities hitherto left to
civilian-military boards. While certain of their functions were vague, it placed
larger control of functional problems in the hands of civilians who were not
responsible to the Services but to the Defense Secretary. One of them, indeed,
represented unified Defense policy on international affairs directly to the National
Security Council. In this context, with the three services so profoundly divided
on strategy and in competition for limited budgetary resources which the civilians
could use to split their ranks, the Joint Chiefs of Staff were unable to stem the

---

[18] Truman, *Memoirs*, 309; Huntington, *The Common Defense*, 47–53, 64–98; Schilling
et al., *Strategy, Politics, and Defense Budgets*, 275–362, 400–76; Ridgway, *Soldier*, 272–77;
U.S. Senate, *Organizing for National Security*, I, 797–98.

[19] Mills, *The Power Elite*, 199.

supremacy of the civilians in the Pentagon. The President usually selected a politically reliable officer to be the head of the Joint Chiefs, and the Air Force was more than willing to break away from the other Services at the sacrifice of a possible common front because, in the showdown, it usually could better protect its own interests against the others. When united, which meant primarily on minor questions, the civilian leaders treated the Joint Chiefs deferentially. In any event, the Defense Reorganization Act of 1958 further strengthened the role of the civilian secretaries, and in that year the Secretary, via the Advanced Research Projects Agency, took over responsibility for all important weapons systems developments.[20]

In the context of the ever-growing dependence of the professional soldiers on the civilian Defense Secretaries, both the soldiers and civilians in the Pentagon in turn increased their reliance on the civilians in business and the universities for the major technological innovations and strategies which are the most grotesquely threatening aspect of the arms race and the condition of the world today. The fact was that the generals and admirals were incapable of managing and developing scientifically sophisticated "hardware" programs with which the United States hoped to compensate for its manpower and ideological disadvantages in a revolutionary world. Most, indeed, were near illiterates in the major critical areas, and alone were patently unable to attain the maximum military impact and resources from the budgets that Congress had allocated. Conscious of these limitations, in 1946 Eisenhower had decided for the Army that ". . . there appears little reason for duplicating within the Army an outside organization which by its experience is better qualified than we are to carry out some of our tasks," which meant the Army would ". . . find much of the talent we need for comprehensive planning in industry and universities."[21] Thus began a vast research and development program and military dependence on industry and universities, and an even larger stake on the part of a vital sector of these institutions in an arms race. In 1948 the Air Force took over the Rand Corporation on contract to secure its advice, and from 1953 to 1958 relied for the direction of its missile program on the Ramo-Wooldridge Corporation, whose ballistic missile staff grew from 18 to 3,269 in five years. After 1953 the Air Force left the co-ordination of its specific weapons systems to its prime contractors, and by 1959 drew 46 percent of its procurement personnel at the supervisory level from private business backgrounds — a figure the Navy and Army almost matched. In the field of missiles almost all of the government's key advisers have been civilians from industry and the universities. By 1955 the Pentagon's in-house Weapons System Evaluation Group was near collapse, and only a contract between M.I.T. and the Defense Department, which led to the

---

[20] Peck and Scherer, *Weapons Acquisition Process*, 72–73; Gene N. Lyons, "The New Civil-Military Relations," *American Political Science Review*, LV (March 1961), 54–55; Burton M. Sapin and Richard C. Snyder, *The Role of the Military in American Foreign Policy* (Garden City, N.Y., 1954), 26–30; Huntington, *The Common Defense*, 115, 155–57.

[21] General Dwight D. Eisenhower, Memo, "Scientific and Technological Resources as Military Assets," April 27, 1946, Henry L. Stimson Papers, Yale University Library.

creation of the multi-university-sponsored Institute for Defense Analysis, saved the undertaking — but in civilian, private hands.[22] By the time the Kennedy Administration took office, civilians had so thoroughly permeated the Military Establishment with their techniques, ideology, and objectives that it was apparent that professional officers were hardly more than docile instruments of the state, less credible to its civilian leadership than even many facile and ambitious Ivy League Ph.D.'s who, in their ability to translate American power into strategies and arms systems, saw the opportunity of becoming advisers to the men already at the top.

The final reorganization of the Defense Department, which Robert McNamara merely completed, utterly depersonalized the distinctive aspects of a military bureaucracy on the premise ". . . that the techniques used to administer these affairs of a large organization are very similar whether that organization be a business enterprise or a Government institution, or an educational institution, or any other large aggregation of human individuals working to a common end."[23] In reality, McNamara's model and experience was the Ford Motor Company, but in the Defense Department he sought to maximize objectives at the lowest possible price rather than accumulate an annual profit. Ph.D.'s managed the resulting "package programs" and increasingly centralized procurement at the further expense of the professional soldiers, who whimpered bitterly but continued to lose vital leverage and administrative functions. Complaints from the generals still often centered on the matter of budgetary allocations for the various Services, or their deflated egos and the roles of officers in ever-narrowing areas, but they did not alter the essential reality of the further "civilianization" of the commanding sectors of the Military Establishment, mainly in the hands of political "liberals" dedicated to civil rights, social welfare, and art centers which have become the liberal's surrogates for a society based on economic foundations of justice.[24]

The collapse of the McNamara empire did not end civilian predominance, even as these civilians chose the new generation of generals more for their technical competence than their military prowess. As a materialist *par excellence*, McNamara eventually realized that the unattainable ideological goals of American policy had outstripped physical resources, turning the war in Vietnam into a seemingly endless series of escalations, each one only further intensifying the defeats America was suffering in the hands of peasants. His elimination came

[22] U.S. House, Committee on Government Operations, *Hearings, Organization and Management of Missile Programs.* 86:1. February–March 1959 (Washington, 1959), 504, 671–74, 689–96, 716, 731–33, 742, 753, 758, 767–69, 775–77; U.S. House, Committee on Government Operations, *Report on Organization and Management of Missile Programs.* 86:1. September 2, 1959 (Washington, 1959), 69–141; U.S. House, Committee on Armed Services, *Hearings, Weapons System Management and Team System Concept in Government Contracting.* 86:1. April–August 1959 (Washington, 1959), 27–29, 563–67.

[23] U.S. Senate, *Organizing for National Security,* I, 1190.

[24] U.S. Senate, Committee on Armed Services, *Hearings, Military Cold War Education and Speech Review Policies.* 87:2. January 1962 (Washington, 1962), 9–12; *Business Week,* July 13, 1963, 56–90; *Wall Street Journal,* March 20, 1961, February 19, 1962; *New York Times,* March 2, 1962, September 5, October 8, 1963, February 2, 1965.

not from his disagreements with the military but with the other civilians who were even more belligerent than he had been throughout his career. Indeed, this episode perhaps more than any other exposed how totally military in means and ends were the ideological premises of those who believed also in the supremacy of civilian authority over the military. It showed how fully, the Military Establishment was merely the instrument of warfare liberalism in the Fair Deal-Great Society period of American history. And Vietnam, in turn, revealed how irrelevant the ingenuity and technical efficiency of American policy had been in a Third World whose fate revolutionary mass movements would determine, despite resistance, repression, and occasional setbacks.

THE END
OF IDEOLOGY?

Pluralists frequently deny that ideology is a primary force in their theory of power. During the fifties their analysis was often tied to the notion that an end of ideology had accompanied the apparent demise of divisive social issues and of disruptive political passions. Pluralism seemed uniquely suited to this new, presumably nonideological climate of mutual tolerance and forbearance. The increase in militant dissent during the sixties, however, shattered this happy illusion that America had achieved a lasting social consensus. As a result, critical scholars now realize that pluralism was never free of ideological bias. Philosopher Robert Paul Wolff here examines certain of these ideological presumptions, focusing on the idea of tolerance, and measures their effect upon the wielding of power.

Although in this essay he is critical of pluralism, Wolff elsewhere has taken issue with some radical analyses. Many critics have at least implied that pluralism, if it existed, would be laudable; the difficulty, these dissenters have suggested, is that "power elites" or "ruling classes" rather than pluralistic groups actually control America. Wolff, on the other hand, believes that pluralism does accurately describe the actual, if not the ideal, distribution of power in the United States. Hence, in his recent book

The Poverty of Liberalism (Boston: Beacon Press, 1968), Wolff concludes that no power elite exists. Leaders, he finds, "are completely vulnerable to popular opposition of even the most peaceful sort," although, admittedly, such opposition is seldom voiced. Though he concedes that pluralists have described power in America more accurately than have many dissident analysts, Wolff, nevertheless, is himself radically critical of the existing political system. Pluralism, as he makes clear in the following indictment, is not justifiable or desirable merely because it exists.

Thus, Wolff charges that pluralist theory is biased against new, unestablished groups and that this severely inhibits progressive social change. Pluralism, in his view, consistently favors the already powerful rather than the disadvantaged and powerless. (Some of this critique is echoed by Theodore Lowi in his article, "The Public Philosophy: Interest-Group Liberalism," The American Political Science Review, LXI [March 1967], pp. 5–24, and in his book, The End of Liberalism [New York: Norton, 1969].) Wolff believes, further, that the theory incorporates no efficacious theory of the common good and that pluralists therefore cannot respond effectively to general social problems transcending the interests of specific groups.

Wolff's lucid and temperate survey uncovers several ideological flaws of liberal pluralism and demonstrates well the close relationship between ideology and power. Moreover, in this essay he speaks for certain radical scholars who believe that the centralization rather than the decentralization of power can best serve the collective interest. (For similar perspectives, see Herbert Marcuse's One Dimensional Man: Studies in the Ideology of Advanced Capitalist Society [Boston: Beacon Press, 1964].) Yet perhaps Wolff does not adequately consider the ideas of those pluralists like Talcott Parsons, who also view power as a "resource" affecting all of society and not just specific interest groups. Some skeptics will also be deeply troubled by Wolff's easily misunderstood exhortation to move "beyond pluralism and beyond tolerance." Without tolerance, they may object, nothing will prevent established groups from consolidating their power and subsequently repressing advocates of unpopular ideas or of beneficial social change. It may be, in fact, that only a companion study detailing the ideological correlates of Wolff's own radical analysis can clarify these ambiguities. David Spitz traces the possible outlines of such an analysis in his polemic, "On Pure Tolerance: A Critique of Criticism," Dissent, XIII (September–October 1966), pp. 510–525; see also the subsequent exchange between Wolff and Spitz, "The Nature of Freedom," ibid., XIV (January–February 1967), pp. 95–98.

ROBERT PAUL WOLFF
Ideology and Power

Democratic pluralism and its attendant principle of tolerance are . . . open to a number of serious criticisms which are, in my opinion, ultimately fatal to pluralism as a defensible ideal of social policy. The weaknesses of pluralism lie not so much in its theoretical formulation as in the covert ideological consequences of its application to the reality of contemporary America. The sense of "ideological" which I intend is that adopted by Karl Mannheim in his classic study *Ideology and Utopia*. Mannheim defines ideology as follows:

> The concept "ideology" reflects the one discovery which emerged from political conflict, namely, that ruling groups can in their thinking become so intensively interest-bound to a situation that they are simply no longer able to see certain facts which would undermine their sense of domination. There is implicit in the word "ideology" the insight that in certain situations the collective unconscious of certain groups obscures the real condition of society both to itself and to others and thereby stabilizes it. (p. 40)

Ideology is thus systematically self-serving thought, in two senses. First, and most simply, it is the refusal to recognize unpleasant facts which might require a less flattering evaluation of a policy or institution or which might undermine one's claim to a right of domination. For example, slave-owners in the antebellum South refused to acknowledge that the slaves themselves were unhappy. The implication was that if they were, then slavery would be harder to justify. Secondly, ideological thinking is a denial of unsettling or revolutionary factors in society on the principle of the self-confirming prophecy that the more stable everyone believes the situation to be, the more stable it actually becomes.

One might think that whatever faults the theory of pluralism possessed, at least it would be free of the dangers of ideological distortion. Does it not accord a legitimate place to all groups in society? How then can it be used to justify or preserve the dominance of one group over another? In fact, I shall try to show that the application of pluralist theory to American society involves ideological distortion in at least three different ways. The first stems from the "vector-sum" or "balance-of-power" interpretation of pluralism; the second arises from the application of the "referee" version of the theory; and the third is inherent in the abstract theory itself.

According to the vector-sum theory of pluralism, the major groups in society compete through the electoral process for control over the actions of the government. Politicians are forced to accommodate themselves to a number of opposed interests and in so doing achieve a rough distributive justice. What are the major groups which, according to pluralism, comprise American society today? First, there are the hereditary groups which are summarized by that catch-phrase of tolerance, "without regard to race, creed, color, or national origin." In addition there are the major economic interest groups among which — so the theory goes — a healthy balance is maintained: labor, business, agriculture, and — a residual category, this — the consumer. Finally, there are a number of voluntary associations whose size, permanence, and influence entitle them to a place in any group-analysis of America, groups such as the veterans' organizations and the American Medical Association.

At one time, this may have been an accurate account of American society. But once constructed, the picture becomes frozen, and when changes take place in the patterns of social or economic grouping, they tend not to be acknowledged because they deviate from that picture. So the application of the theory of pluralism always favors the groups in existence against those in process of formation. For example, at any given time the major religious, racial, and ethnic groups are viewed as permanent and exhaustive categories into which every American can conveniently be pigeonholed. Individuals who fall outside any major social group — the non-religious, say — are treated as exceptions and relegated in practice to a second-class status. Thus agnostic conscientious objectors are required to serve in the armed forces, while those who claim even the most bizarre religious basis for their refusal are treated with ritual tolerance and excused by the courts. Similarly, orphanages in America are so completely dominated by the three major faiths that a non-religious or religiously-mixed couple simply cannot adopt a child in many states. The net effect is to preserve the official three-great-religions image of American society long after it has ceased to correspond to social reality and to discourage individuals from officially breaking their religious ties. A revealing example of the mechanism of tolerance is the ubiquitous joke about "the priest, the minister, and the rabbi." A world of insight into the psychology of tolerance can be had simply from observing the mixture of emotions with which an audience greets such a joke, as told by George Jessel or some other apostle of "interfaith understanding." One senses embarrassment, nervousness, and finally an explosion of self-congratulatory laughter as though everyone were relieved at a difficult moment got through without incident. The gentle ribbing nicely distributed in the story among the three men of the cloth gives each member of the audience a chance to express his hostility safely and acceptably, and in the end to reaffirm the principle of tolerance by joining in the applause. Only a bigot, one feels, could refuse to crack a smile!

Rather more serious in its conservative falsifying of social reality is the established image of the major economic groups of American society. The emergence of a rough parity between big industry and organized labor has been paralleled by the rise of a philosophy of moderation and cooperation between them, based on mutual understanding and respect, which is precisely similar to the achieve-

ment of interfaith and ethnic tolerance. What has been overlooked or suppressed is the fact that there are tens of millions of Americans — businessmen
and workers alike — whose interests are completely ignored by this genial give-
and-take. Non-unionized workers are worse off after each price-wage increase, as
are the thousands of small businessmen who cannot survive in the competition
against great nationwide firms. The theory of pluralism does not espouse the
interests of the unionized against the non-unionized, or of large against small
business; but by presenting a picture of the American economy in which those
disadvantaged elements do not appear, it tends to perpetuate the inequality by
ignoring rather than justifying it.

The case here is the same as with much ideological thinking. Once pluralists
acknowledge the existence of groups whose interests are not weighed in the
labor-business balance, then their own theory requires them to call for an altera-
tion of the system. If migrant workers, or white-collar workers, or small businessmen are genuine *groups*, then they have a legitimate place in the system of
group-adjustments. Thus, pluralism is not explicitly a philosophy of privilege or
injustice — it is a philosophy of equality and justice whose *concrete application*
supports inequality by ignoring the existence of certain legitimate social groups.

This ideological function of pluralism helps to explain one of the peculiarities
of American politics. There is a very sharp distinction in the public domain
between legitimate interests and those which are absolutely beyond the pale. If
a group or interest is within the framework of acceptability, then it can be sure
of winning some measure of what it seeks, for the process of national politics is
distributive and compromising. On the other hand, if an interest falls *outside*
the circle of the acceptable, it receives no attention whatsoever and its proponents are treated as crackpots, extremists, or foreign agents. With bewildering
speed, an interest can move from "outside" to "inside" and its partisans, who
have been scorned by the solid and established in the community, become
presidential advisers and newspaper columnists.

A vivid example from recent political history is the sudden legitimation of
the problem of poverty in America. In the post-war years, tens of millions of
poor Americans were left behind by the sustained growth of the economy. The
facts were known and discussed for years by fringe critics whose attempts to
call attention to these forgotten Americans were greeted with either silence or
contempt. Suddenly, poverty was "discovered" by Presidents Kennedy and Johnson, and articles were published in *Look* and *Time* which a year earlier would
have been more at home in the radical journals which inhabit political limbo
in America. A social group whose very existence had long been denied was now
the object of a national crusade.

A similar elevation from obscurity to relative prominence was experienced by
the peace movement, a "group" of a rather different nature. For years, the
partisans of disarmament labored to gain a hearing for their view that nuclear
war could not be a reasonable instrument of national policy. Sober politicians
and serious columnists treated such ideas as the naive fantasies of bearded peace-
niks, communist sympathizers, and well-meaning but hopelessly muddled clerics.
Then suddenly the Soviet Union achieved the nuclear parity which had been
long forecast, the prospect of which had convinced disarmers of the insanity of

nuclear war. Sober reevaluations appeared in the columns of Walter Lippmann, and some even found their way into the speeches of President Kennedy — what had been unthinkable, absurd, naive, dangerous, even subversive, six months before, was now plausible, sound, thoughtful, and — within another six months — official American policy.

The explanation for these rapid shifts in the political winds lies, I suggest, in the logic of pluralism. According to pluralist theory, every genuine social group has a right to a voice in the making of policy and a share in the benefits. Any policy urged by a group in the system must be given respectful attention, no matter how bizarre. By the same token, a policy or principle which lacks legitimate representation has no place in the society, no matter how reasonable or right it may be. Consequently, the line between acceptable and unacceptable alternatives is very sharp, so that the territory of American politics is like a plateau with steep cliffs on all sides rather than like a pyramid. On the plateau are all the interest groups which are recognized as legitimate; in the deep valley all around lie the outsiders, the fringe groups which are scorned as "extremist." The most important battle waged by any group in American politics is the struggle to climb onto the plateau. Once there, it can count on some measure of what it seeks. No group ever gets all of what it wants, and no *legitimate* group is completely frustrated in its efforts.

Thus, the "vector-sum" version of pluralist theory functions ideologically by tending to deny new groups or interests access to the political plateau. It does this by ignoring their existence in practice, not by denying their claim in theory. The result is that pluralism has a braking effect on social change; it slows down transformation in the system of group adjustments but does not set up an absolute barrier to change. For this reason, as well as because of its origins as a fusion of two conflicting social philosophies, it deserves the title "conservative liberalism."

According to the second, or "referee," version of pluralism, the role of the government is to oversee and regulate the competition among interest groups in the society. Out of the applications of this theory have grown not only countless laws, such as the antitrust bills, pure food and drug acts, and Taft-Hartley Law, but also the complex system of quasi-judicial regulatory agencies in the executive branch of government. Henry Kariel, in a powerful and convincing book entitled *The Decline of American Pluralism*, has shown that this referee function of government, as it actually works out in practice, systematically favors the interests of the stronger against the weaker party in interest-group conflicts and tends to solidify the power of those who already hold it. The government, therefore, plays a conservative, rather than a neutral, role in the society.

Kariel details the ways in which this discriminatory influence is exercised. In the field of regulation of labor unions, for example, the federal agencies deal with the established leadership of the unions. In such matters as the overseeing of union elections, the settlement of jurisdictional disputes, or the setting up of mediation boards, it is the interests of those leaders rather than the competing interests of rank-and-file dissidents which are favored. In the regulation of agriculture, again, the locally most influential farmers or leaders of farmers' organizations draw up the guidelines for control which are then adopted by the federal inspectors. In each case, ironically, the unwillingness of the government to impose its own standards or rules results not in a free play of competing groups, but in the enforcement of the preferences of the existing predominant interests.

In a sense, these unhappy consequences of government regulation stem from a confusion between a theory of interest-conflict and a theory of power-conflict. The government quite successfully referees the conflict among competing *powers* — any group which has already managed to accumulate a significant quantum of power will find its claims attended to by the federal agencies. But legitimate *interests* which have been ignored, suppressed, defeated, or which have not yet succeeded in organizing themselves for effective action, will find their disadvantageous position perpetuated through the decisions of the government. It is as though an umpire were to come upon a baseball game in progress between big boys and little boys, in which the big boys cheated, broke the rules, claimed hits that were outs, and made the little boys accept the injustice by brute force. If the umpire undertakes to "regulate" the game by simply enforcing the "rules" actually being practiced, he does not thereby make the game a fair one. Indeed, he may actually make matters worse, because if the little boys get up their courage, band together, and decide to fight it out, the umpire will accuse them of breaking the rules and throw his weight against them! Precisely the same sort of thing happens in pluralist politics. For example, the American Medical Association exercises a stranglehold over American medicine through its influence over the government's licensing regulations. Doctors who are opposed to the A.M.A.'s political positions, or even to its medical policies, do not merely have to buck the entrenched authority of the organization's leaders. They must also risk the loss of hospital affiliations, specialty accreditation, and so forth, all of which powers have been placed in the hands of the medical establishment by state and federal laws. Those laws are written by the government in cooperation with the very same A.M.A. leaders; not surprisingly, the interests of dissenting doctors do not receive favorable attention.

The net effect of government action is thus to weaken, rather than strengthen, the play of conflicting interests in the society. The theory of pluralism here has a crippling effect upon the government, for it warns against positive federal intervention in the name of independent principles of justice, equality, or fairness. The theory says justice will emerge from the free interplay of opposed groups; the practice tends to destroy that interplay.

Finally, the theory of pluralism in all its forms has the effect in American thought and politics of discriminating not only against certain social groups or interests, but also against certain sorts of proposals for the solution of social problems. According to pluralist theory, politics is a contest among social groups for control of the power and decision of the government. Each group is motivated by some interest or cluster of interests and seeks to sway the government toward action in its favor. The typical social problem according to pluralism is therefore some instance of distributive injustice. One group is getting too much, another too little, of the available resources. In accord with its modification of traditional liberalism, pluralism's goal is a rough parity among competing groups rather than among competing individuals. Characteristically, new proposals originate with a group which feels that its legitimate interests have been slighted, and the legislative outcome is a measure which corrects the social imbalance to a degree commensurate with the size and political power of the initiating group.

But there are some social ills in America whose causes do not lie in a maldistribution of wealth, and which cannot be cured therefore by the techniques of pluralist politics. For example, America is growing uglier, more dangerous, and less pleasant to live in, as its citizens grow richer. The reason is that natural beauty, public order, the cultivation of the arts, are not the special interest of any identifiable social group. Consequently, evils and inadequacies in those areas cannot be remedied by shifting the distribution of wealth and power among existing social groups. To be sure, crime and urban slums hurt the poor more than the rich, the Negro more than the white — but fundamentally they are problems of the society as a whole, not of any particular group. That is to say, they concern the general good, not merely the aggregate of private goods. To deal with such problems, there must be some way of constituting the whole society a genuine group with a group purpose and a conception of the common good. Pluralism rules this out in theory by portraying society as an aggregate of human communities rather than as itself a human community; and it equally rules out a concern for the general good in practice by encouraging a politics of interest-group pressures in which there is no mechanism for the discovery and expression of the common good.

The theory and practice of pluralism first came to dominate American politics during the depression, when the Democratic party put together an electoral majority of minority groups. It is not at all surprising that the same period saw the demise of an active socialist movement. For socialism, both in its diagnosis of the ills of industrial capitalism and in its proposed remedies, focuses on the structure of the economy and society as a whole and advances programs in the name of the general good. Pluralism, both as theory and as practice, simply does not acknowledge the possibility of wholesale reorganization of the society. By insisting on the group nature of society, it denies the existence of society-wide interests — save the purely procedural interest in preserving the system of group pressures — and the possibility of communal action in pursuit of the general good.

A proof of this charge can be found in the commissions, committees, institutes, and conferences which are convened from time to time to ponder the "national interest." The membership of these assemblies always includes an enlightened business executive, a labor leader, an educator, several clergymen of various faiths, a woman, a literate general or admiral, and a few public figures of unquestioned sobriety and predictable views. The whole is a microcosm of the interest groups and hereditary groups which, according to pluralism, constitute American society. Any vision of the national interest which emerges from such a group will inevitably be a standard pluralist picture of a harmonious, cooperative, distributively just, *tolerant* America. One could hardly expect a committee of group representatives to decide that the pluralist system of social groups is an obstacle to the general good!

Pluralist democracy, with its virtue, tolerance, constitutes the highest stage in the political development of industrial capitalism. It transcends the crude

"limitations" of early individualistic liberalism and makes a place for the com-
munitarian features of social life, as well as for the interest-group politics which
emerged as a domesticated version of the class struggle. Pluralism is humane,
benevolent, accommodating, and far more responsive to the evils of social injustice than either the egoistic liberalism or the traditionalistic conservatism from
which it grew. But pluralism is fatally blind to the evils which afflict the entire
body politic, and as a theory of society it obstructs consideration of precisely
the sorts of thoroughgoing social revisions which may be needed to remedy those
evils. Like all great social theories, pluralism answered a genuine social need
during a significant period of history. Now, however, new problems confront
America, problems not of distributive injustice but of the common good. We
must give up the image of society as a battleground of competing groups and
formulate an ideal of society more exalted than the mere acceptance of opposed
interests and diverse customs. There is need for a new philosophy of community,
beyond pluralism and beyond tolerance.

Suggested Reading

The debate over power in postwar America still pivots, with remarkable consistency, about the work of a few great thinkers who first sketched the outlines of pluralist, class, and elite theory. Students interested in pursuing the problem of power might well begin with the important writings of these early theoretical adepts. Pluralists still draw upon the classic study by Alexis de Tocqueville, *Democracy in America* (2 vols., 1835–1840), now available in several editions. Both pluralists and anti-pluralists have relied selectively on the work of James Madison in *The Federalist Papers*, especially the celebrated 10th Federalist. Karl Marx never completed his projected Chapter 52, "The Classes," in volume III of *Capital*, but a few of his shorter tracts give the flavor of Marx's theory of class and of class struggle: *The Communist Manifesto* (1848), *The Class Struggle in France* (1850), *The Eighteenth Brumaire of Louis Bonaparte* (1852), among others. For Max Weber's most important thought on power, see Part II: "Power" in Hans H. Gerth and C. Wright Mills, *From Max Weber: Essays in Sociology* (New York: Oxford University Press, 1946). Certain works by Thorstein Veblen — *The Theory of the Leisure Class* (1899), *The Theory of Business Enterprise* (1904), *The Engineers and the Price System* (1921), and *Absentee Ownership* (1923) — are invaluable. The work of major European elite thinkers is now available in English translation: Robert Michels, *Political Parties* (New York: Dover, 1959); Gaetano Mosca, *The Ruling Class* (New York: McGraw-Hill, 1939); and Vilfredo Pareto, *The Mind and Society*, 4 vols. (New York: Dover, 1963).

Several secondary works clarify some of the theoretical issues bearing upon the study of power. Three books by T. B. Bottomore — *Classes in Modern Society* (New York: Pantheon, 1966), *Critics of Society: Radical Thought in North America* (New York: Pantheon, 1968), *Elites and Society* (Baltimore: Pelican Books, 1966) — briefly summarize the traditions of class and elite theory. Ralf Dahrendorf, in *Class and Class Conflict in Industrial Society* (Stanford: Stanford University Press, 1959), discusses Marxist and post-Marxist theories of class. James Meisel, *The Myth of the Ruling Class* (Ann Arbor: University of Michigan Press, 1958) is a helpful survey, focusing on the work of Gaetano Mosca. Franz Neumann's *The Democratic and the Authoritarian State: Essays in Political and Legal Theory* (New York: The Free Press, 1957), Herbert Marcuse, ed., contains a number of important essays by a brilliant theorist, in particular "Approaches to the Study of Power," pp. 3–21. Raymond Aron, "Social Structure and the Ruling Class," *British Journal of Sociology*, I (March 1950), pp. 1–17, critically discusses and summarizes the theories of Marx and of Pareto. Aron's *Main Currents in Sociological Thought*, 4 vols. (New York: Basic Books, 1965 —) is also relevant, as is Norman Birnbaum's *The Crisis of Industrial Society*

(New York: Oxford University Press, 1969). A number of sources help to clarify intellectual developments in the American social sciences pertinent to the current debate over power. Excellent introductions to the field of political sociology are Reinhard Bendix and Seymour Martin Lipset, "Political Sociology — A Trend Report and Bibliography," *Current Sociology*, VI, 2 (1957), pp. 79–169 and Seymour M. Lipset, "Political Sociology," in Robert K. Merton *et al.*, eds., *Sociology Today* (New York: Harper & Row, 1965), vol. I, 81–114. The student, further, should not overlook the stimulating criticisms of American social science advanced by Barrington Moore, Jr., *Political Power and Social Theory* (Cambridge: Harvard University Press, 1958), especially chapters 3 and 4; by dissenting political scientists in Philip Green and Sanford Levinson, eds., *Power and Community: Dissenting Essays in Political Science* (New York: Pantheon, 1970); and by C. Wright Mills, *The Sociological Imagination* (New York: Oxford University Press, 1959). Hans L. Zetterberg, *Sociology in the United States of America* (Paris: UNESCO, 1956) and Dwight Waldo, *Political Science in the United States* (Paris: UNESCO, 1956) are useful surveys of particular disciplines.

Milton M. Gordon, *Social Class in American Sociology* (Durham: Duke University Press, 1958), Joseph A. Kahl, *The American Class Structure* (New York: Rinehart, 1957), Leonard Riessman, *Class in American Society* (Glencoe: The Free Press, 1959), and W. Lloyd Warner, *et al.*, *Social Class in America* (Gloucester, Mass.: Peter Smith, 1957) discuss the various uses of the "class" concept in American social science. H. D. Lasswell, Daniel Lerner, and C. Easton Rothwell, *The Comparative Study of Elites* (Stanford: Stanford University Press, 1952) is an important early consideration of elite analysis. Richard Merelman, "On the Neo-Elitist Critique of Community Power," *American Political Science Review*, 62 (June 1968), pp. 451–462, challenges many assumptions of elite theorists.

Two good introductions to the immense literature on community power are Nelson W. Polsby, *Community Power and Political Theory* (New Haven: Yale University Press, 1963) and Robert Presthus, *Men at the Top: A Study in Community Power* (New York: Oxford University Press, 1964). Maurice Stein, *The Eclipse of Community* (Princeton: Princeton University Press, 1960) and Arthur Vidich, Joseph Bensman, and Maurice Stein, eds., *Reflections on Community Studies* (New York: John Wiley, 1964) are also valuable. Linton C. Freeman *et al.*, *Local Community Leadership* (Syracuse: University College, 1960) lists over five hundred studies that had appeared since 1953, when Floyd Hunter inspired new interest in the study of community power. John Walton, "Substance and Artifact: The Current Status of Research on Community Power Structure," *American Journal of Sociology*, LXXI (January 1966), pp. 430–438 discusses thirty-three studies dealing with fifty-five communities. Also useful is William J. Gore and Fred S. Silander, "A Bibliographical Essay on Decision-Making," *Administrative Science Quarterly*, 4 (June 1959), pp. 106–121.

Two articles by Peter Rossi provide additional bibliographic and interpretive guides to the study of community power: "Community Decision Making," *Administrative Science Quarterly*, I (June 1957) pp. 415–443, and "Power and Community Structure," *Midwest Journal of Political Science*, 4 (November 1960), pp. 390–401. The surveys of recent literature by Lawrence J. R. Herson, "In the Footsteps of Community Power," *American Political Science Review*, LV (December 1961), pp. 817–830 and Herbert M. Danzger, "Community Power Structure: Problems and Continuities," *American Sociological Review*, 29 (October 1964), pp. 707–717 are generally critical of the Hunter school. On the other hand, the thoughtful essays by Thomas J. Anton, "Power, Pluralism, and Local Politics," *Administrative Science Quarterly*, 7 (March 1963), pp. 425–457 and Allan Rosenbaum, "Community Power and Political Theory: A Case of Misperception," *Berkeley Journal of Sociology*, XII (Summer 1967), pp. 91–116 criticize pluralist analyses. In a section of his challenging article, "Neutrality, Legitimacy, and the Supreme Court: Some Interactions

Between Law and Political Science," *Stanford Law Review*, 20 (November 1967), especially pp. 250ff., Jan G. Deutsch raises questions about the community power analyses of Robert Dahl and Nelson Polsby; Polsby himself replies to this attack in his essay, "On Interactions Between Law and Political Science," *Stanford Law Review*, 21 (November 1968), pp. 142–151.

William V. D'Antonio and William H. Form, *Influentials in Two Border Cities* (Notre Dame: University of Notre Dame Press, 1965) and Carol Estes Thometz, *The Decision Makers: The Power Structure of Dallas* (Dallas: Southern Methodist University Press, 1963) are specific studies reflecting the influence of Floyd Hunter. Ritchy K. Lowry, *Who's Running This Town?* (New York: Harper & Row, 1965), on the other hand, provides some cheer for those of pluralist sympathies. Arthur Vidich and Joseph Bensman, *Small Town in Mass Society* (Princeton: Princeton University Press, 1958) account for subtle factors such as mobilization of bias in their study of community power. Robert E. Agger, Daniel Goldrich, and Bert Swanson, *The Rulers and the Ruled: Political Power and Influence in American Communities* (New York: John Wiley and Sons, 1964) study four communities in two regions, the South and the West, and discover two types of power structure, consensual elite and competitive mass.

Sociologist Robert O. Schulze, "The Role of Economic Dominants in Community Power Structure," *American Sociological Review*, 23 (February 1958), pp. 3–9 finds, in a midwestern community, that economic power no longer coincides with political power. These findings are not supported, however, by Delbert C. Miller, "Industry and Community Power Structure: A Comparative Study of an American and an English City," *American Sociological Review*, 23 (February 1958), pp. 9–15; or by Roland J. Pellegrin and Charles H. Coates, "Absentee-Owned Corporations and Community Power Structure," *American Journal of Sociology*, LXI (March 1956), pp. 413–419. Further, C. Wright Mills and Melville J. Ulmer, "Small Business and Civic Welfare," Report of the Special Committee to Study Problems of American Small Business, U.S. Senate, 79th Congress, 2nd Session (Washington, D.C., 1946) suggest that economic dominants may exercise subtle, indirect control over political leaders. Schulze concedes this point, in part, in his longer study, "The Bifurcation of Power in a Satellite City," in Morris Janowitz, ed., *Community Political Systems* (New York: The Free Press, 1961), pp. 19–80.

The history of the current debate over decentralization of power is as yet unwritten. Daniel P. Moynihan, however, does explore the War on Poverty's commitment to community action in his recent book, *Maximum Feasible Misunderstanding* (New York: The Free Press, 1969). Stephan Thernstrom, *Poverty, Planning and Politics in the New Boston* (New York: Basic Books, 1969) is a useful history of Boston's 1961 antipoverty program written from the viewpoint of grassroots participants. In addition, the hearings on the Economic Opportunity Act, held before the Committee on Education and Labor, House of Representatives, June 12 to August 1, 1967 (4 volumes) and the new hearings before the Ad Hoc Task Force on Poverty of the Committee of Education and Labor, House of Representatives, March 24 to June 2, 1969 (4 volumes) are themselves a treasury of information about the issue of decentralization and community participation in the exercise of power.

The confusing debate over methodology and over definitions of power, relevant to the study of community power and of national power, is partly summarized in the exchange between Nelson Polsby, "Community Power Structure: Some Reflections on the Recent Literature," Raymond E. Wolfinger, "A Plea for a Decent Burial," and William V. D'Antonio, Howard J. Ehrlich, and Eugene C. Erickson, "Further Notes on the Study of Community Power," *American Sociological Review*, 27 (December 1962), pp. 838–854. In a lengthy review article, "American Business, Public Policy, Case Studies and Political Theory," *World Politics*, XVI (July 1964), pp. 677–715, Theodore J. Lowi develops a useful analytical framework for the study of power. Bertrand Russell, *Power* (New York: Norton, 1938),

Bertrand de Jouvenel, *On Power* (New York: Viking, 1949), and Harold Lasswell and Abraham Kaplan, *Power and Society* (New Haven: Yale University Press, 1950) are older, more general studies with contemporary relevance. Adolph A. Berle's *Power* (New York: Harcourt, Brace, 1969) is a stimulating, if not always persuasive, attempt to develop general laws of power. Roderick Bell, David V. Edwards, and R. Harrison Wagner, eds., *Political Power: A Reader on Theory and Research* (New York: The Free Press, 1969) is a helpful collection of articles containing a useful bibliography.

Three recent collections clarify a number of general issues pertinent to the study of power: William E. Connolly, ed. *The Bias of Pluralism* (New York: Atherton Press, 1969), Norman L. Crockett, ed. *The "Power Elite" in America* (Boston: D. C. Heath, 1970), and Charles A. McCoy and John Playford, eds. *Apolitical Politics: A Critique of Behavioralism* (New York: Crowell, 1967). Robert Dahl, "Further Reflections on 'The Elitist Theory of Democracy,' " *American Political Science Review*, LX (June 1966), pp. 296–305, Irving Louis Horowitz, "Consensus, Conflict and Cooperation: A Sociological Inventory," *Social Forces*, 41 (December 1962), pp. 177–188, Herbert McClosky, "Consensus and Ideology in American Politics," *American Political Science Review*, LVIII (June 1964), Peter Y. Medding, " 'Elitist' Democracy: An Unsuccessful Critique of a Misunderstood Theory," *Journal of Politics*, 31 (August 1969), pp. 641–654, and Jack Walker, "A Critique of the Elitist Theory of Democracy," *American Political Science Review*, LX (June 1966), pp. 285–295, are important theoretical critiques by scholars of divergent persuasions.

Arthur F. Bentley, *The Process of Government* (Chicago: University of Chicago Press, 1908) is a classic pluralist study, and so is V. O. Key, Jr., *Politics, Parties and Pressure Groups* (New York: Crowell, 1942 and 1959). Robert A. Dahl, *Pluralist Democracy in the United States: Conflict and Consent* (Chicago: Rand McNally, 1967), Wilfred Binkley and Malcolm Moos, *A Grammar of American Politics* (New York: Knopf, 1950), David Truman, *The Governmental Process* (New York: Knopf, 1951), and Edward Banfield, *Political Influence* (New York: The Free Press, 1961) are more recent studies in the same tradition. These works, by political scientists, may be supplemented by Seymour Martin Lipset's *Political Man* (Garden City, N.Y.: Doubleday & Co., 1960), a pluralist interpretation by a sociologist. In addition, the fine collection of essays edited by Lipset and Reinhard Bendix, *Class, Status and Power* (New York: The Free Press, 1953, 1966) is worth consulting.

Richard A. Schermerhorn, *Society and Power* (New York: Random House, 1961) is a good, brief survey of the literature on national (and community) power. Milton Mankoff, "Power in Advanced Capitalist Society: A Review Essay on Recent Elitist and Marxist Criticism of Pluralist Theory," *Social Problems*, 17 (Winter 1970), pp. 418–430, also gives a good overview of some significant recent studies. E. E. Schattschneider, *The Semi-Sovereign People* (New York: Holt, Rinehart and Winston, 1960) finds many weaknesses in pluralist theory; "the flaw in the pluralist heaven," he writes, "is that the heavenly chorus sings with a strong upper-class accent." Henry Kariel, *The Decline of American Pluralism* (Stanford: Stanford University Press, 1961) maintains that "the organizations which the early theorists of pluralism relied upon to sustain the individual against a unified government have themselves become oligarchically governed hierarchies, and now place unjustifiable limits on constitutional democracy." Grant McConnell, *Private Power and American Democracy* (New York: Knopf, 1966) is a penetrating study contending that pluralism has no theory of the public interest. Andrew McFarland, *Power and Leadership in Pluralist Systems* (Stanford: Stanford University Press, 1969) criticizes pluralism, yet is unwilling to abandon the theory completely. Arthur Kornhauser, ed., *Problems of Power in American Democracy* (Detroit: Wayne State University Press, 1957) contains provocative papers by Robert Lynd and C. Wright Mills, among others. Michael Paul Rogin, *The Intellectuals and McCarthy: The Radical Specter* (Cambridge: The M.I.T. Press, 1967) is a significant critique of pluralist theory and interpretation. Finally, students should consult two arresting essays by young leftists: Todd Gitlin, "Local Pluralism as Theory and Ideology," *Studies on the Left*, 5, 3 (1965), pp. 21–45, and Shin'ya Ono, "The Limits of Bourgeois Pluralism," *ibid.*, pp. 46–72.

David Riesman's work is critically reviewed in S. M. Lipset and Leo Lowenthal, eds., *Culture and Social Character: The Work of David Riesman Reviewed* (New York: The Free Press, 1961). Especially relevant is William Kornhauser's essay, " 'Power Elite' or 'Veto Groups'?" which compares Riesman and Mills; in the same volume, Ralf Dahrendorf, "Democracy Without Liberty: An Essay on the Politics of Other-Directed Man" intelligently discusses Riesman's "fallacy of the state that runs itself."

Students interested in the state of American Marxism may profitably peruse the pages of *The Monthly Review*. Paul Sweezy further elaborates his views in *The Future as History: Essays and Reviews on Capitalism and Socialism* (New York: Monthly Review Press, 1953), "Has Capitalism Changed?" in *Has Capitalism Changed?* ed. Shigeto Tsuru (Tokyo: Twanami Shotin, 1961), and in *Monopoly Capital* and *The Theory of Capitalist Development*, previously cited. William Appleman Williams' *The Great Evasion* (Chicago: Quadrangle, 1964) deplores the neglect of Marxism by American intellectuals. See, however, Eugene Genovese's critical review, "William Appleman Williams on Marx and America," *Studies on the Left*, VI (January–February, 1966), pp. 70–86. Ernest Mandel, *Marxist Economic Theory* (New York: Monthly Review Press, 1969, rev. ed.) is a masterful exposition of Marxist economics by a well-known Belgian scholar. Donald R. Matthews, *Social Background of the Political Decision Makers* (Garden City, N.Y.: Doubleday, 1954), David T. Stanley, Dean E. Mann, and Jameson W. Doig, *Men Who Govern* (Washington: The Brookings Institution, 1967), and Gabriel Kolko, Chapter 1, "The Men of Power," in *The Roots of American Foreign Policy* (Boston: Beacon Press, 1969), pp. 3–26, all probe the social backgrounds and career lines of decision makers.

Social mobility has been at the center of the debate over America's class structure and over the character of American elites. Some of the literature, as it relates to business leaders, is reviewed by Morroe Berger, "The Business Elite: Then and Now," *Commentary*, 22 (October 1956), pp. 367–374. Reinhard Bendix and Frank W. Howton, "Social Mobility and the American Business Elite," in Seymour M. Lipset and Reinhard Bendix, *Social Mobility in Industrial Society* (Berkeley: University of California Press, 1959) find some increase in upward mobility into the business elite. Students may also profit from W. Lloyd Warner and James C. Abegglen, *Occupational Mobility in American Business and Industry* (Minneapolis: University of Minnesota Press, 1955); Mabel Newcomer, *The Big Business Executive* (New York: Columbia University Press, 1955); Suzanne Keller, *Beyond the Ruling Class* (New York: Random House, 1963); and C. Wright Mills, "The American Business Elite: A Collective Portrait," *The Journal of Economic History*, 4, Supplement V (December 1945), pp. 20–44. More recently historian Stephen Thernstrom has challenged such studies of social mobility that focus primarily upon the upper class: "Is There Really a New Poor?" *Dissent*, XV (January–February 1968).

As yet there is no adequate intellectual biography of C. Wright Mills. Nevertheless, the memorial volume edited by Irving Louis Horowitz, *The New Sociology: Essays in Social Science and Social Theory in Honor of C. Wright Mills* (New York: Oxford University Press, 1963) is sometimes useful, as is the flawed study by Herbert Aptheker, *The World of C. Wright Mills* (New York: Marzani and Munsell, Inc., 1960). Mills' own essay, "The Power Elite: Comment on Criticism," *Dissent*, V (Winter 1957), pp. 22–34, is especially helpful in assessing *The Power Elite*. William Kornhauser, *The Politics of Mass Society* (New York: The Free Press, 1963) takes issue with Mills' interpretation of the mass society. Harold Cruse, *The Crisis of the Negro Intellectual: From Its Origins to the Present* (New York: William Morrow and Company, Inc., 1967) praises many of Mills' insights but suggests that he neglects the role of race.

Talcott Parsons has further elaborated his views on power in "The Concept of Political Power," *American Philosophical Society, Proceedings*, CVII (June 1963), pp. 232–262, and "On the Concept of Influence," *Public Opinion Quarterly*, 27 (Spring 1963), pp. 37–92 (with a comment by James S. Coleman and a rejoinder by Parsons). The best general assessment of Parsons' work is Tom Bottomore's essay, "Out of This World," *The New York Review of Books*, XIII (November 6, 1969), pp. 34–39. Other overviews are Max Black, ed., *The Social Theories of Talcott Parsons* (Englewood Cliffs, N.J.: Prentice-Hall, 1961) and William C. Mitchell, *Sociological Analysis and Politics: The Theories of Talcott Parsons* (Englewood Cliffs, N.J.: Prentice-Hall, 1967). Jeffrey M. Schevitz's helpful review, "The Shadow Knows: A Synthetic Review of Domhoff's *Who Rules America?* and Parsons' 'On the Concept of Political Power,' " may be found in the *Berkeley Journal of Sociology*, XIII (1968), pp. 82–96. An elaborate and telling assault on Parsons' entire theoretical edifice has been mounted by Alvin W. Gouldner in his magisterial study, *The Coming Crisis of Western Sociology* (New York: Basic Books, 1970).

Scholars of quite different intellectual persuasions have made use of two important studies by sociologist E. Digby Baltzell, *Philadelphia Gentlemen: The Making of a National Upper Class* (New York: The Free Press, 1958) and a sequel, *The Protestant Establishment: Aristocracy and Caste in America* (New York: Random House, 1964). In his first study, Baltzell pictured the rise of an American business aristocracy; in the second he argued that the institutions and authority of the old upper class had declined since 1940 and called for the establishment of a new upper class cutting across ethnic and religious lines. Andrew Hacker, "Liberal Democracy and Social Control," *American Political Science Review*, LI (September 1957), pp. 1009–1026 also argues that the old ruling class has declined in power, although Hacker suggests that a new ruling group—the "new engineers"—may now dominate national affairs. Hacker should be supplemented by Samuel Dubois Cook, "Hacker's 'Liberal Democracy and Social Control': A Critique," *ibid.*, pp. 1027–1039. Allan Potter, a British scholar, rejects the contention that governing class power has declined during the present century: in "The American Governing Class," *British Journal of Sociology*, XIII (December 1962), pp. 309–319, Potter argues that if "1939 was the year in which the American governing class was born, 1960 was, indeed, the year in which it came of age."

Beyond the work of Adolph Berle and Gardiner Means, students may wish to examine James Burnham's study of *The Managerial Revolution: What Is Happening in the World* (New York: John Day, 1941), which helped to popularize the notion of a managerial revolution, a concept earlier implicit in some of Thorstein Veblen's work. Robert J. Larner, "Ownership and Control in the 200 Largest Nonfinancial Corporations, 1929 and 1963," *The American Economic Review*, 56 (September 1966), pp. 777–787 agrees with the hypothesis that managerial control has increased dramatically since 1929. For other views similar to those of Berle, Means, and Galbraith, see Peter Drucker, *The Concept of the Corporation* (New York: John Day, 1946) and David Lilienthal, *Big Business: A New Era* (New York: Harper & Bros., 1953). Carl Kaysen develops his theory of the "soulful corporation" in "The Social Significance of the Modern Corporation," *The American Economic Review*, XLVII (May 1957), pp. 311–319. Robert Gordon, *Business Leadership in the Large Corporation* (Washington, D.C.: The Brookings Institution, 1945) argues that corporation executives are controlled by their boards of directors and that management, in turn, often controls a majority of the directors.

Earl F. Cheit, ed., *The Business Establishment* (New York: John Wiley & Sons, 1964) and Andrew Hacker, ed. *The Corporation Take-Over* (New York: Harper & Row, 1964) are useful collections of articles relating to business power. In *Steel and the Presidency*, 1962 (New York: Norton, 1963), Grant McConnell examines the clash between President Kennedy and United States Steel. In addition to previously cited analyses by Kolko and Villarejo, the student should consult Victor Perlo, "Peoples' Capitalism and Stock Ownership," *American Economic Review*, XLVIII (June 1958), pp. 333–347, which is critical of many generalizations derived from the concept of a managerial revolution. Ben B. Seligman, "The American Corporation: Ideology and Reality," *Dissent*, XI (Summer 1964), pp. 316–327 also assails pluralist interpretations of corporate power. A government report, *Interlocks in Corporate Management* (Washington, D.C., 1965) contains data suggesting the extent of corporate unity and influence.

The symposium, "Fundamental Characteristics of the American Economy: Degrees of Competition, of Monopoly, and of Countervailing Power; Theoretical Significance," *American Economic Review, Papers and Proceedings*, XLIV (May 1954), pp. 1–34 is a good summary of the debate over countervailing power. Arthur Schweitzer, "A Critique of Countervailing Power," *Social Research*, 21 (October 1954), pp. 253–285 is important too. In *Monopoly in America: The Government as Promoter* (New York: Macmillan, 1955), Walter Adams and Horace Grey argue that monopoly and the growth of corporate power arise from misguided public policies. Irv Beller, "American Behemoth: The Concentration of U.S. Corporate Power," *Dissent*, XIV (November–December 1967), pp. 742–756 (reprinted from the AFL–CIO *American Federationist*) believes that by "1977, the 100 largest manufacturing corporations will control more than two-thirds of the nation's net manufacturing assets." Useful for comparative purposes is David Lynch's summary of the research carried out by the Temporary National Economic Committee during the late thirties, *The Concentration of Economic Power* (New York: Columbia University Press, 1946). "The Merger Movement: A Study in Power," *Monthly Review*, 21 (June 1969) surveys the recent trend of conglomerate mergers.

The article by Marc Pilisuk and Thomas Hayden cited elsewhere in this volume contains a good bibliography on the military-industrial complex. Two other publications also survey this literature: The Social Science Research Council, *Civil-Military Relations: An Annotated Bibliography, 1940–1952* (New York: Columbia University Press, 1954); and Morris Janowitz and Robert Little, *Sociology and the Military Establishment* (New York: Russell Sage Foundation, 1964). Fred Cook, *The Warfare State* (New York: Macmillan, 1962) is a journalistic account echoing Mills' more scholarly analysis. The renewed alarm of American liberals over the growth of military power is reflected in several recent publications: John Kenneth Galbraith, "How to Control the Military," *Harper's*, 238 (June 1969), pp. 31–46, also available in book form (New York: The New American Library, 1969); Richard J. Barnet, *The Economy of Death* (New York: Atheneum, 1970); and a special issue of *The Progressive*, 33 (June 1969), entitled "The Power of the Pentagon." H. L. Nieburg, *In the Name of Science* (Chicago: Quadrangle, 1966) laments the involvement of American scientists in the military-industrial complex. Jack Raymond, *Power at the Pentagon* (New York: Harper & Row, 1964) is another critical study, as is Marxist Victor Perlo's *Militarism and Industry* (New York: International Publishers, 1963), an examination of corporate profits arising from defense contracts. In *The Soldier and the State* (Cambridge: Harvard University Press, 1957), Samuel P. Huntington develops a conservative interpretation of civil-military relations. David Horowitz, ed., *Corporations and the Cold War* (New York: Monthly Review Press, 1969) contains essays by radical scholars convinced that corporate interests are served by American foreign policy. Harry Magdoff, *The Age of Imperialism: The Economics of U.S. Foreign Policy* (New York: Monthly Review Press, 1969), presents a similar analysis. However, Raymond A. Bauer, Ithiel de Sola Pool, and Lewis Anthony Dexter, *American Business and Public Policy: The Politics of Foreign Trade* (New York: Atherton Press, 1963) vindicate pluralism. In one of the better recent studies on the subject, *Pentagon Capitalism, The Political Economy of War* (New York: McGraw-Hill, 1970), Seymour Melman makes the controversial argument that the military establishment is now an independent entity able to dominate economic and political interests.

In two articles, "The 'Industrial-Military Complex' in Historical Perspective: World War

I," *Business History Review*, XLI (Winter 1967), pp. 378–403, and "The 'Industrial-Military Complex' in Historical Perspective: The InterWar Years," *Journal of American History*, LVI (March 1970), pp. 819–839, Paul A. C. Koistinen traces the roots of today's military and industrial establishment to the pre-World War II era. Barton J. Bernstein has closely studied several episodes pertinent to C. Wright Mills' thesis that, during World War II, "the merger of the corporate economy and the military bureaucracy came into its present-day significance": see especially, "The Debate on Industrial Reconversion: The Protection of Oligopoly and Military Control of the War Economy," *American Journal of Economics and Sociology*, XXVI (April 1967), pp. 159–172; and "The Removal of War Production Controls on Business, 1944–1946," *Business History Review*, XXXIX (Summer 1965), pp. 243–260.

The classic study of ideology is Karl Mannheim's *Ideology and Utopia* (New York: Harcourt, Brace, 1936), Louis Wirth and Edward Shils, translators. The notion of an end of ideology was originally championed by a group of intellectuals associated with the British journal, *Encounter*, and then argued systematically by the French sociologist Raymond Aron in his book *The Opium of the Intellectuals* (New York: Norton, 1962). The thesis was popularized in America by Daniel Bell (among others): "The End of Ideology in the West," in *The End of Ideology*, *op. cit.*, pp. 393–407. It is also discussed by Seymour Martin Lipset, "The End of Ideology?" in *Political Man*, *op. cit.*, pp. 439–456. Various positions on this issue are presented in Chaim Isaac Waxman, ed., *The End of Ideology Debate* (New York: Funk & Wagnalls, 1969), whereas Norman Birnbaum discusses the general notion of ideology itself in "The Sociological Analysis of Ideology, 1940–60," *Current Sociology*, 9, 2 (1960). James Petras, "Ideology and United States Political Scientists," *Science and Society*, XXIX (Spring 1965), pp. 192–216 is an impassioned yet perceptive analysis of a particular discipline.